The Campus History Series

NEW ENGLAND COLLEGE

On the Cover: Pictured is the 1963 Winter Carnival Queen with some brothers of Lambda Epsilon Delta in front of the Administration Building. From left to right are William Meeker, Charles P. Lucas IV, Robert Seaman, Georgia Taggart, Michael Mullavey, Irwin Friedman, Clint McMahon, Queen Lynne Hiscock, Bruce Pettibone, Madge Evans, William Pennington. Seaman ('65) later joined the engineering faculty. (Courtesy of Hillsborough Historical Society.)

Cover Background: This image shows the iconic covered bridge that spans the Contoocook River, which runs through the Henniker campus of New England College. (Courtesy of New England College archives.)

The Campus History Series

NEW ENGLAND COLLEGE

CYNTHIA BURNS MARTIN
FOREWORD BY ALEXANDER "LEX" SCOURBY

ARCADIA
PUBLISHING

ISBN 978-1-4671-2431-7

Published by Arcadia Publishing
Charleston, South Carolina

Printed in the United States of America

Library of Congress Control Number: 2016950037

For all general information, please contact Arcadia Publishing:
Telephone 843-853-2070
Fax 843-853-0044
E-mail sales@arcadiapublishing.com
For customer service and orders:
Toll-Free 1-888-313-2665

Visit us on the Internet at www.arcadiapublishing.com

This book is dedicated to the New England College community of the past, present, and future.

Contents

FOREWORD

Hello Readers!

This eclectic collection of candid and informal images speaks eloquently of the caring, collaborative, and enduring relationships that are the community of New England College.

For 70 years, New England College has been known and respected for innovative academic programs that transform the lives of students. The magic ingredients to this transformation are a supportive and inspiring environment and the hands-on engagement of students and faculty.

New England College has always recognized that learning can happen in many different places. During the college's first few years, students took classes on a makeshift campus cobbled together from rented buildings, sparse and unheated rooms, and the great outdoors. New England College still uses its vibrant natural surroundings to encourage creativity and conversation. Faculty also inspire students in classrooms and offices, labs, online forums, theaters, galleries, and experiential workshops. Regardless of location, New England College students experience personal transformation.

With 30 years of experience teaching and witnessing the evolution at New England College, author and professor Cynthia Burns Martin is the perfect storyteller. She begins with the passing of the federal GI Bill, which almost immediately changed the quiet ebb and flow of Henniker, New Hampshire. She leaves readers smiling with the realization that the same warm community exists today.

As for me, I arrived at New England College unsure of what I was capable, but I left with the skills and confidence that helped me and a fellow NEC alumnus start a business. Because of the impact my experience had on me and so many others, I chose to join the board of trustees and lead development efforts to advance the school. Looking at the rich history represented in this commemorative book, I couldn't be more proud of New England College's past and present, nor more optimistic about its future.

Enjoy!

—Alexander Scourby, BA '75, MBA
Chairman-Elect, New England College Board of Trustees

ACKNOWLEDGMENTS

I hope this small collection of images will awaken fond memories and strengthen connections for the entire New England College community. It is not intended to be a comprehensive history, which I hope will be written by someone else before too many more icebergs float down the Contoocook during spring thaw.

Henniker Historical Society and Hillsborough Historical Society generously shared a significant number of images from their collections. Many individuals contributed images, historical memory, financial support, access, patience, and problem-solving to make this book possible, including Christine and Steve Burritt, Daniel DaCosta, David Deziel, Shirley English-Whitman, Dan Freese, Melissa Gardiner, Nina Giannotti, Peter and Marie Gilbert, Dorothy Greenly, Frank Hall, Meghan Hallock, Chelsea Hanrahan, Brian Hopkins, Ryan Hornblower, Sue Lewey, Kevin Martin, Neal Brian Martin, Gary McGrath, John O'Connor, Michele Perkins, Samantha Piehl, Deborah Spring Reed, Catherine Ryan, Anne Sayce, Lex Scourby, Gilman Shattuck, Morgan Smith, Andrea Stickney, Martha C. Taylor, Jim Walsh, Mark Watman, and Nancy Weinheimer Wilson. At every stage of production, I received outstanding support from title manager Henry Clougherty. Pei-Sien Poh ('16) helped me locate art resources and assess feasibility of this project. Yuman He ('16) scanned and organized hundreds of images. James Carlson ('16) identified most of the athletes in chapter 3 and people pictured on the cover. I am grateful for invaluable encouragement from mentors Ethel Brindle Cross, Dorothy Burton Fairman, Sandra Hawkes, Roy Heisler, and John Lyons. Thank you all!

Unless otherwise noted, all images in this book are from the archives of New England College.

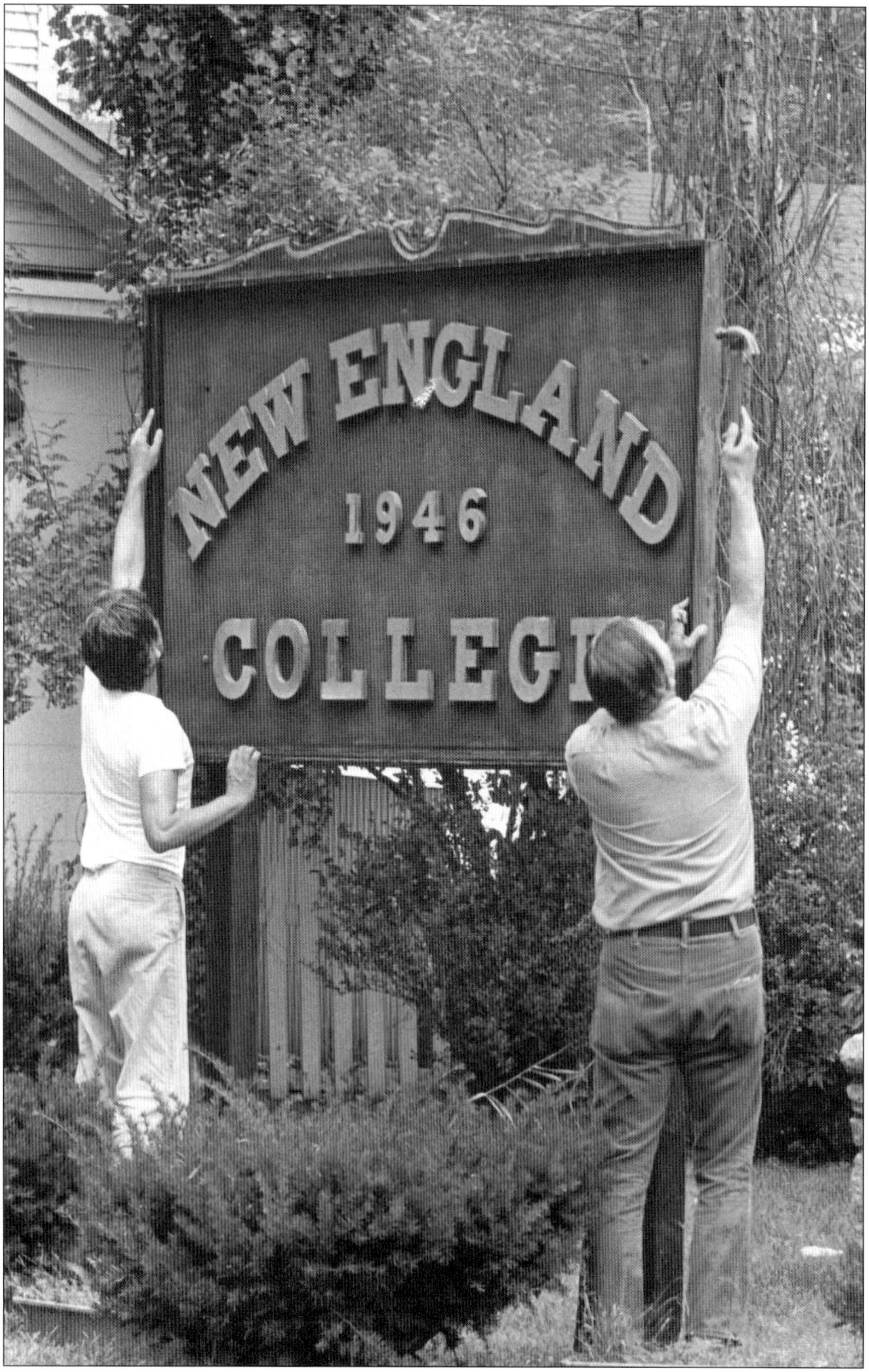

The New England College sign was installed in the late 1950s next to the Administration Building to greet visitors to campus. (Courtesy of Henniker Historical Society.)

INTRODUCTION

The entrepreneur Boone Doudy Tillett started from modest beginnings. Born in 1895 at Nags Head, a fishing village on North Carolina's windswept and sandy Outer Banks, the eldest of eight children and son of a fisherman, Tillett tried fishing for an occupation. Ambitious, he taught school in Georgia, worked as a bookkeeper for a tobacco company, opened a law practice in a time and place when approval by the Supreme Court of North Carolina was the sole criterion necessary to enter the profession, and taught briefly for the University of Maryland at College Park, where a 1936 yearbook lists his credentials as DCL (doctorate in civil law), normally an honorary degree. He was still involved in higher education as dean of Hofstra University's school of business administration when he realized that the country's colleges could not meet the looming demand from veterans who wanted to exercise their GI Bill education rights after the Second World War.

During the spring of 1946, Boone Tillett and young Hofstra professor Charles Weber scouted New England for locations to establish a new college that would be wholly owned by Tillett. Tillett gave a presentation in Manchester, New Hampshire, where his plan was heard by the chair of the Henniker Board of Selectmen, Fred Taylor Connor, a prominent citizen who was deeply concerned about the economic future of Henniker, which had lost farms and population to western migration. He and other Henniker citizens also anticipated a federal flood-control project that would close most of the town's small mills on the Contoocook River. Townspeople were eager to gain rental income from spare rooms and vacant buildings. The board of selectmen and Tillett agreed that Connor would make local arrangements for housing and classrooms, while Tillett would recruit students and faculty.

Boone Tillett sent his brother Walter R. Tillett to manage the startup operation. A prosperous merchant and landowner named Max Israel agreed to persuade local businesspeople to extend credit to the new business. Israel was a self-made man who arrived in this country in 1905 as a teenaged refugee from present-day Lithuania, earned a living as an itinerant peddler, settled in Henniker, and started a business in "junk" and iron, which evolved into an antiques dealership with a national reputation for quality. He also invested wisely in real estate.

From the start to the present day, New England College has responded with alacrity to opportunities in a changing marketplace. Six months after Boone Tillett first visited Henniker, New England College opened its doors, ready for business. According to local historian Peter Gilbert, "It appears that faculty and students were rounded up and sent to Henniker by a roaming Boone Tillett. Since there was no actual accredited school, the fact that these people came at all is a testimony to Tillett's convincing nature."

Unfortunately, the Tillett brothers underestimated startup costs and overextended lines of credit, so by the end of the first semester, their creditors were anxious about bad debt. On March 20, 1947, the *Manchester Union Leader* reported that Boone D. Tillett had severed his connections with New England College and turned over its assets and liabilities to a board of five local resident trustees: undertaker Harry L. Holmes, grocery store owner George M. Chase, former legislator Fred T. Connor, New England College professor Charles M. Weber, and registrar Mary S. Jameson. A Methodist minister from Hillsboro, New Hampshire, named Milo Farmer agreed to serve as interim president. On May 1, 1947, Dr. Laurie Davidson Cox, a longtime summer resident and recently retired from the faculty of Syracuse University, was appointed president of New England College.

To establish a competitive advantage for the fledgling institution, Cox announced plans for a unique three-year degree program on June 16, 1947. The *Manchester Union Leader* recounted that "under the streamlined, three-year program, the four year course would be divided into nine semesters, with only a week's vacation between the first and second, and second and third. Each semester will comprise 14 college credits, making a total of 126 semester credit hours for the four years, which exceeds the usual credits received in a four-year college course. . . . Monthly examinations would replace ordinary semester exams and that for the sake of college social life the freshman, sophomore and junior years would each comprise two semesters while the senior year would have three semesters." Andy Holton recalled that for faculty like him, "This meant 12 preparations a year, a real slave driver, no rest day or night." New England College's innovative year-round program was later copied by nearby Dartmouth College and many other institutions.

From the earliest years, the college relied on a significant number of part-time faculty who were active professionals in their fields. This was innovation that saved costs and better met the needs of older veteran students who were eager to begin careers, but it was not a commonly accepted practice in higher education at that time and so was likely to attract close scrutiny during accreditations. "These professionals and special lecturers not only teach the required content of their courses but keep the students in touch with current developments in their special field. The cost to the college is far less than that of hiring fulltime faculty members," noted the *Christian Science Monitor*.

The college was incorporated on June 20, 1947, when Gov. Charles M. Dale signed Chapter 376, Laws of 1947, an Act of Incorporation for New England College. According to Gilbert, "this act allowed the college to operate under the supervision of the State Board of Education and approved the first two years of courses, allowing New England College to grant Associate degrees 'when and during the period it is approved by the State Board of Education'. It further stated 'upon approval of the State Board of Education it may, after meeting adequate academic standards, grant degrees of Bachelor of Arts or Bachelor of Science.' "

The college responded to rapid growth by creative use of existing buildings in town.

In September 1947, the *Manchester Union Leader* reported, "The Henniker Inn has been purchased by the townspeople and half of the building has been turned over for the use of the school. . . . The town and Grange halls have been taken over and fitted for classrooms while a former grain warehouse has been converted into a 66 man dormitory." The grain store was located on the lot later occupied by the Science Building. The town agreed to share the high school gymnasium, public library, and baseball field. Soon, the inn's carriage sheds were converted to laboratories. According to Gilbert, the college also purchased an old farmhouse with a large barn on Hall Avenue, named it Faculty Hall, and planned to use it for classrooms, laboratories, and faculty offices.

Conditions in some of those repurposed buildings were rustic, to say the least. Faculty member Andy Holton reports in his memoirs that "in the early years . . . classes were held in the old town hall. This was a large second floor room with two pot bellied stoves and lone smoke stacks to either side of the stage. If we had an eight o'clock class we had to start a wood fire in these to keep warm. Often two classes met at the same time in opposite corners of the room. . . . The students were all GI's at the time, much older and more eager to learn than later students."

Dr. Cox, who was a nationally recognized landscape engineer, stated, "We would not want to exchange this friendly, informal atmosphere and rich community life for that of a formal campus, set apart from the town. As we build, we hope to fit our buildings into the general architectural and landscaping plan of the town, rather than alter its traditional New England loveliness."

Townspeople welcomed students in their homes, and the college reciprocated. The first Winter Carnival weekend began on Friday, February 11, 1949, and the *Boston Post* reported that "a huge statue of a Puritan in snow is going up in front of the Town Inn. . . . Saturday is the big day. Drop by Moody's Meadow about noon and you'll find everybody in Henniker lined up at a canvas covered chuck wagon for baked beans, ham and biscuits."

The *New Englander* was on the beat from the college's first year, when staff signed off on the first issue at midnight on April 17, 1947. There was optimistic news to report about growth in the college's buildings and cocurricular programs. For example, the January 15, 1948, *New Englander* reports that "the new college library, located in the rear wing of Henniker Inn, has opened its doors to students of New England College. The library is to be open all day on Monday and Wednesday and from 3 to 5 on Tuesday, Thursday and Friday." In the same issue, the paper reports that New England College sent a seven-man ski team to an intercollegiate meet in Jackson, New Hampshire. "Hopes for success rest chiefly upon the captain, Neil Dearborn, who . . . served in the Army with the Ski Troops and supervised instruction at Camp Hale, Colorado, attached to the famous 10th Mountain Division. Upon return to civilian life he became a member of the ski patrol on Cannon Mountain and last winter taught skiing at the Franconia Ski School."

At 10:30 a.m. on Tuesday, June 29, 1948, New England College held its first commencement at Henniker Congregational Church. President Cox awarded 27 associate's degrees. The academic procession included the faculty, trustees, and graduates. The alma mater, "Hail Thee New England," was sung for the first time by combined choirs of the church and New England College. It has been sung at the college's graduations ever since.

Athletics have always been an integral part of New England College. By the college's third year, it had men's teams for winter sports, baseball, basketball, soccer, football, and lacrosse, according to an article in *New Hampshire Sunday News*. The football team, the Pilgrims, practiced in a field near campus. According to the *New Hampshire News* on September 14, 1949, "An advantage of a small college like this is that the 'ham and egg' athletes have as much chance to play in the games as the star players." The same article notes, "The rural atmosphere and the smallness combine to bring a closer relationship between students and faculty than at the bigger colleges." The first new building ever constructed by New England College was a 44-by-18-foot wood-frame fieldhouse, erected in 1949 at the playing fields on what is today called Old Concord Road. A sportsmen's club actively promoted interest in golf, swimming, skiing, skating, fishing, hunting, and hiking for students not involved in team sports. The college also had a glee club, which appeared on the radio and in public concerts.

Experiential learning, or "hands-on" education, has always been a distinguishing hallmark of a New England College education. The *Boston Sunday Globe* commended the college in 1953 because "seniors in the engineering department, for instance, laid out two miles of new highway, for which they received engineers' salaries from the state of New Hampshire, turning over their earnings for the good of the college," while *Country Correspondence* remarked in 1955 that "the college boys, under supervision of state officials, take over the actual engineering work of a strip of new road or the remodeling and widening of an older highway. The boys get actual experience planning bridges, culverts, road grades and all the other technical aspects of building roads."

At the college's first homecoming on Armistice Day, Friday, November 11, 1949, more than 60 percent of the first year's graduating class returned to witness both the college's first football victory and the dedication of the athletic field, according to the *New Hampshire Sunday News*.

New England College has survived and thrived because it adapted, time and time again, to changes in the environment. When veteran demand for higher education funded by the GI Bill was nearly depleted and revenues were falling, Dr. William H. Mandrey was appointed president after Laurie D. Cox returned to retirement in the summer of 1950. The *Hillsborough Messenger* reported that "President Mandrey, on his assumption of office, instituted rigid economies in the business operations of the college. He also argued against college monies being used to support the Henniker Inn, which he insisted should stand on its own feet. His cleaning up of the college's business practices, as well as his insistence on the separation of the inn's finances from those of the college, reportedly were not popular with some of the local trustees who operate local businesses." Faculty member Andy Holton recalled: "I think it was under Dr. Mandrey when all things possible were converted to cash to meet the payroll. Even the typewriters from the course in typing were sold. We were not paid for two periods back then but somehow most of us stayed on."

Just as it appeared the end was near, a generous benefactor with no prior ties to New England College, except friendship with former president Cox, offered a loan (that became a de facto gift) of much-needed cash in exchange for control over business operations of the organization. The trustees dismissed president Mandrey and relinquished control to a small emergency committee, chaired by benefactor Stephen Phillips. According to the *Manchester Union Leader*, "Mr. Phillips and his wife and a close friend were named to the committee at a special meeting of the trustees, at which Dr. Laurie D. Cox was renamed college president."

Efforts of the Mollie Pitchers, a group of local Henniker women who pledged to promote the college, began to yield a flurry of positive articles in regional newspapers. The *Christian Science Monitor* noted that "the freshman class which entered in 1952 included students from all New England states, as well as Rhode Island, New York and New Jersey, as well as students from Venezuela and Haiti. Only 5 of the 90 freshmen were veterans."

The college began to acquire buildings and property across the river from the town center. According to Gilbert, "By March of 1953 . . . Sigma Phi Delta fraternity had purchased the so-called Bailey Property, later referred to as the Fred Davis land. And they had agreed to sell or donate that land not occupied by the buildings to the college (where Colby, West and Simon Center stand today). . . . Mr. Phillips purchased the Reynolds property, a house and land on Grove Street that abutted the land that he had received from Fred. T. Connor. He gave this property to the college and they proposed to use it as a residence for college presidents. The . . . library is now located on this property." The adjacent Robertson house and property were also acquired for a women's dormitory and became the second student residence to be called Connor Hall. The Morrison house was acquired and renamed as the college's third Connor Hall, later called Tower House. In 1956, the Brady house was purchased for library space and renamed Spaulding House. The Brady purchase included land behind the house, where the quadrangle of Charter Hall, East Hall, and Connor Hall were eventually constructed. Having overseen significant improvements in the physical plan, Dr. Laurie Cox retired for the third time in his academic career.

By the end of the first decade, New England College had proved it was a resilient and entrepreneurial institution with a reputation for innovations, including an accelerated degree program, "learning by doing," and full-time professionals on the faculty. New England College fosters values that allowed the institution to survive against the odds: creative and frugal use of limited resources, taking chances, working hard, and striving for excellence. In the following pages are glimpses of some people, places, and events that will bring back memories for many thousands of members of the New England College community.

One

Hail Thee New England!

Early Campus, East of the River

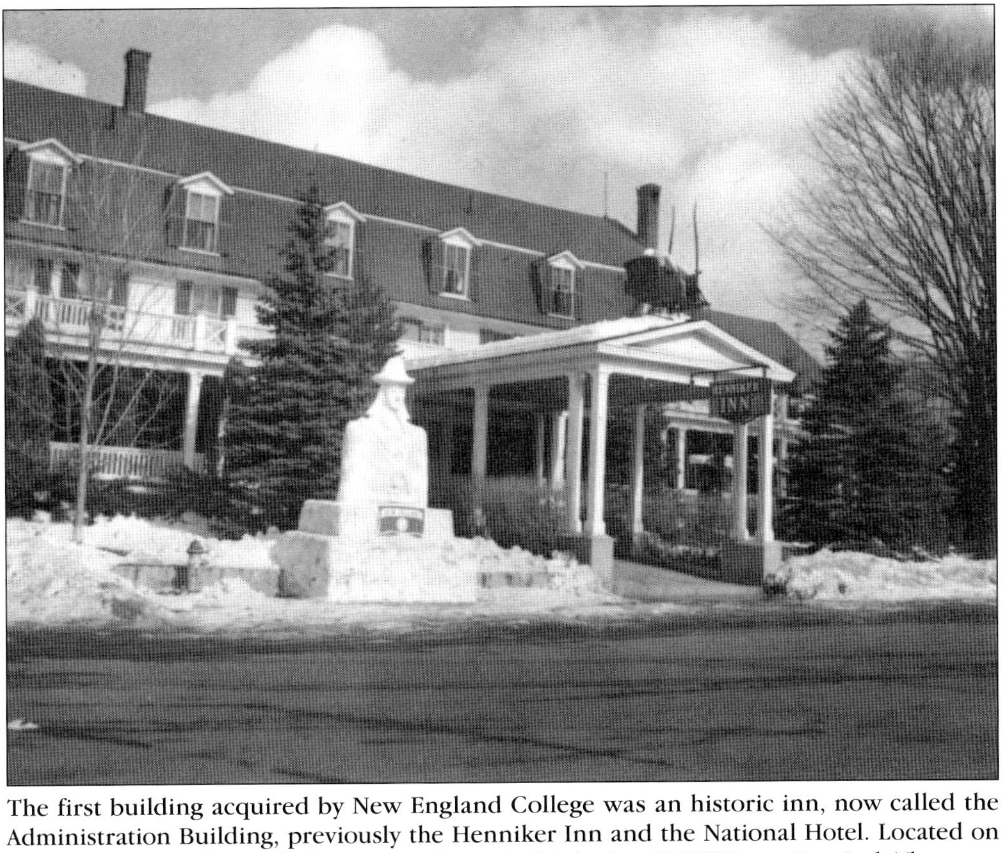

The first building acquired by New England College was an historic inn, now called the Administration Building, previously the Henniker Inn and the National Hotel. Located on Main Street, it looks much the same today as it did during 1950 Winter Carnival. The snow sculpture in front of the Henniker Inn features the Pilgrim mascot. The sign on the front of the sculpture displays the college's first logo. (Courtesy of George Landry.)

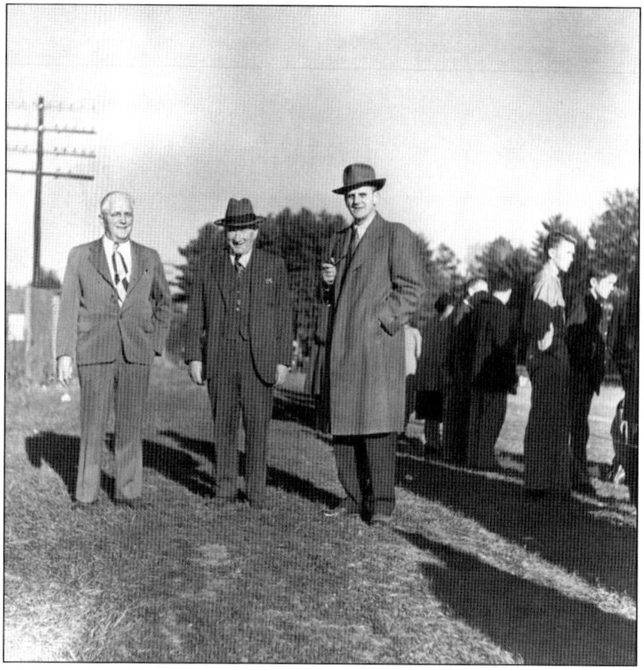

From left to right are George W. Boynton, Hillsboro, New Hampshire, trustee (1947–1954); Max Israel, trustee (1947–1953); and William H. Mandrey, trustee (1949–1952) and president (1950–March 1951). (Courtesy of Henniker Historical Society.)

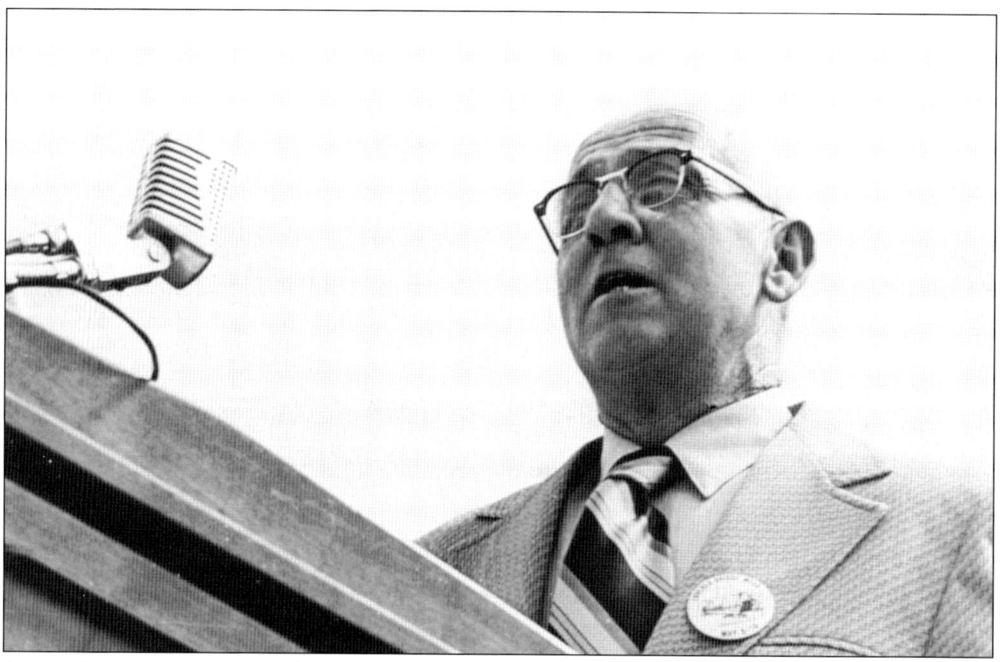

Lester Connor is the son of Fred T. Connor, one of the college's founders and a member of the state legislature who provided political advice to the institution in critical early years.

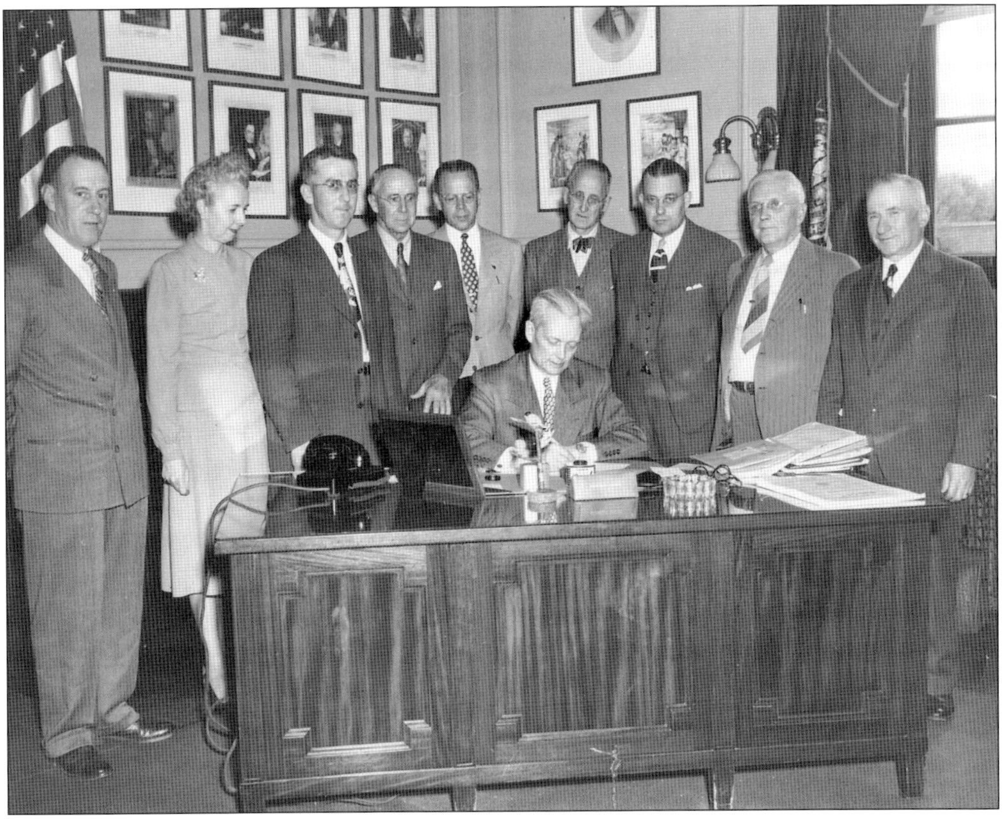

Gov. Sherman Adams signed an act on May 4, 1949, that enabled New England College to grant baccalaureate degrees. From left to right are Franklin Flanders, Mary Jameson, Lester Connor, Fred Connor, Philip Butterfield, Laurie Cox, George Chase, George Boynton, and Max Israel. (Courtesy of Henniker Historical Society.)

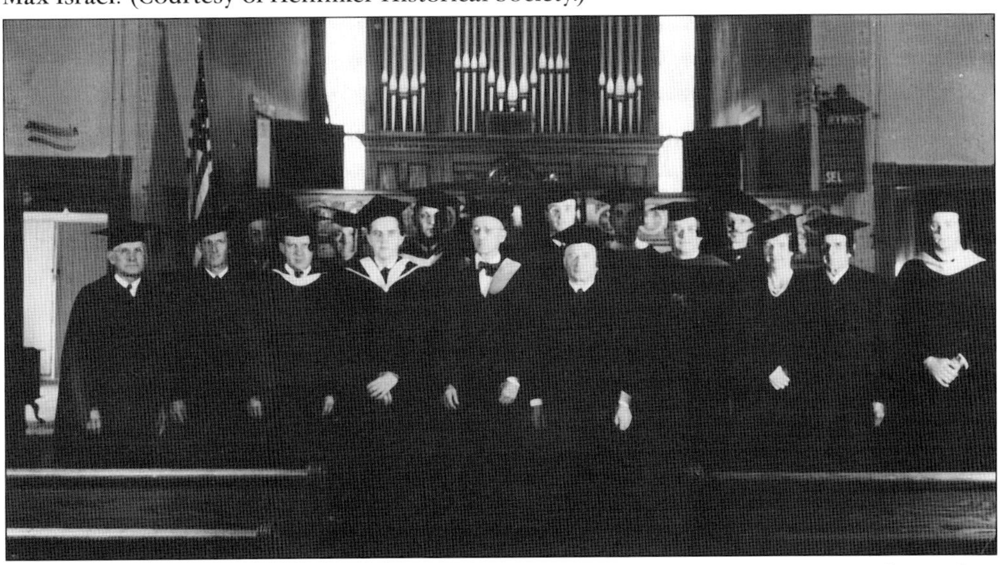

This early image of New England College faculty may have been taken at the college's first graduation, celebrated in Henniker Congregational Church.

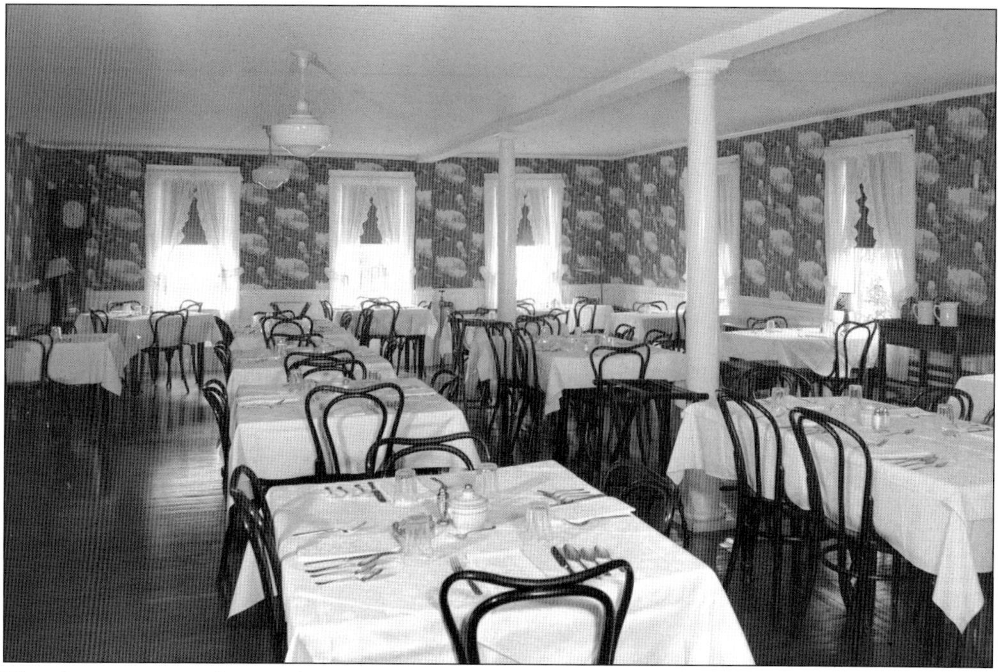

The dining room of Henniker Inn is pictured in 1942. For a few years after acquisition by the college, Henniker Inn continued to welcome business travelers and tourists while also providing residential space and dining commons for students. (Courtesy of Hillsborough Historical Society.)

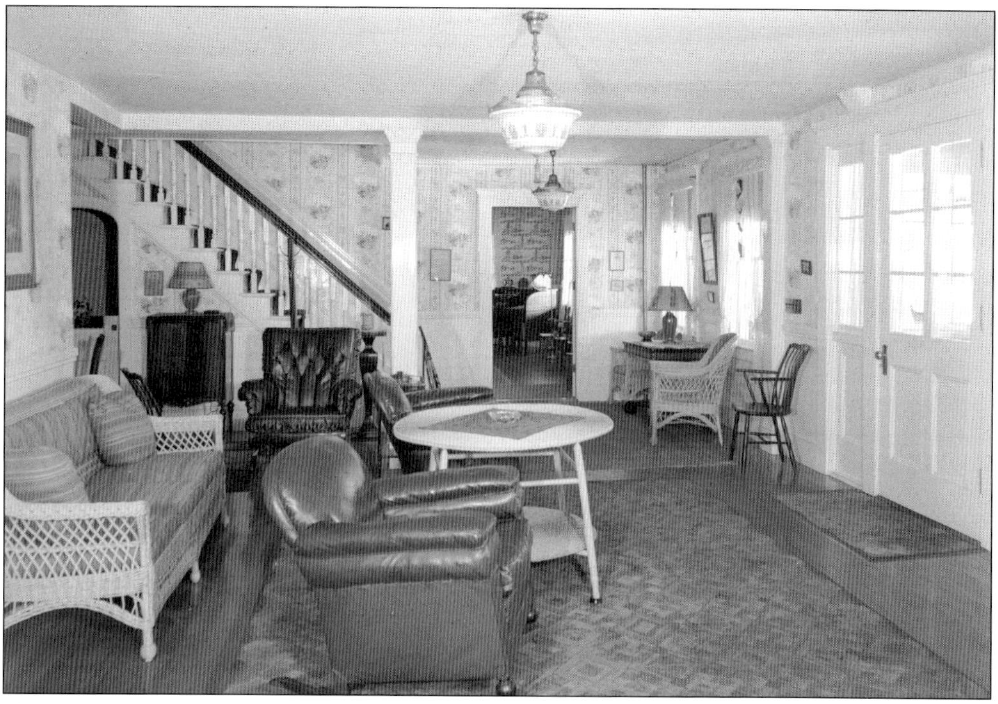

This is the lobby of the Henniker Inn as it appeared in 1942. (Courtesy of Hillsborough Historical Society.)

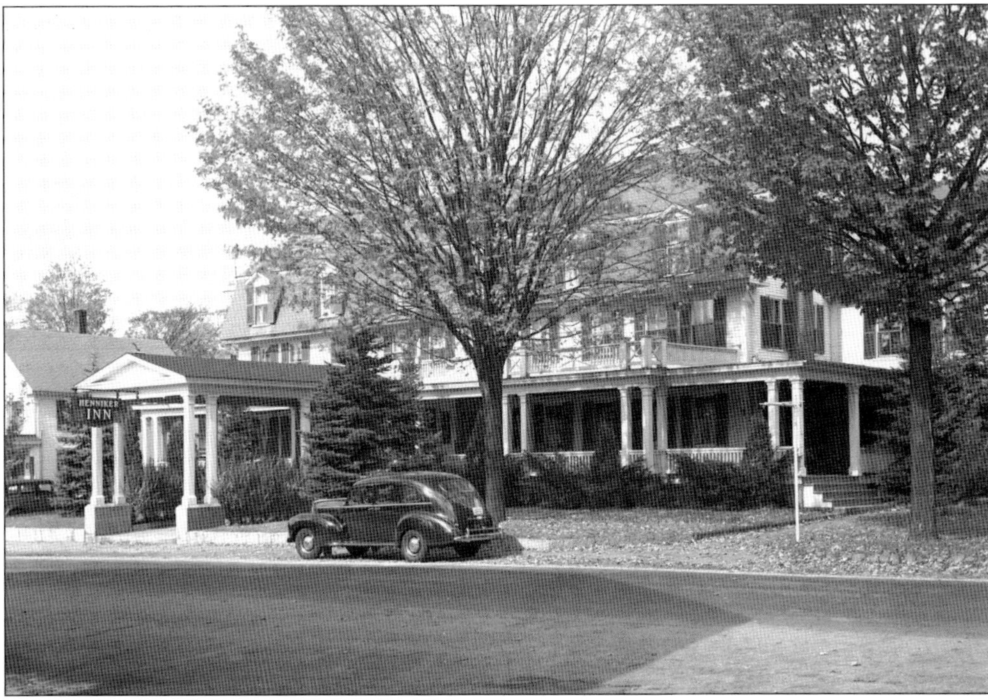

This early image of the Henniker Inn was taken on November 19, 1942, by the Manahan-Phelps Studio and probably used for publicity purposes. (Courtesy of Hillsborough Historical Society.)

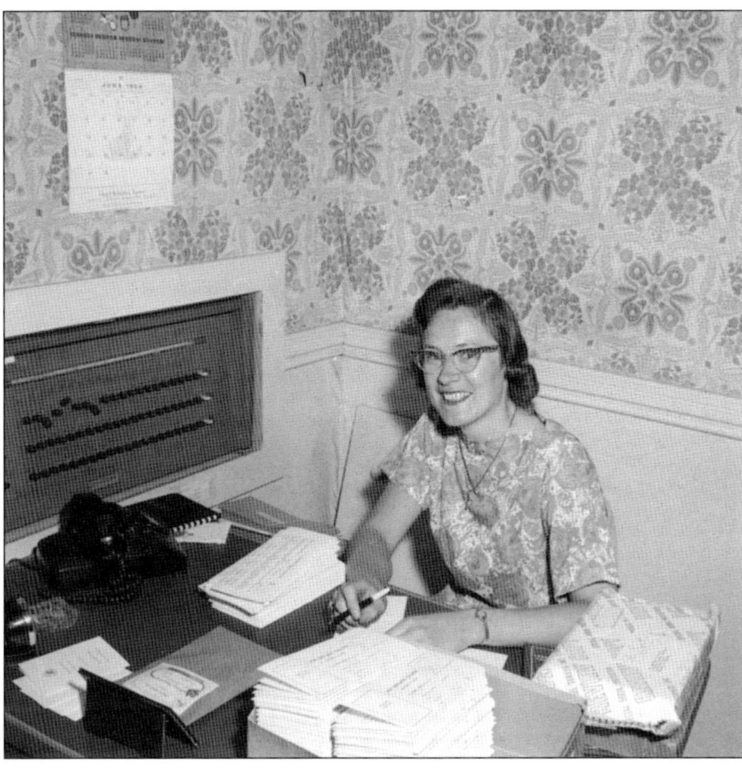

From the 1940s through the mid-1980s, the college telephones were operated through a switchboard located in the lobby of the Administration Building. Shown here is Mildred Davis, admissions secretary in 1964. One alumna recalled that "the plus side of having an operator was that she frequently could say where the person was that you were trying to call." (Courtesy of Hillsborough Historical Society.)

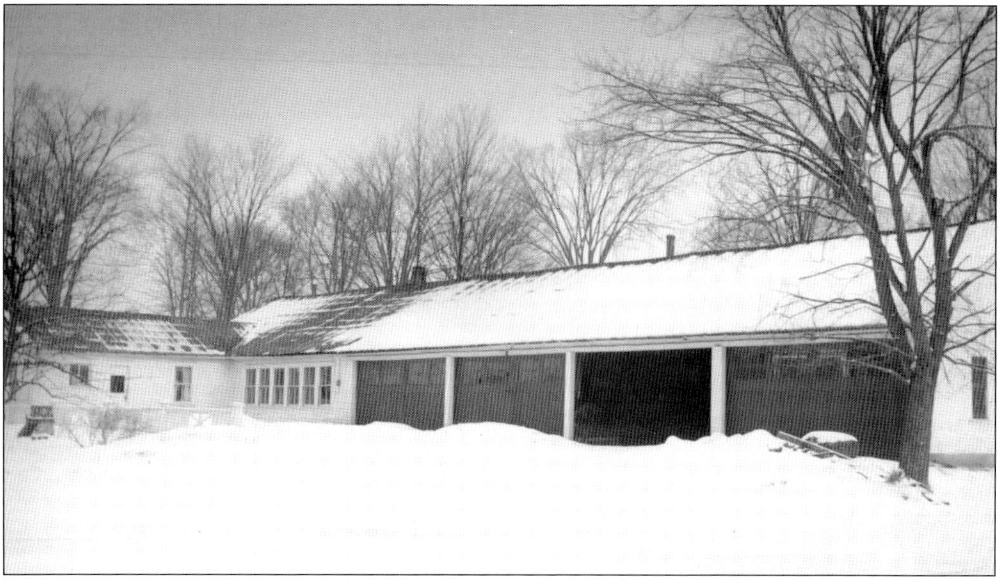

Carriage House is behind the Administration Building. This long structure was built to house horses and carriages and, later, automobiles for the inn's paying guests. The college converted the carriage shed to classrooms and laboratory space. This image was taken by faculty member Gerda Peterich, who taught at the college from 1958 to 1961 and was a photographer of national renown. (Courtesy of Henniker Historical Society.)

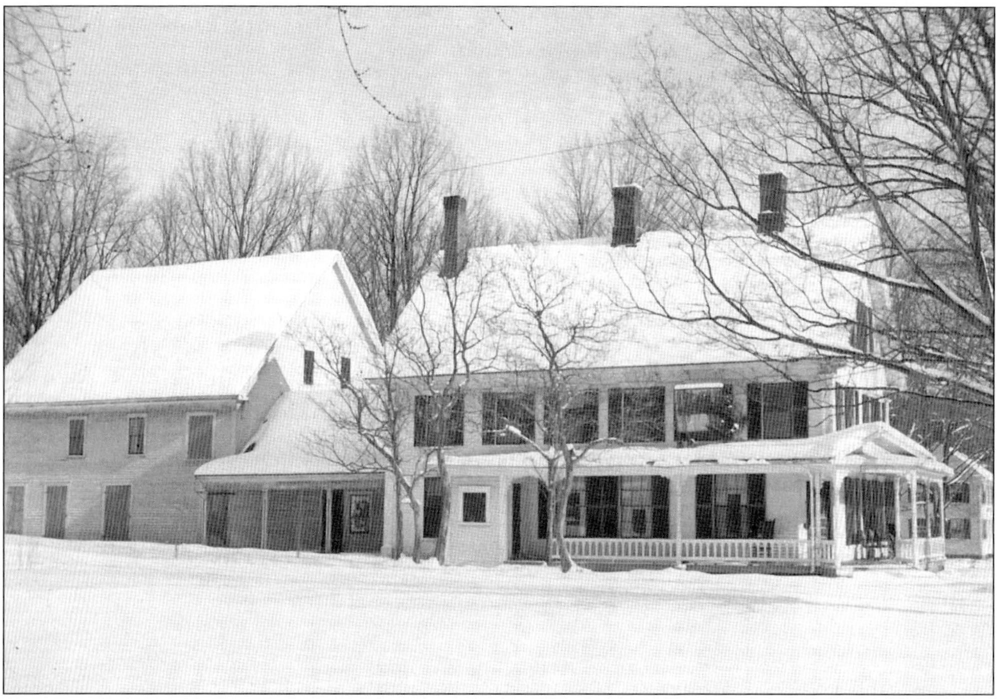

Preston House and Barn, built around 1880, are located on Main Street, east of the Administration Building. The former home of George C. Preston, this house has been the college bookstore and a costume workshop for the theatre department. Preston Barn was converted to gallery display space. (Courtesy of Henniker Historical Society.)

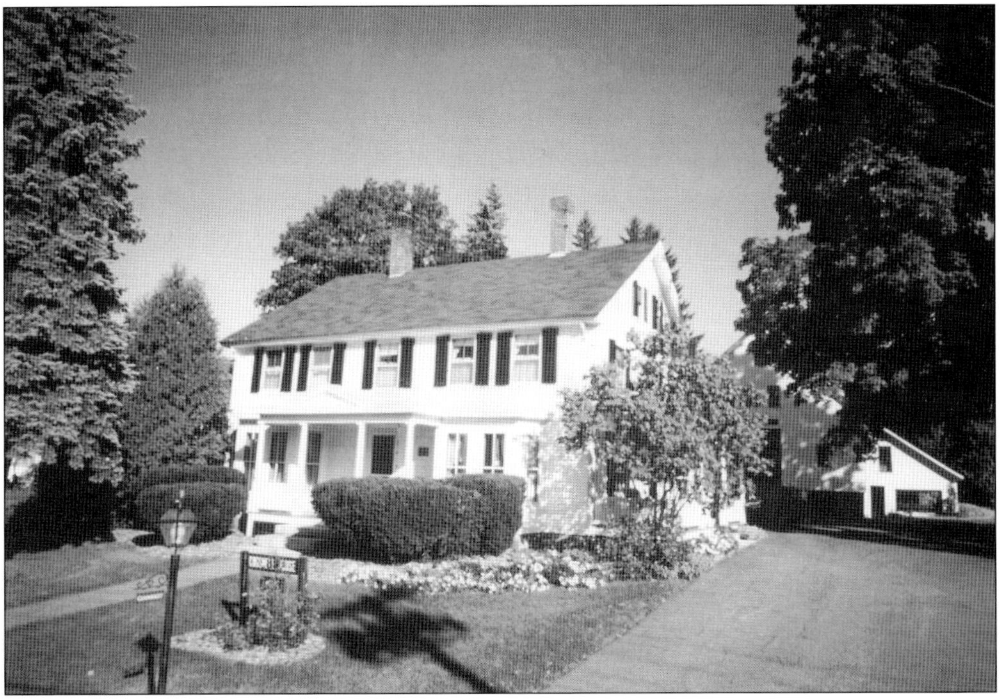

Farther east on Main Street is Cogswell House, built around 1820 by David Cogswell and later owned by his son, David W. Cogswell. This house is now owned by New England College and has been the official residence of recent presidents.

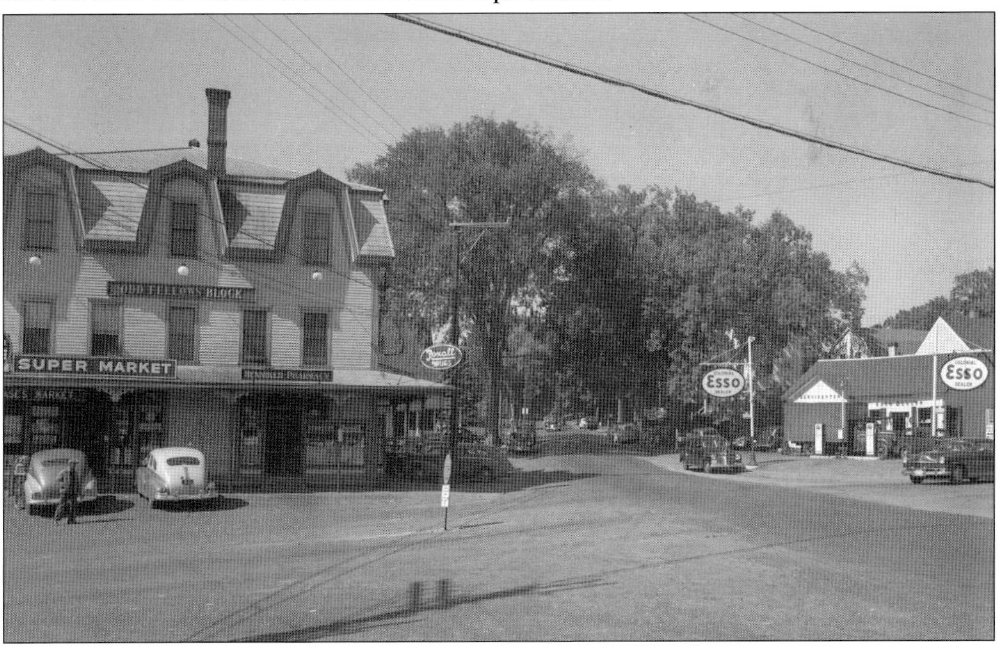

Proctor Square, at the intersection of Maple and Main Streets, has changed little since this image was taken on August 23, 1949, three years after the founding of New England College. Many residents are glad there is not yet need for a traffic light in the center of town. (Courtesy of Hillsborough Historical Society.)

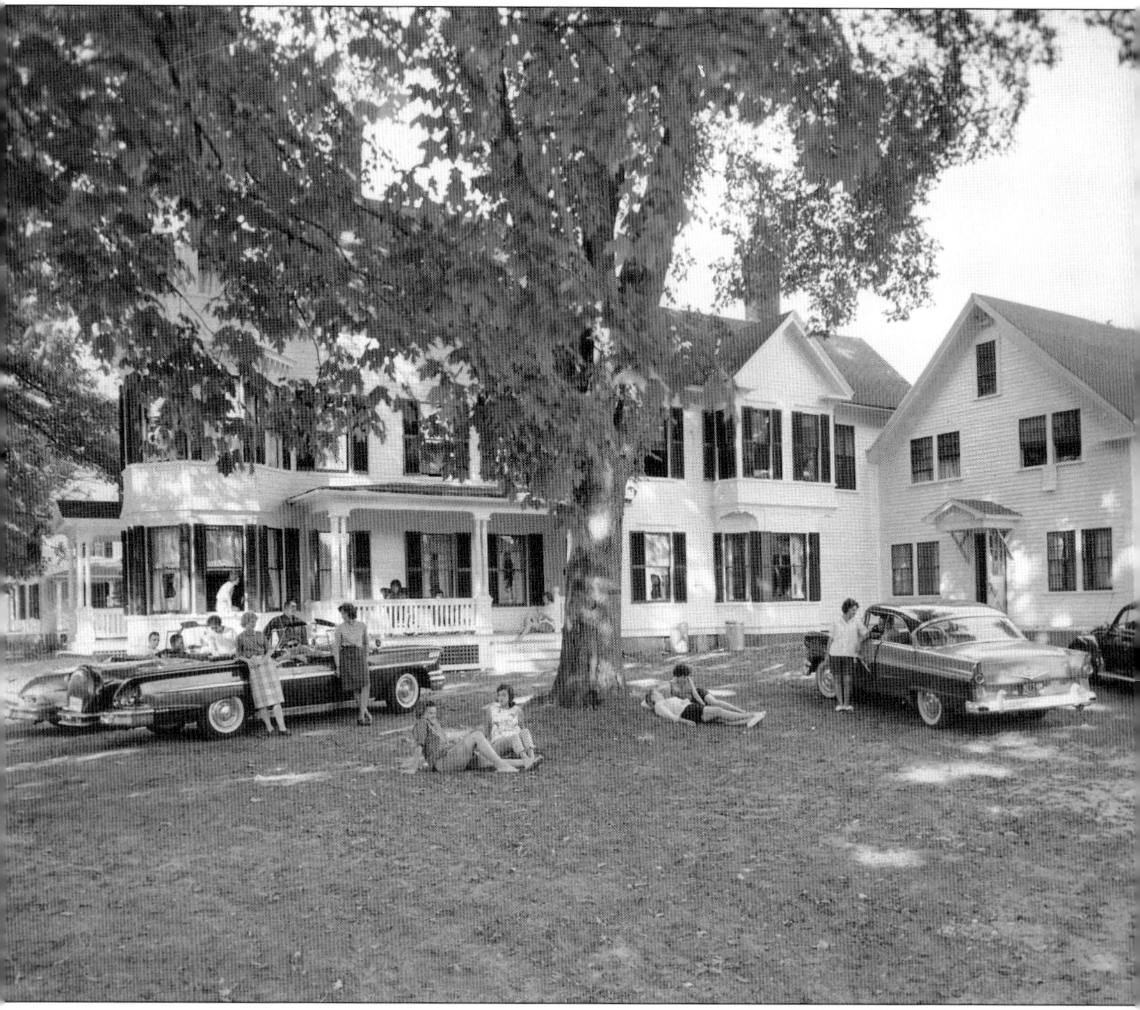

Sanborn Hall, on Rush Road, was built in the mid-19th century, sometime after 1858. The former residence of Dr. George H. Sanborn, it was acquired by the college for a women's residence. Alumna Deborah Spring Reed recalled that Sanborn House had a dining hall for women, who were not allowed to share a commons with male students. Gerda Peterich took this picture of Sanborn House in 1964. (Courtesy of Henniker Historical Society.)

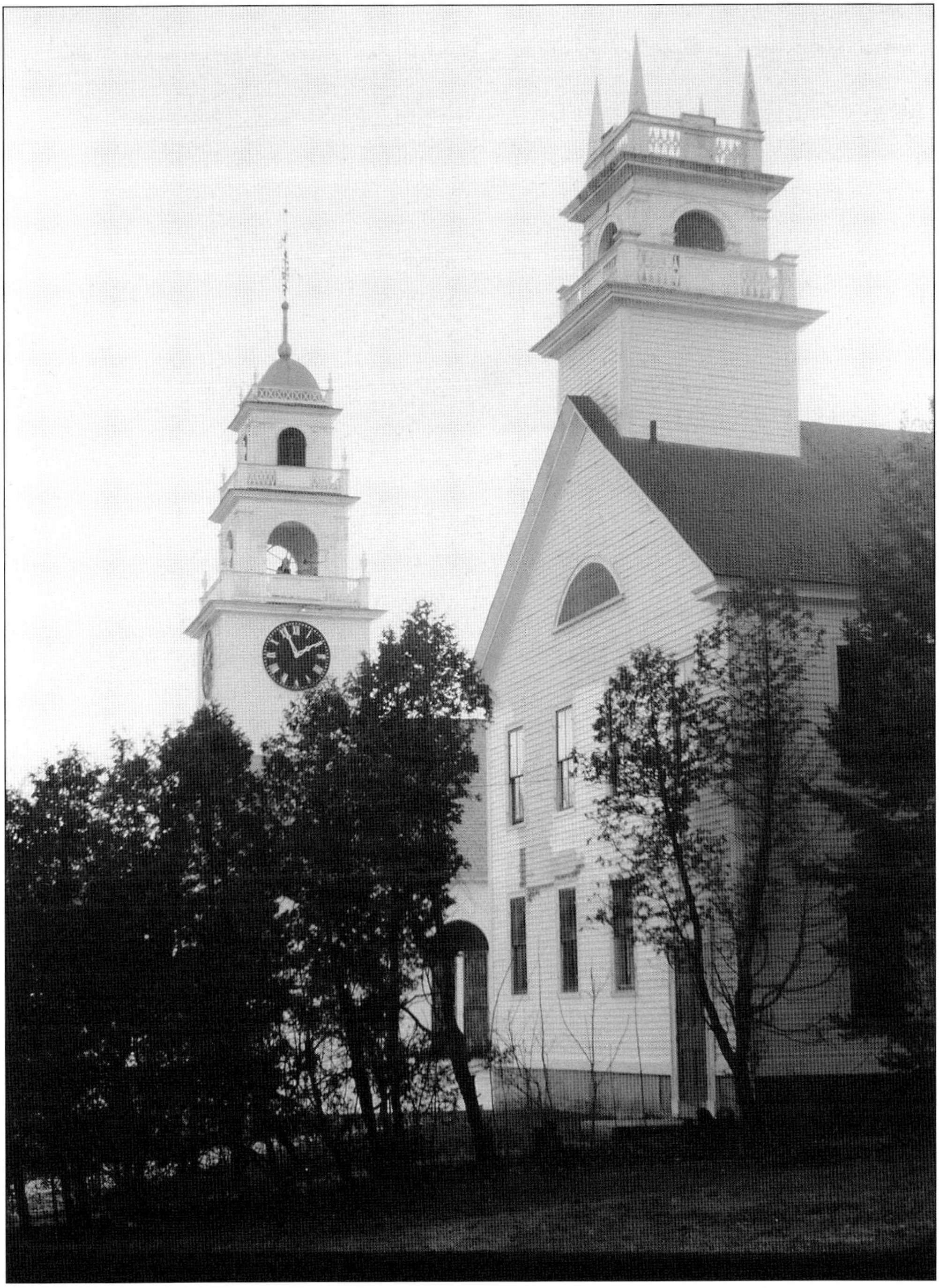

On the left, Henniker Congregational Church, built around 1800, is located on Maple Street. The congregation allowed the college to use the church for commencements and inaugurations of new presidents. Ralph Edwards, church choir director, was also music instructor at the college and founder of the student glee club, the Pilgrimaires. On the right is Academy Hall, built around 1800, which was rented to the college for many years for classroom and meeting space. It now houses Henniker Historical Society.

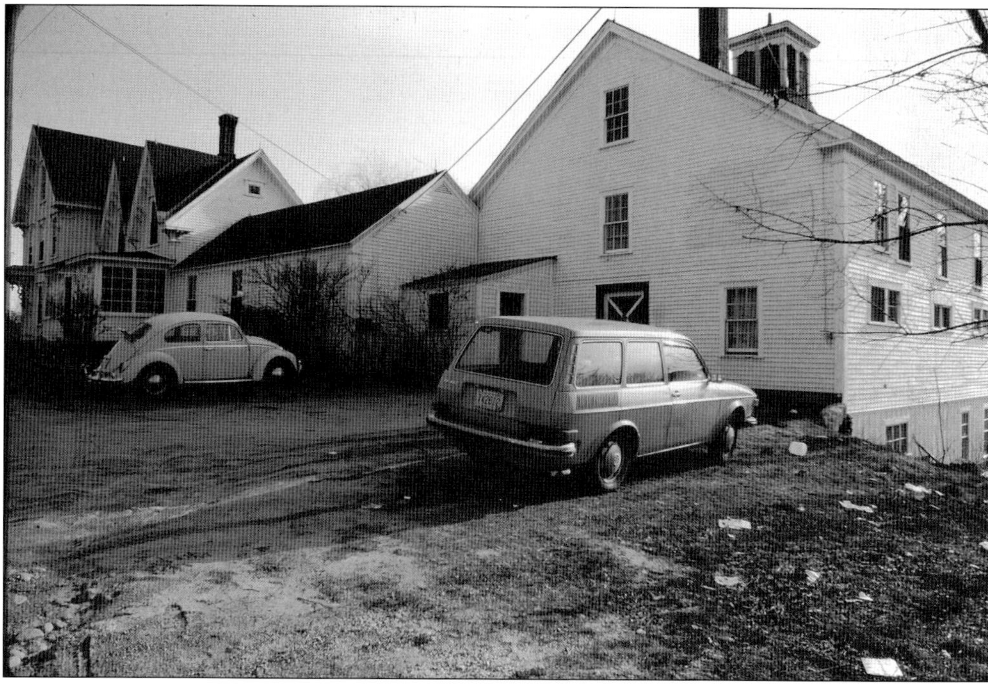

Rowe House and Barn, located at 234 Western Avenue, are named for the family of former owner Alden Rowe. The farmhouse and barn were constructed around 1880.

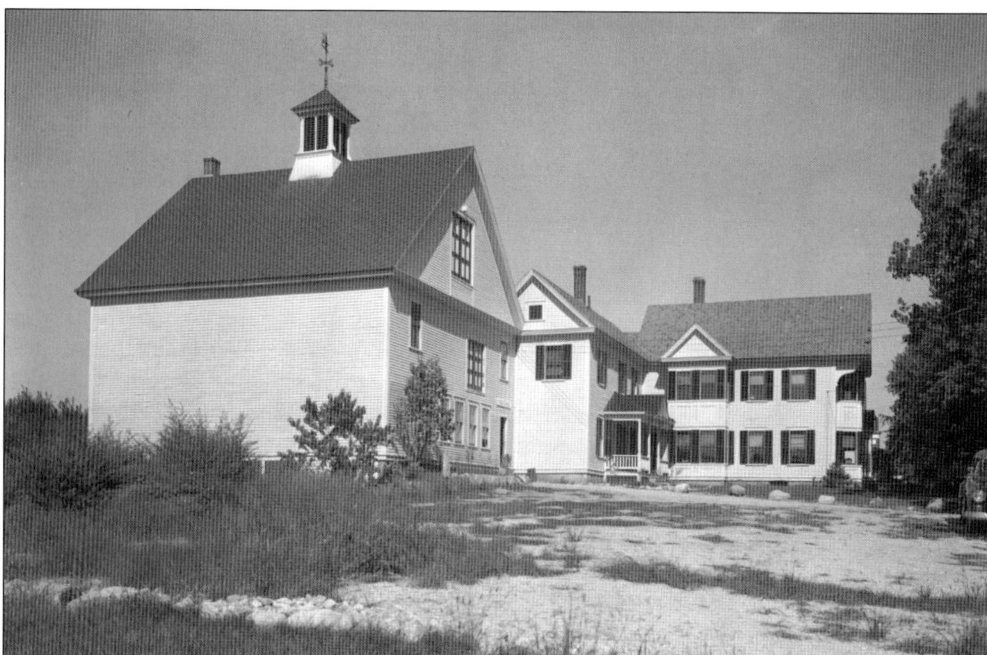

This house on Hall Avenue was once a college building and now is White Birch Community Center. Built around 1860 as a private residence, the house was converted to laboratories and offices and called Faculty Hall. (Courtesy of Hillsborough Historical Society.)

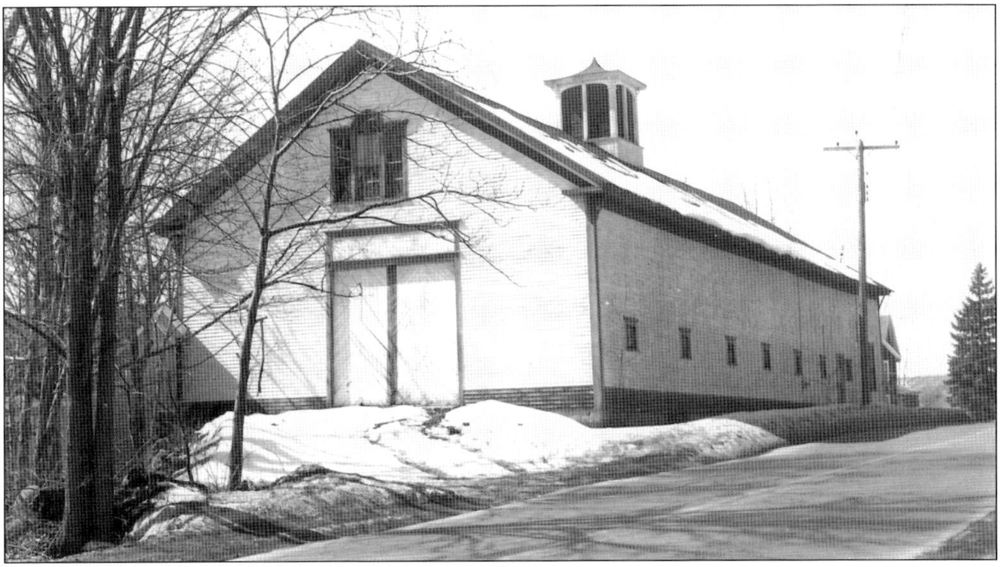

This classic dairy barn, formerly on Western Avenue, was built after 1892 and owned by Fannie Worthen Bennett, wife of Mark Heber Bennett, who used the barn to keep cows in town during the winter months. During summers, the cows went to pasture outside the village center. Mrs. Bennett rented the barn to Louis and Charles Damour, for use as a garage. New England College acquired the property and eventually named it Theatre Barn. (Courtesy of Henniker Historical Society.)

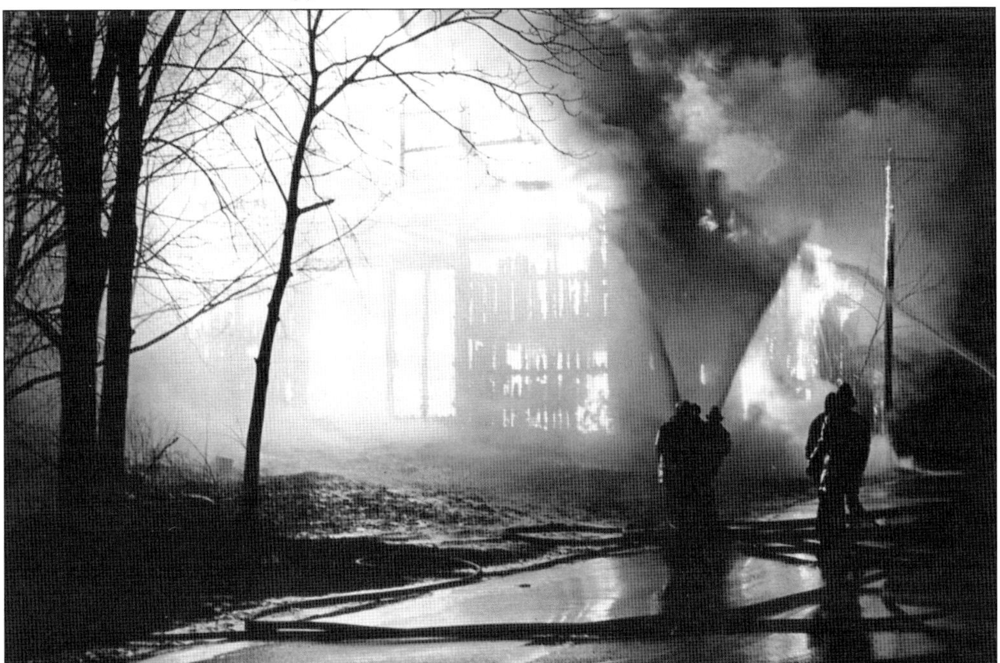

During a town meeting in 1974, the alarm was raised and Henniker's volunteer firefighters responded to fight a fire at what was by then known as Theatre Barn. The town meeting was postponed, but despite valiant efforts, the building was a total loss. (Courtesy of Henniker Historical Society.)

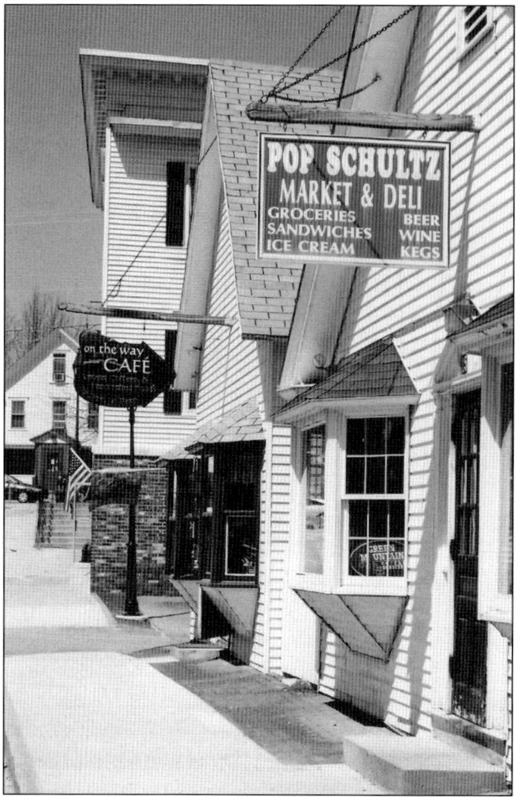

The college has provided many business opportunities for entrepreneurs like Brad and Rindy Routon, who owned and operated Pop Schultz Market & Deli, which was very popular with students. The storefront seen below, on Bridge Street near the stone bridge, has been occupied by the Muddy River Playhouse (pictured) and On the Way Café (shown at right) and today is once again a popular café. Buildings near campus are repurposed fairly frequently to meet changing needs and interests of the student population.

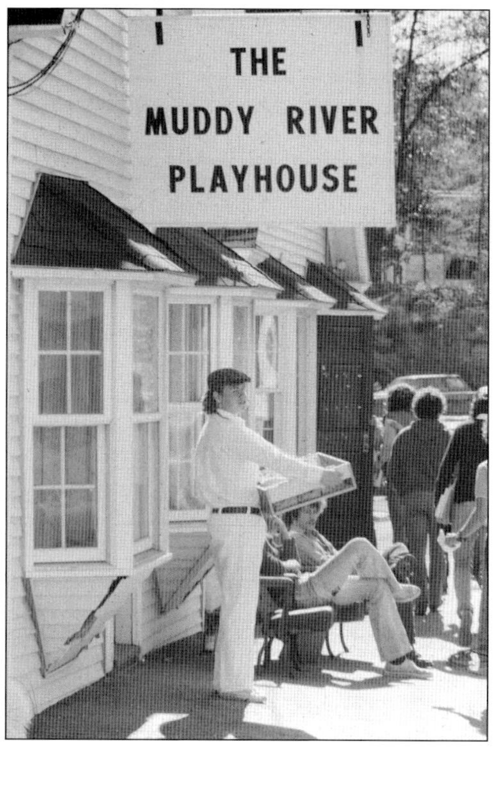

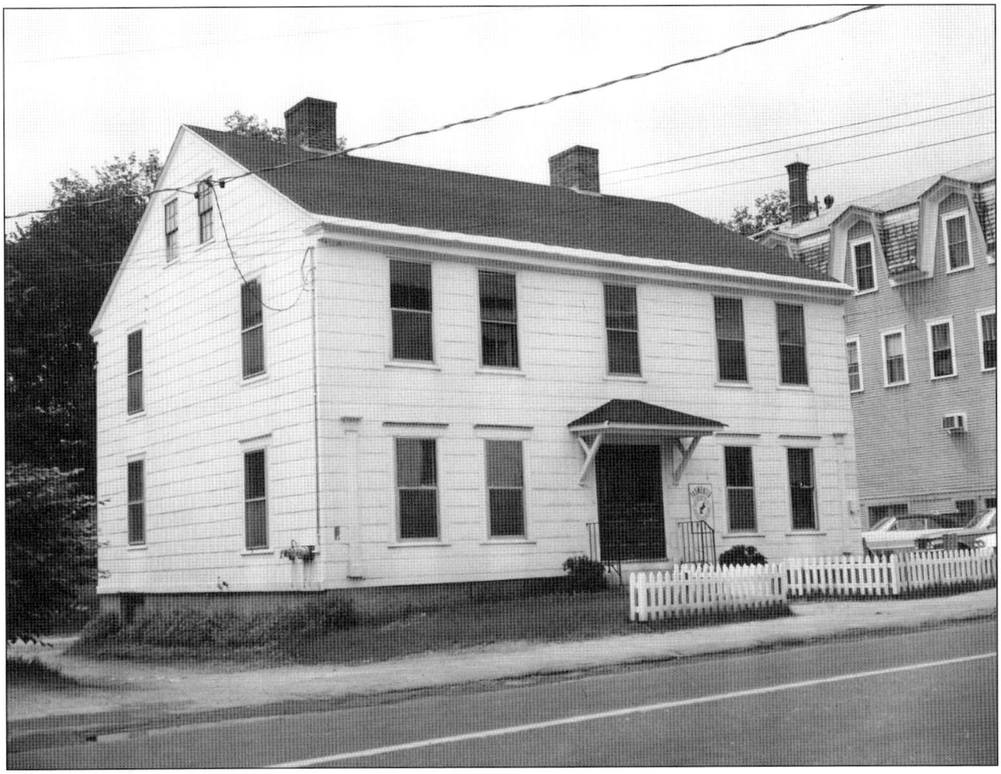

This building, constructed around 1800 and known in the early 1900s as Riverside Hotel, is located between Proctor Square and the Contoocook River. It housed a doctor's office for many years. The college's health center was briefly located in this building.

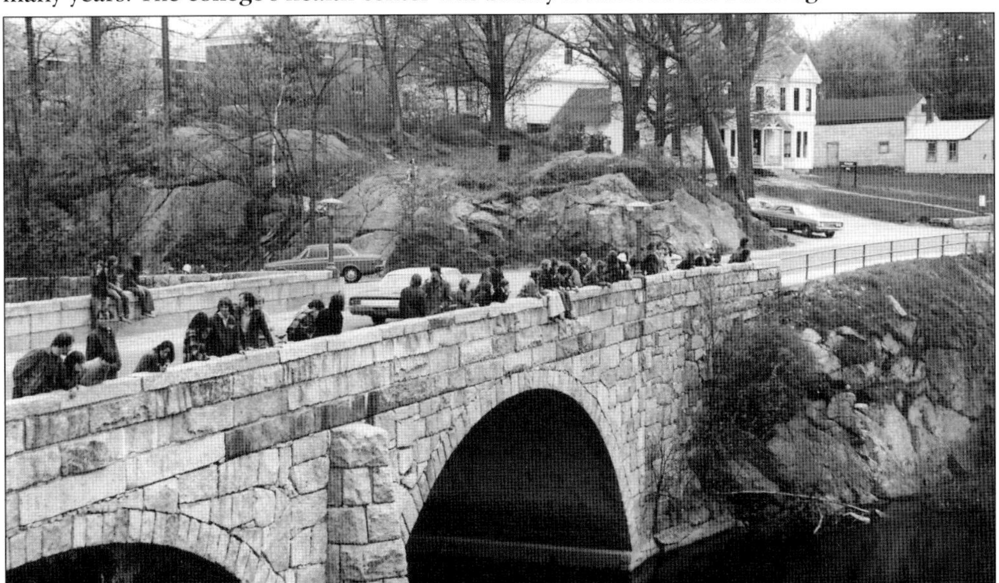

A historic stone bridge spans the Contoocook River, which winds through the center of campus. Every day, hundreds of students, employees, and townspeople cross the bridge from the center of town to the campus across the river.

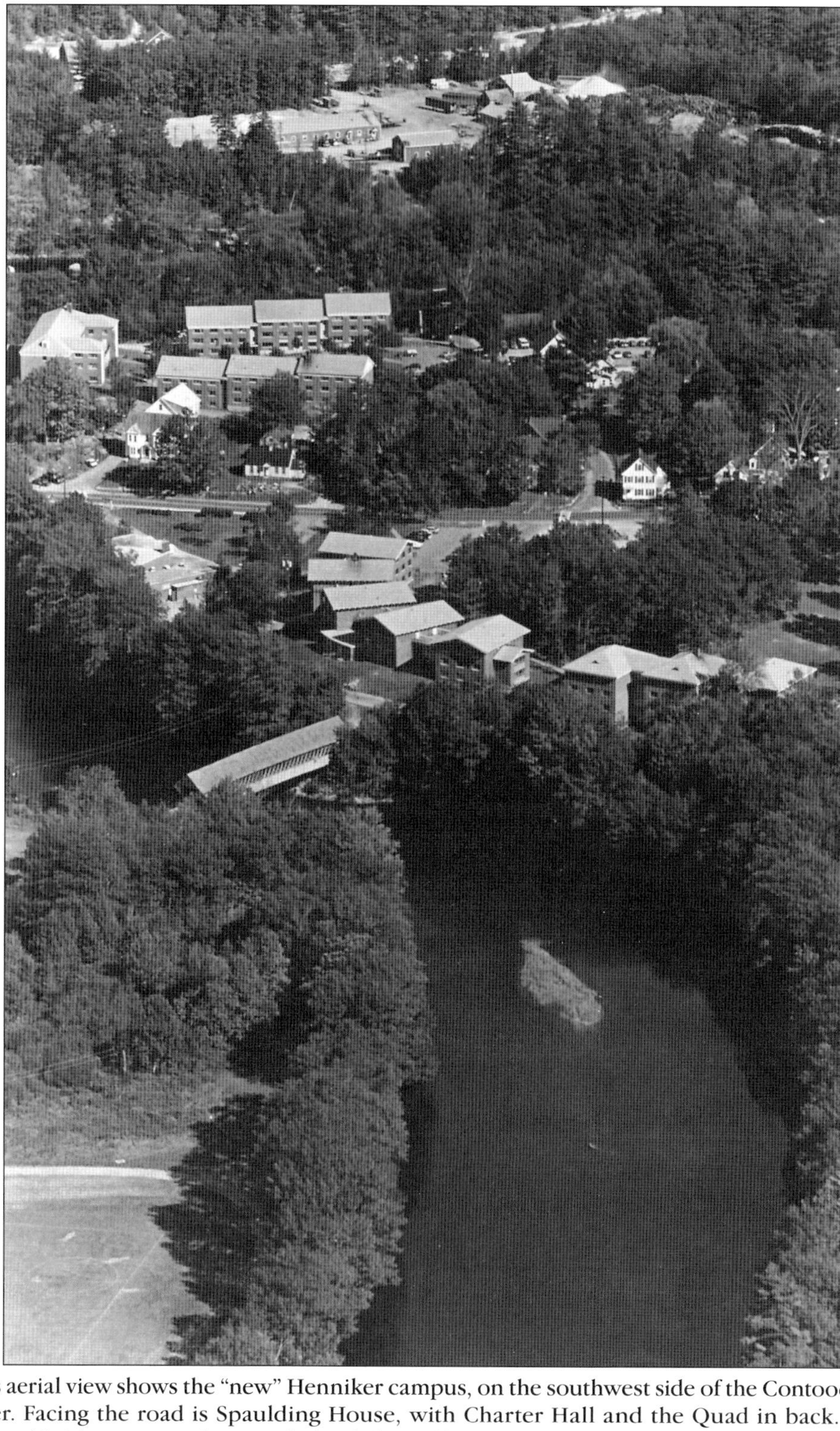

This aerial view shows the "new" Henniker campus, on the southwest side of the Contoocook River. Facing the road is Spaulding House, with Charter Hall and the Quad in back. The covered bridge crosses the river behind the Colby and West dormitories.

Two

To Thy Dear Portals

New Campus, West of the River

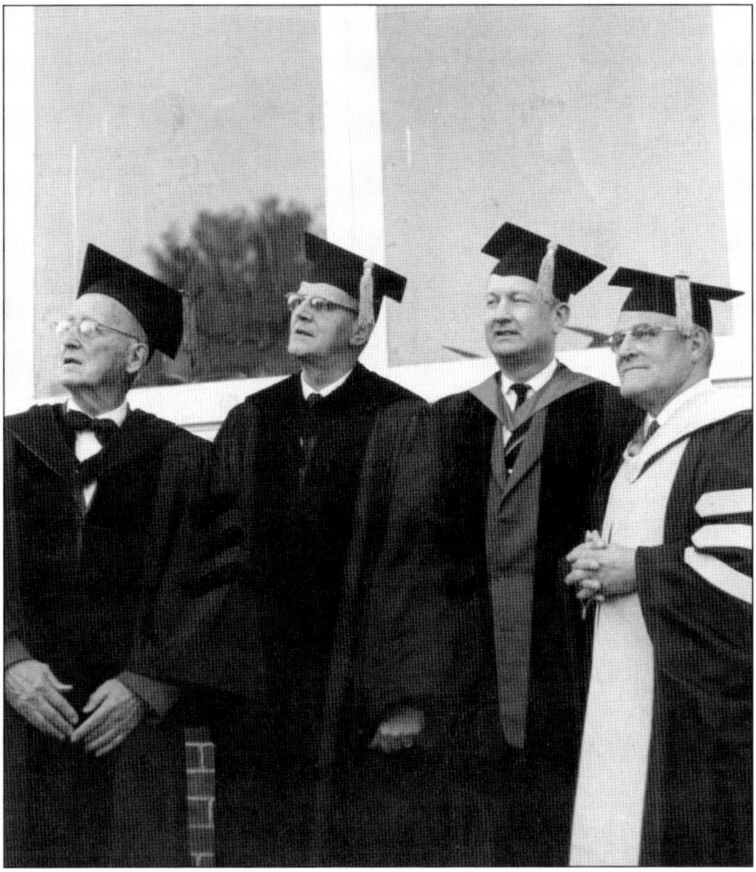

The first four presidents of New England College are pictured; they are, from left to right, Dr. Laurie D. Cox, Dr. William Mandery, Dr. Robert L Campbell, and Dr. H. Raymond Danforth. By the time this image was taken in 1964, the still-young college had a traditional campus with buildings on both sides of the Contoocook River. (Courtesy of Henniker Historical Society.)

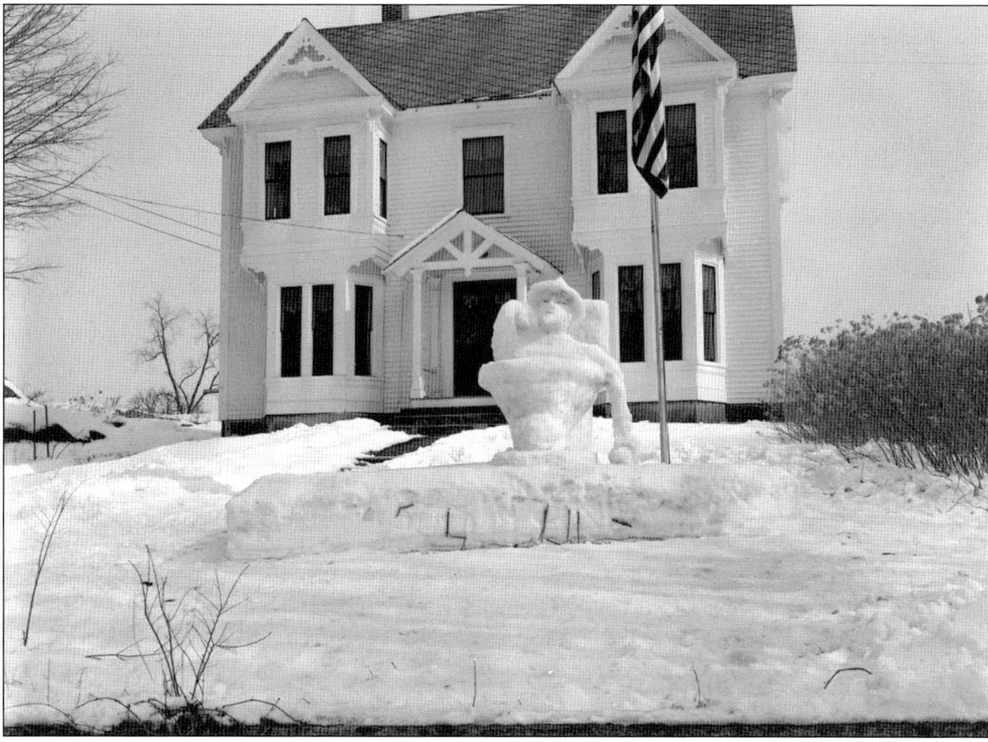

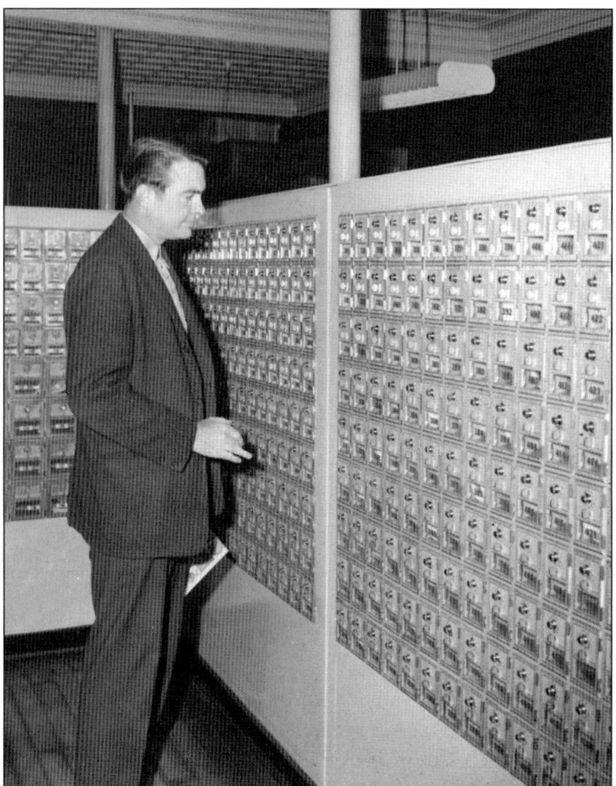

Spaulding Hall, on Bridge Street, was built around 1880. This Victorian house was occupied by the Brady family until it was acquired by the college for use as a library. The Brady farmland behind Spaulding Hall was used for construction of dormitories and the Charter Hall student union. This early image dates from the winter of 1959. (Courtesy of Hillsborough Historical Society.)

The college's first mailroom was located in Spaulding Hall. Subsequently, the mail room was located in Charter Hall for many years. Here is W. Clapham "Cope" Murray checking his mailbox. Murray joined the faculty in 1962 and served as professor of theatre at the British Campus during his career.

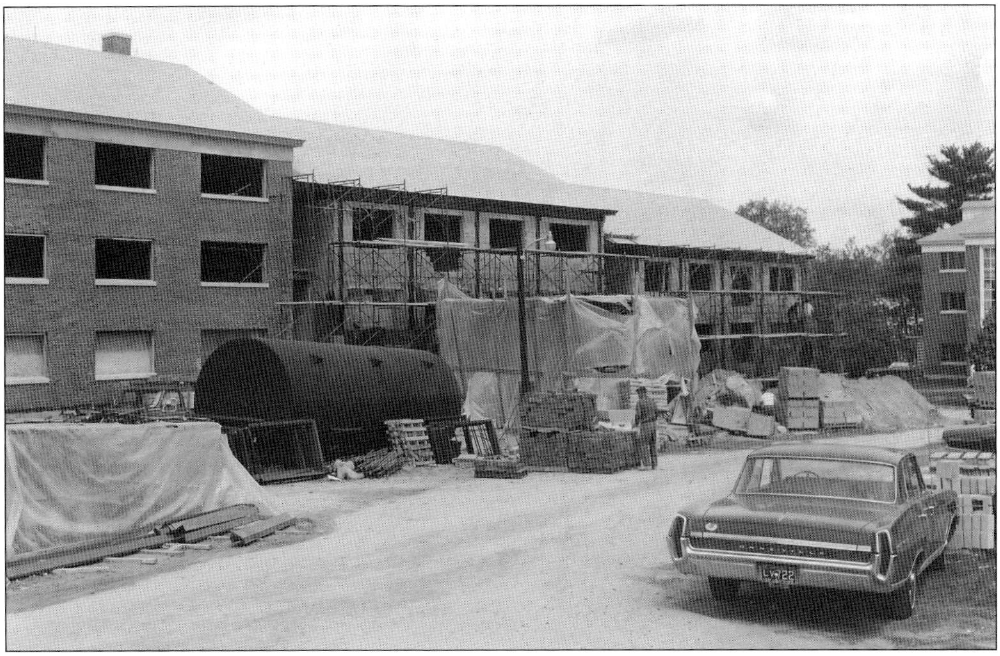

Construction of the Quadrangle dormitories, East and Connor (IV), greatly increased residential space and allowed enrollments to increase. Shown here on the left is East Hall during construction.

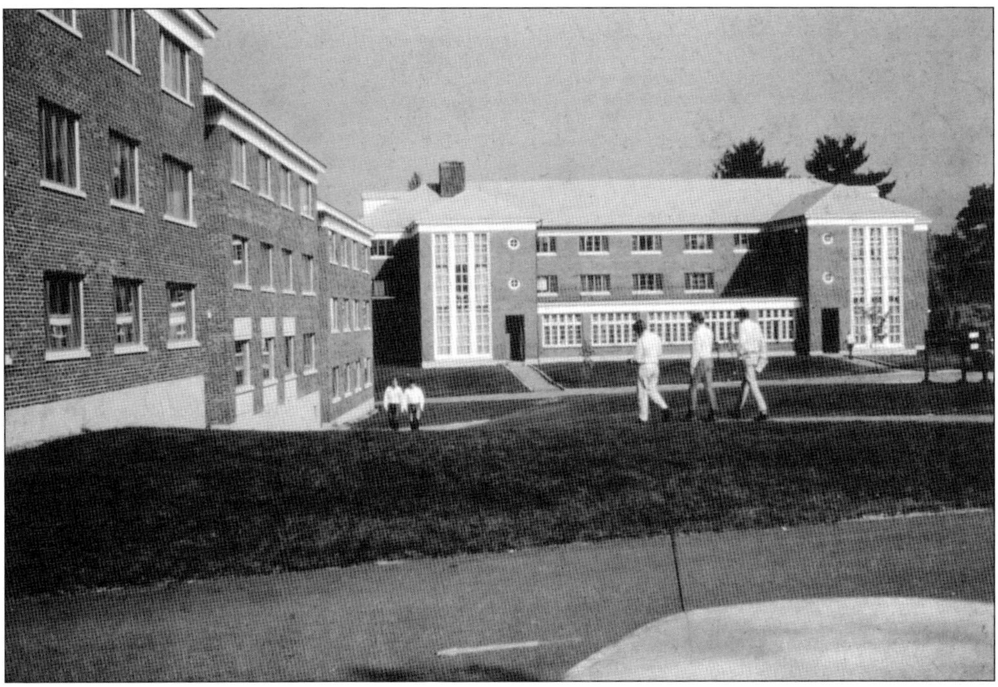

Charter Hall formed one side of the quadrangle bounded by East and Connor dormitories and Union Street. Charter has served as a residence hall and student union. Behind the ground-floor windows is the former James Doon café, where employees and students mingled at lunchtime, now used for a coffee house and dance studio.

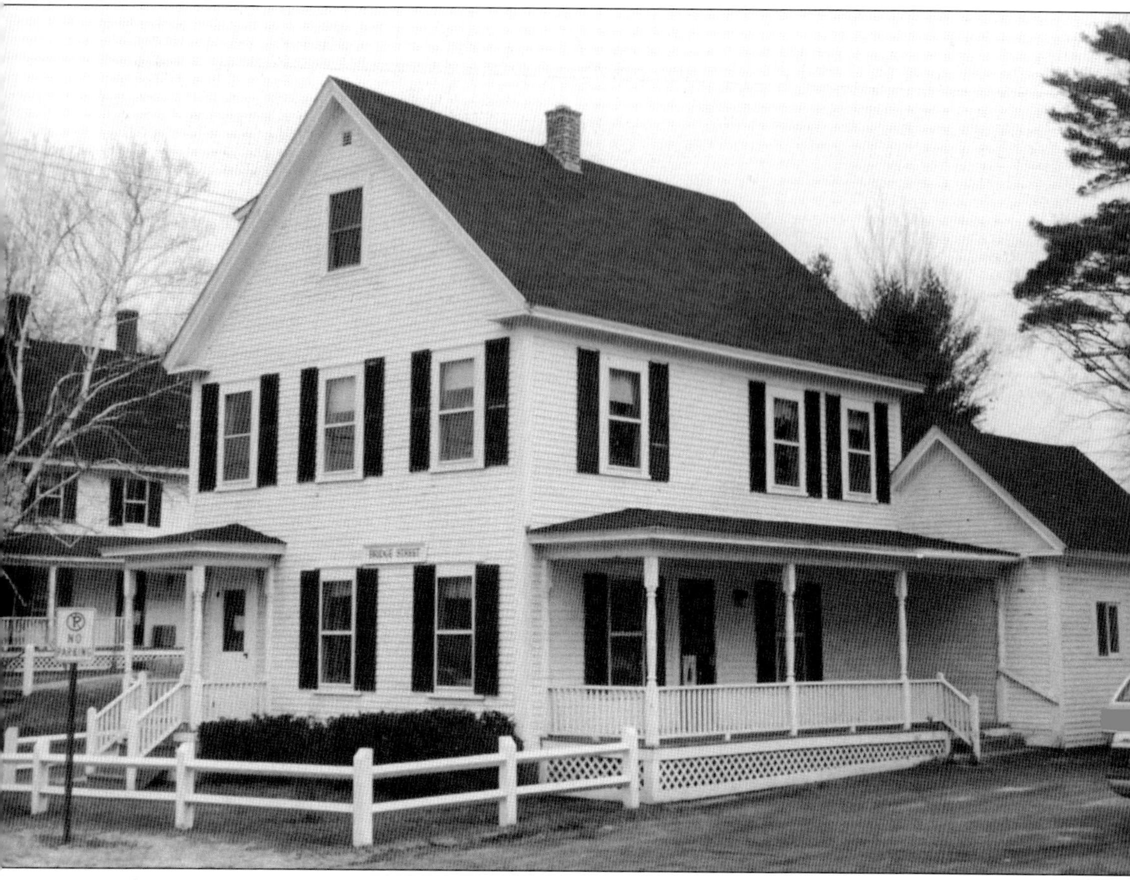

College student John "Jay" Maragon ('77) purchased this house at the corner of Bridge and Union Streets, renovated it with help from Prof. John Lyons, and rented rooms to classmates while he completed his degree. Now called Bridge Street House, the building was acquired by the college for office and classroom space. Just visible on the left is Lewin House, which was built in the early 20th century and provides office space for faculty and paraprofessional staff.

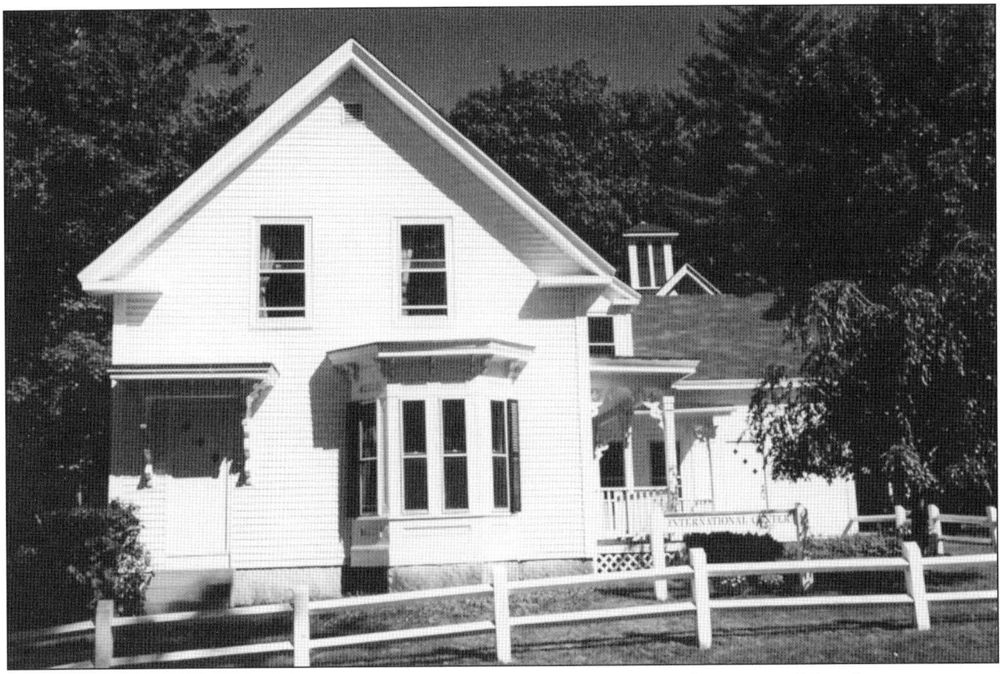

Fitch House, also on Bridge Street, dates from about 1880 and is named for former owner Clarence Fitch. The bay-windowed office of Dr. Montford "Bunny" Sayce was left open around the clock as a lounge for dedicated "Sayceans," who gathered there to enjoy a cup of tea and endless spirited debates about literature, philosophy, culture, international relations, and politics. Sayce created the international administration major and coached many successful teams for intercollegiate Model United Nations.

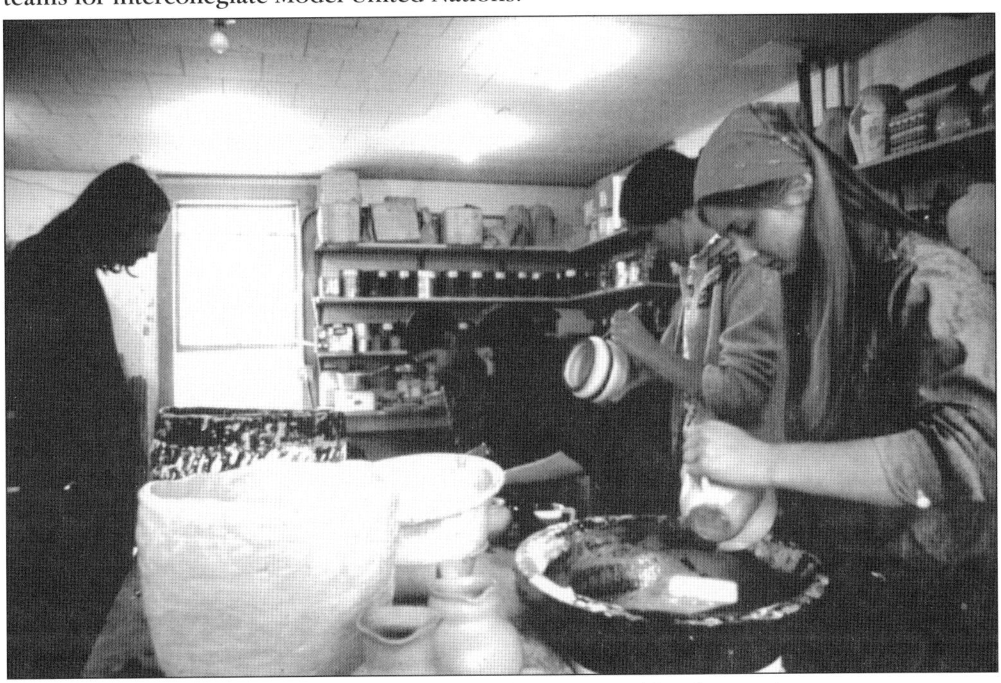

Fitch Barn housed the pottery studio and darkrooms used by the art department.

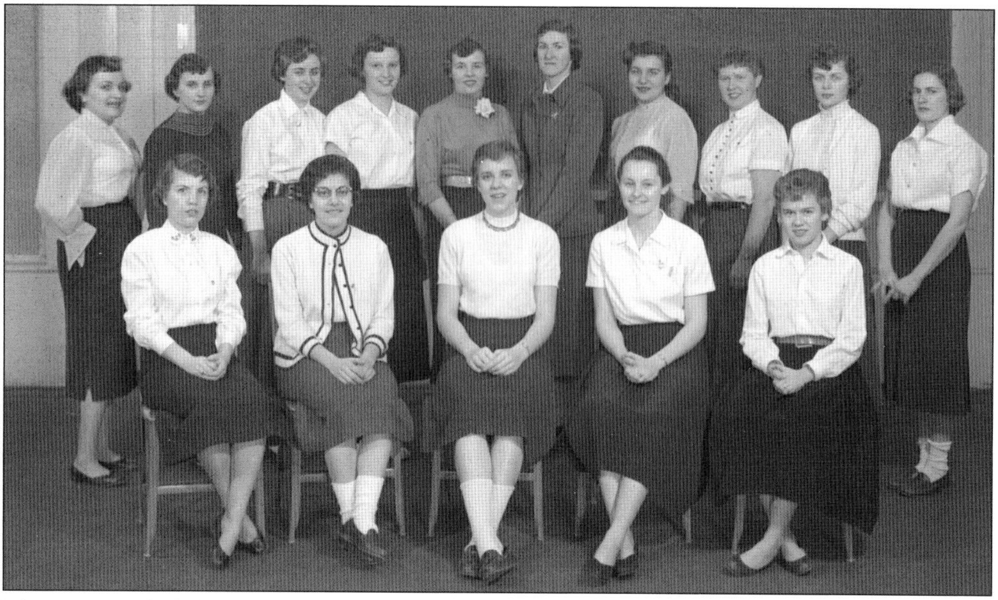

The sisters of Alpha Epsilon sorority in 1954 are, from left to right, (first row) Marianne Vincent, Patricia Mauro, Kathleen French, Carolee Cleveland, and Sandra White; (second row) Frances Tedesco, Isabelle Laundrie, Ruth Moore, Ann Willey, Barbara Hunter, Virginia Estes, Lorraine Tedesco, Jane Sawyer, Charlotte Vigue, and Donita Holder Lane. (Courtesy of Hillsborough Historical Society.)

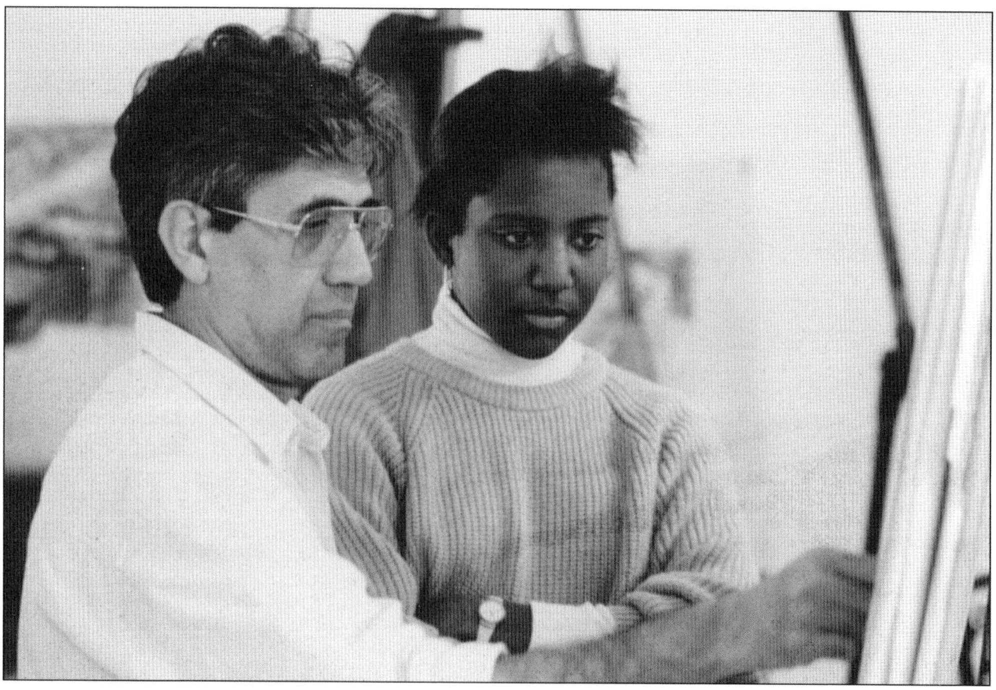

Farid Haddad, professor of art, joined the faculty in 1979. Many students selected his foundational drawing course to meet a college requirement and discovered to their surprise that they had creative talents they had not recognized. Many of these courses were in Tower Hall studios.

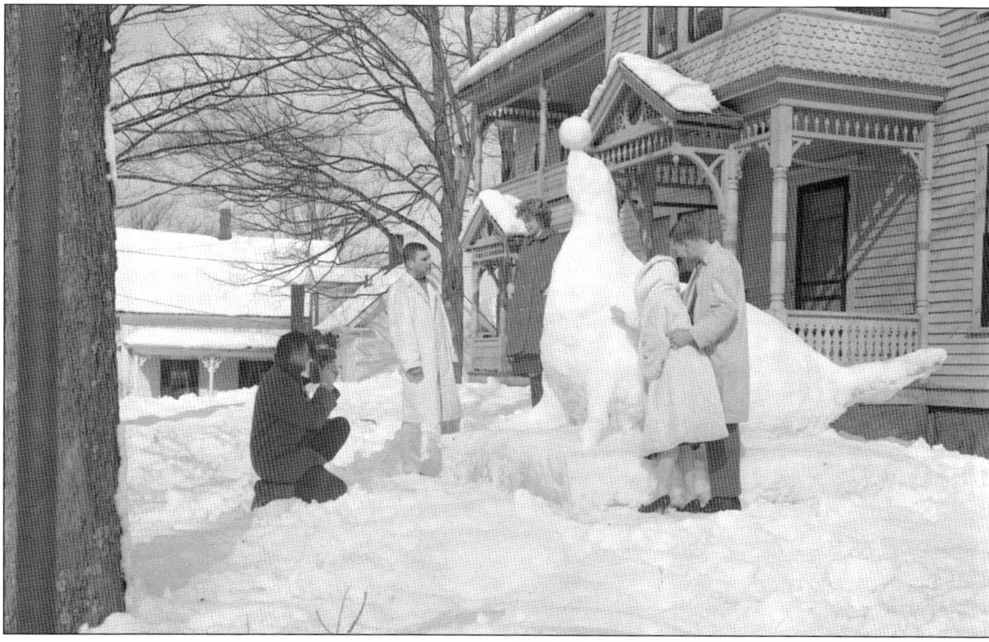

Pictured in front of Tower Hall admiring a Winter Carnival sculpture of a seal balancing a ball on its nose are, from left to right, an unidentified photographer from a Boston television station, John Flannigan, Debbie Spring Reed ('61), and an unidentified couple. (Courtesy of Hillsborough Historical Society.)

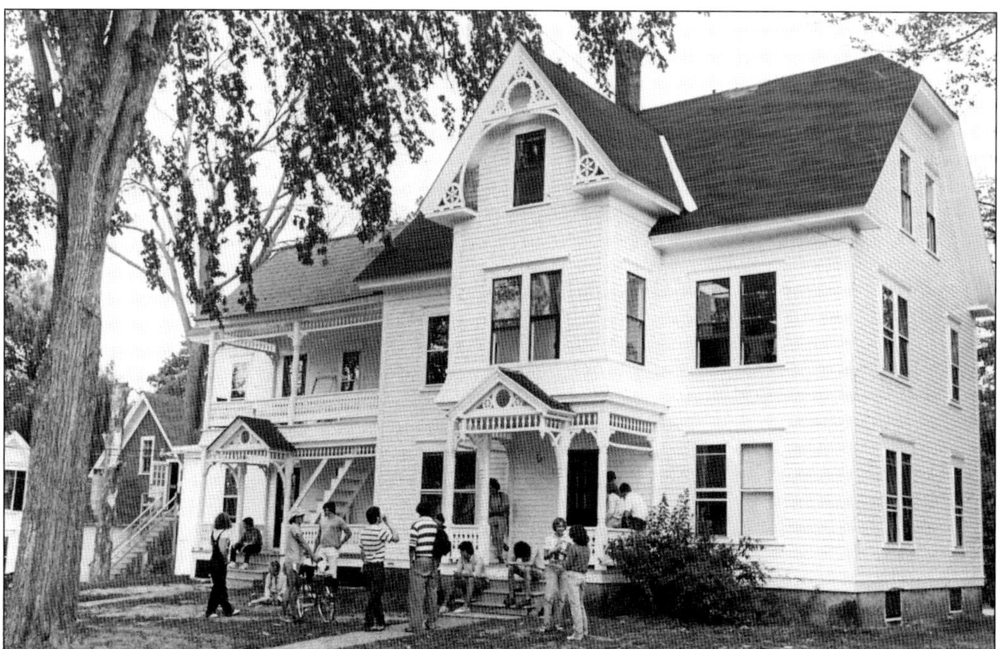

Tower Hall was built around 1880. In the early 1900s, the house was owned by Dean Morrison. In good weather, students linger outside Tower, hoping the art professors will announce a day outdoors rather than in the studio.

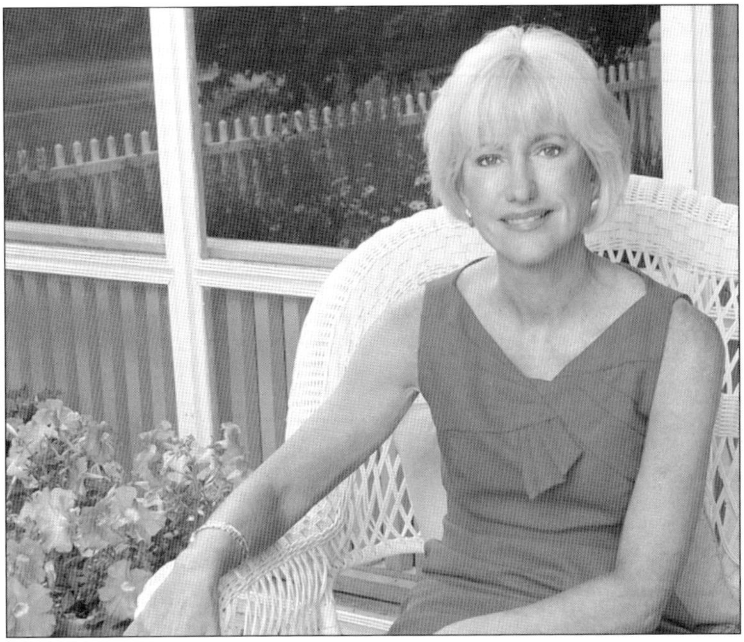

Dr. Michele D. Perkins, college president and professor of theatre, joined the college in 2001 and was appointed as president in 2007. Among her many accomplishments are significant growth in online program enrollment and a successful capital campaign enabling numerous campus improvements and construction of the John Lyons Center.

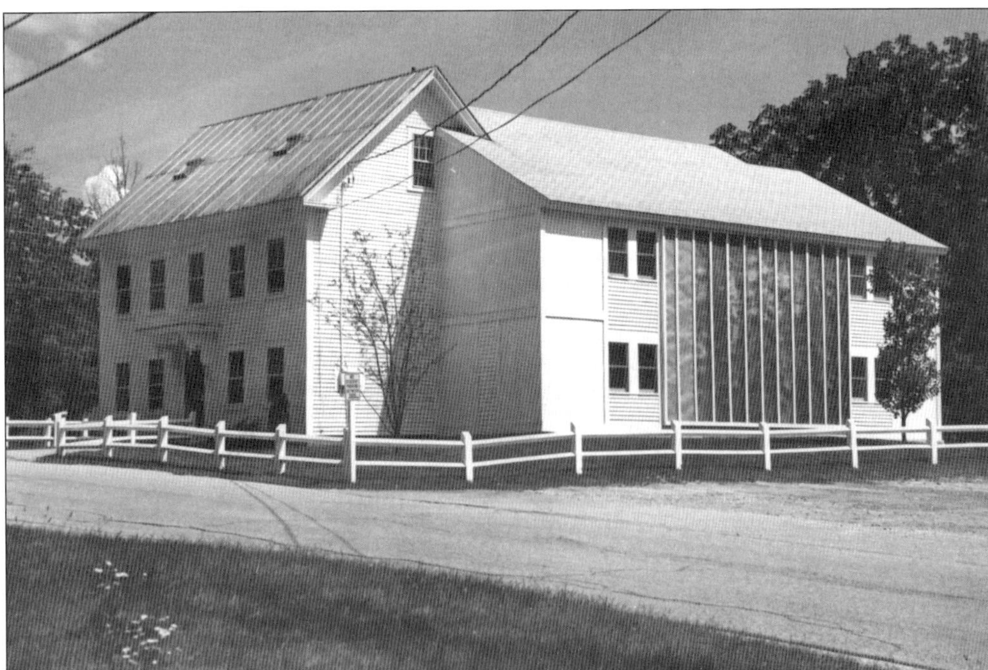

Gone from Depot Hill Road now is Larter Hall. Constructed in 1880, it was the Hiram Twiss farm house. It served as a classroom and office building for management and business programs for several decades until it was razed to make room for the John Lyons Center, a more modern educational building. Visible on the side of the building are early solar panels, installed before the technology was perfected.

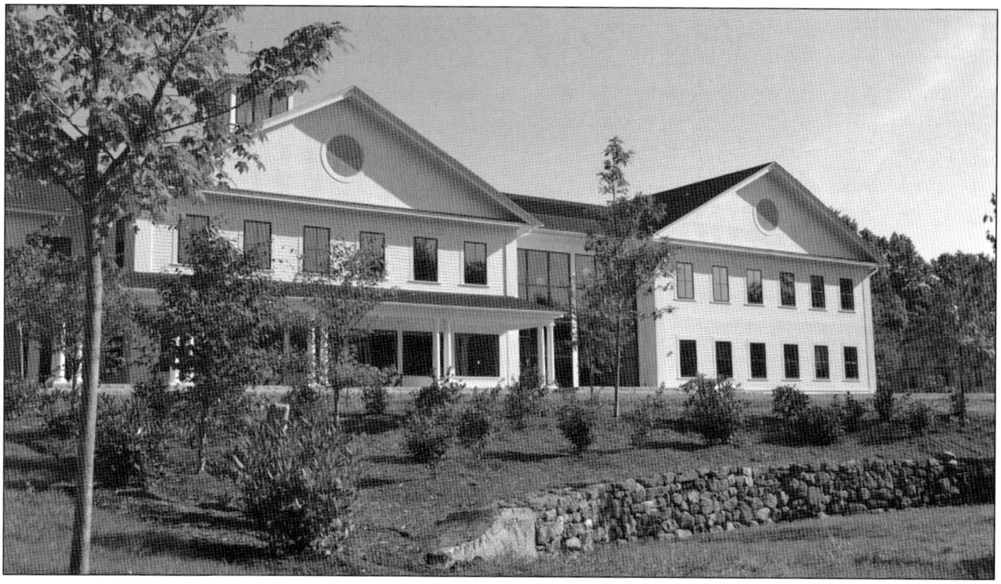

John Lyons Center, a new academic building dedicated in 2016, includes academic, meeting, and faculty space. Built to LEED standards, the building features a two-story learning commons and café surrounded by classrooms, seminar rooms, group study spaces, and offices. Professor Lyons joined the faculty in 1973.

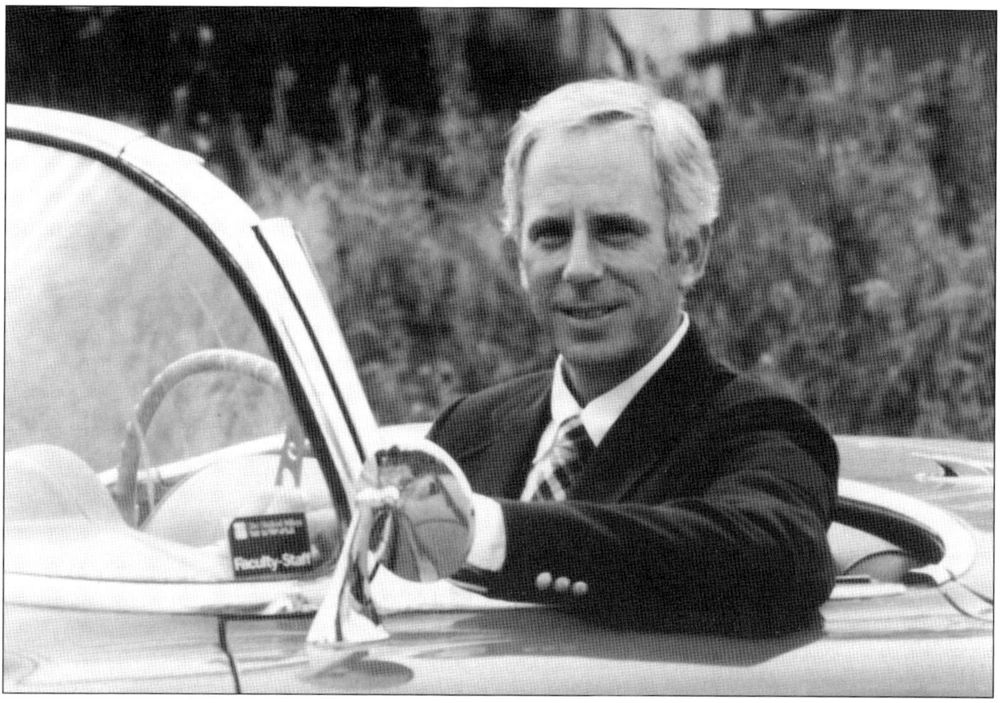

Every year, on the first warm spring day, Prof. John Lyons drove to school in his bright red Corvette. He found the car abandoned behind a barn in 1970, three years before he began teaching at New England College. With help from alum Philip "Skip" Hustis ('70), Professor Lyons completely restored the car and gave it the memorable license plate "57Vett." (Courtesy of John Lyons.)

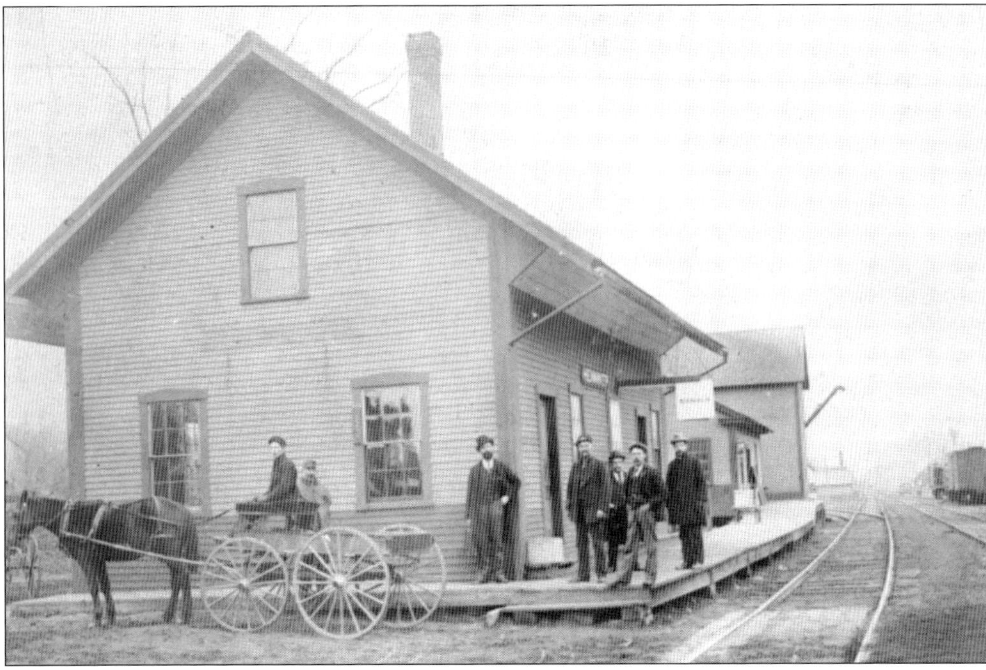

The original Henniker Railroad Station (pictured), was constructed in 1850. Per Gilbert, this building was moved to a nearby location around 1900, when the Boston and Maine Railroad built the present depot, which now houses the Currier Alumni Center. (Courtesy of Hillsborough Historical Society.)

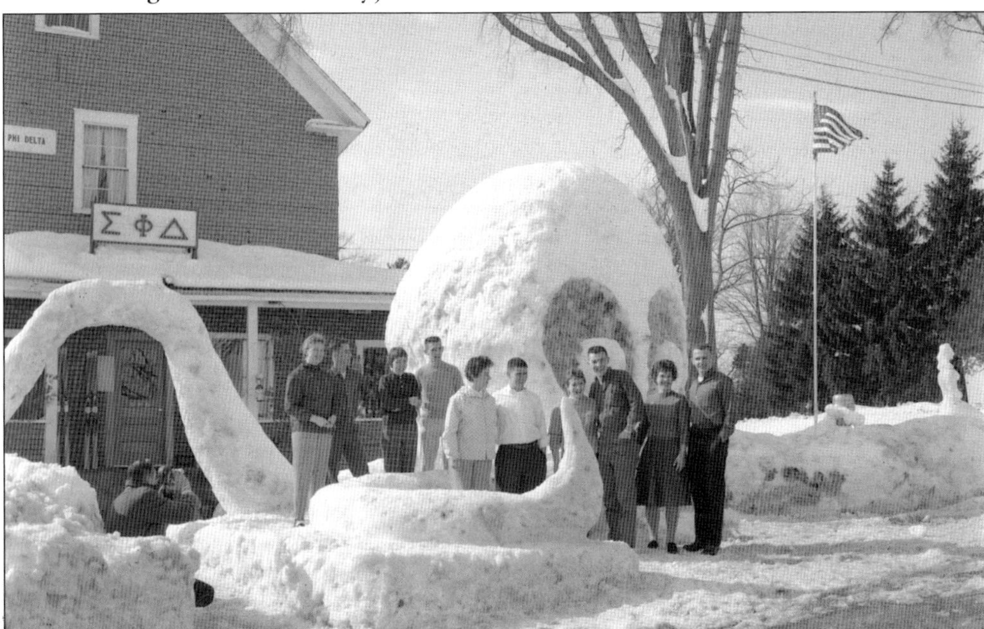

On the opposite side of Depot Hill Road, across the road from Currier Alumni Center, is the Science Building. It was constructed on the site where this Sigma Delta fraternity house was formerly located. This is the fraternity house that was repurposed from a grain store, as described in the introduction.

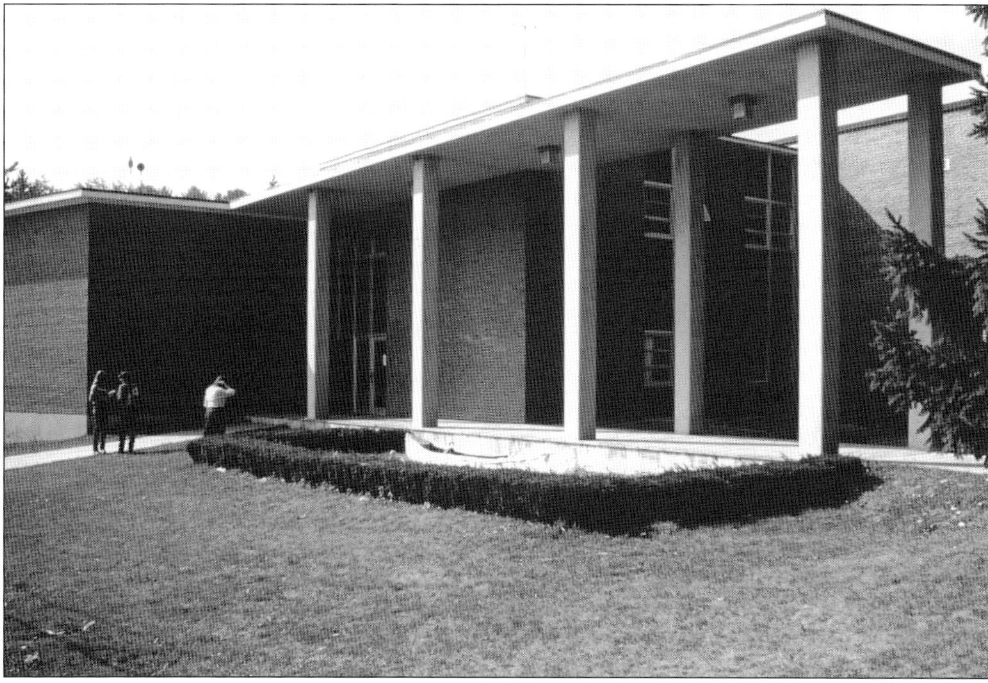

The Science Building, formerly called the New Science Building, is located on Depot Hill Road and houses a theater, classrooms, and laboratories for courses in graphic design, information systems, and the sciences.

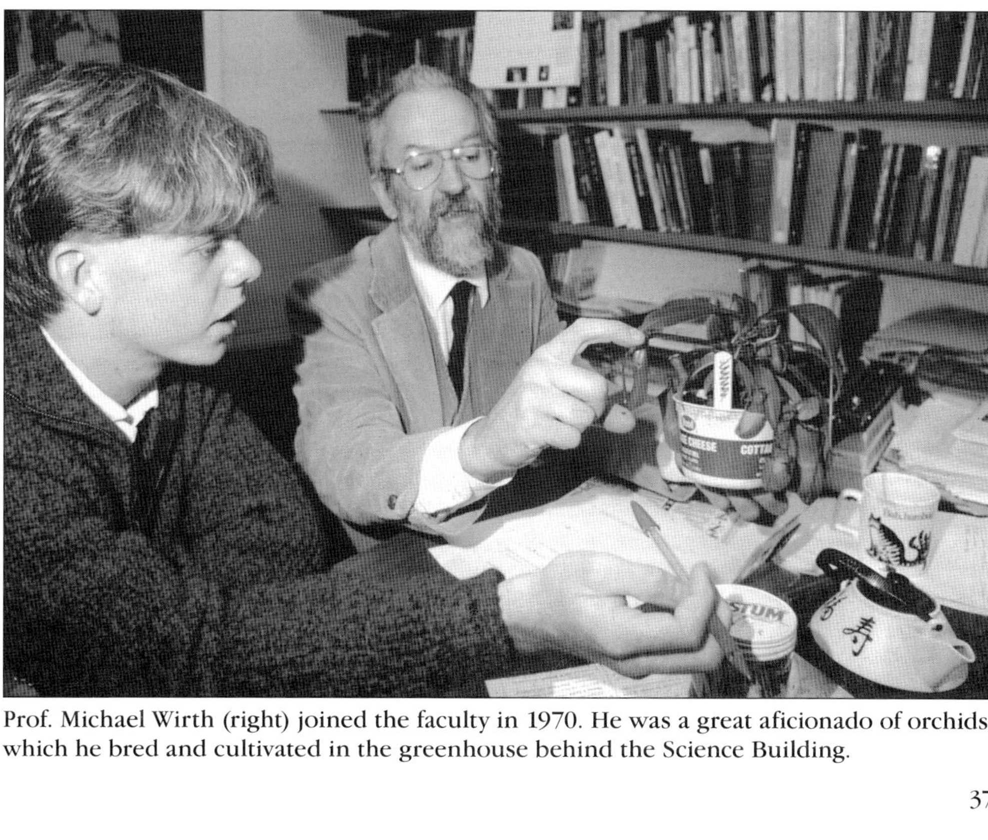

Prof. Michael Wirth (right) joined the faculty in 1970. He was a great aficionado of orchids, which he bred and cultivated in the greenhouse behind the Science Building.

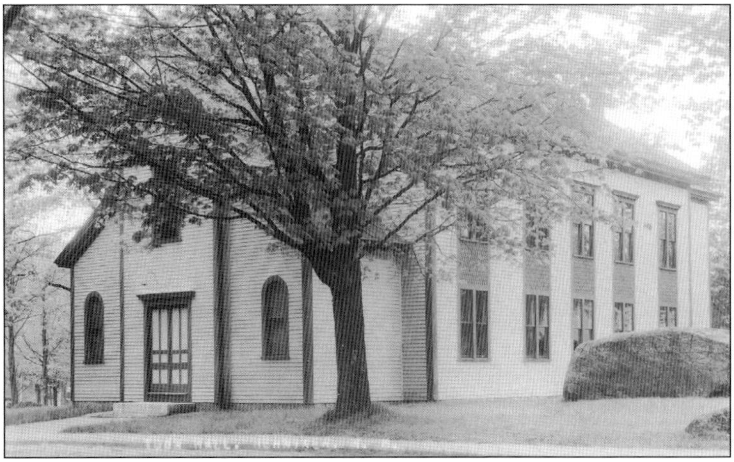

Henniker Town Hall, located on Depot Hill Road, was formerly a meetinghouse, constructed in 1787. In the college's earliest years, this building was rented and used for classroom space and college gatherings. (Courtesy of Henniker Historical Society.)

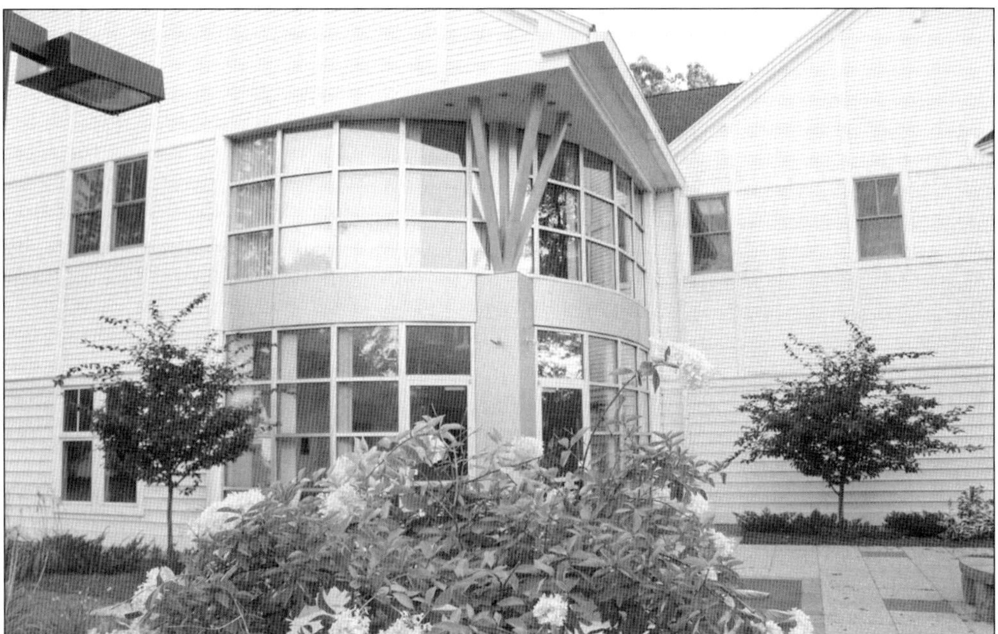

The Center for Educational Innovation was taken from dream to reality under the leadership of Ellen S. Hurwitz, president from 1999 to 2004. This building is located at the corner of Circle Street and Depot Hill Road.

Don W. Melander joined the faculty as a member of the English department at New England College in 1969. He is an author and poet who has shared his great love of literature, particularly Shakespeare, with generations of New England College students.

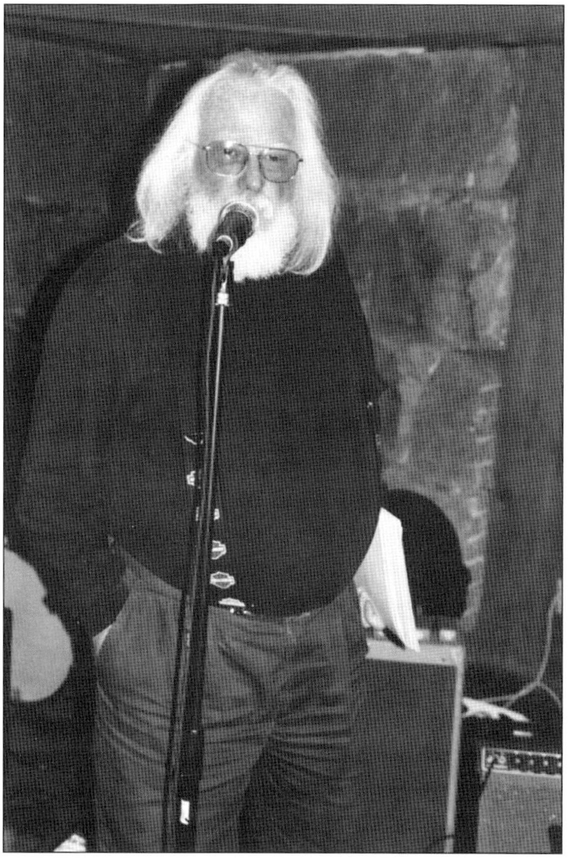

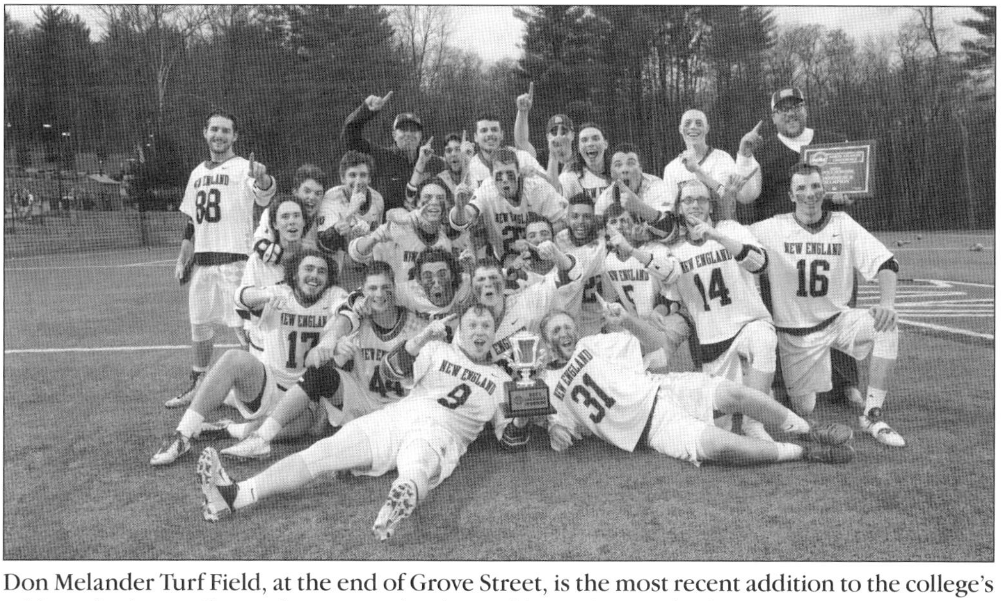

Don Melander Turf Field, at the end of Grove Street, is the most recent addition to the college's athletic facilities. Shown here at Melander Field are the 2016 Pilgrims after winning their third North Atlantic Conference championship in five years. Cocaptain James Carlson, No. 23, was research assistant for this book.

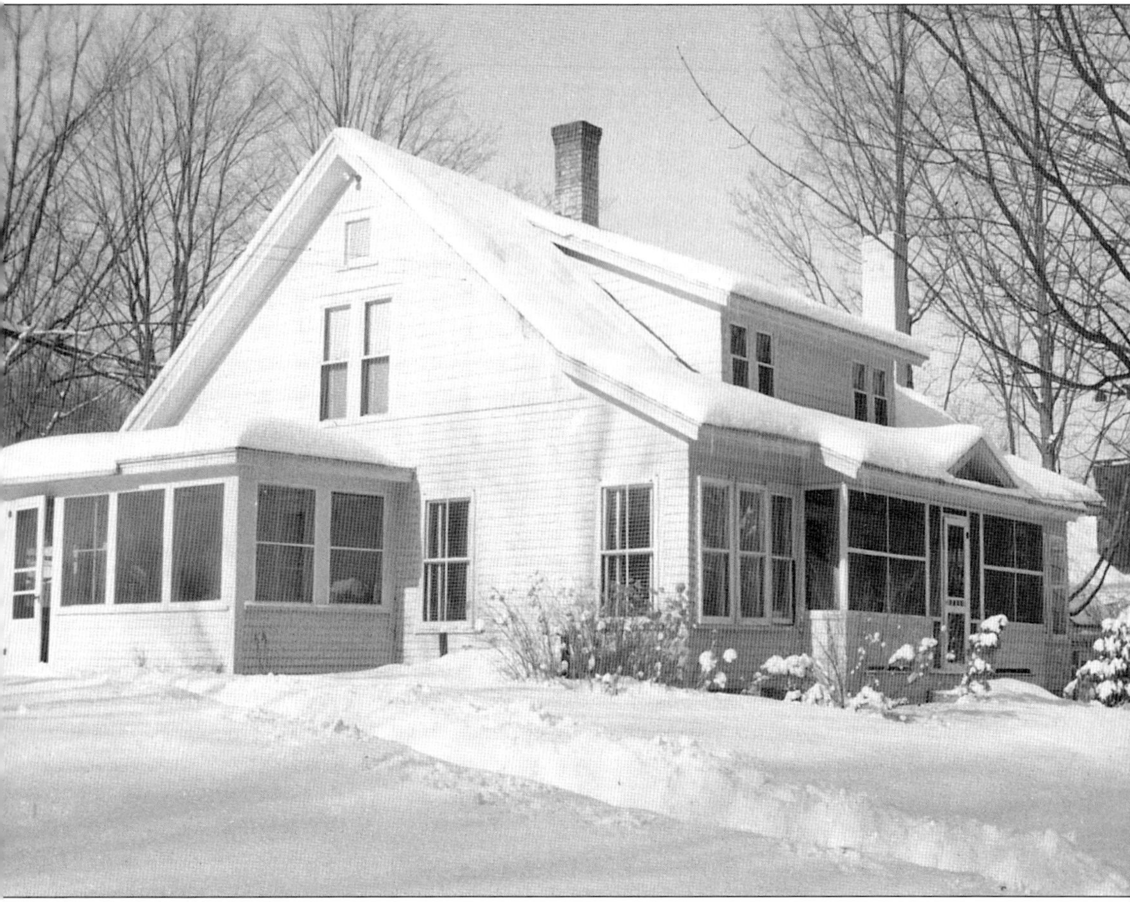

The house pictured here was located at the corner of Bridge and Grove Streets. It was occupied by college presidents Robert Campbell (1956–1958) and Dr. H. Raymond Danforth (1958–1969), then was torn down to make room for the construction of Danforth Library. (Courtesy of Henniker Historical Society.)

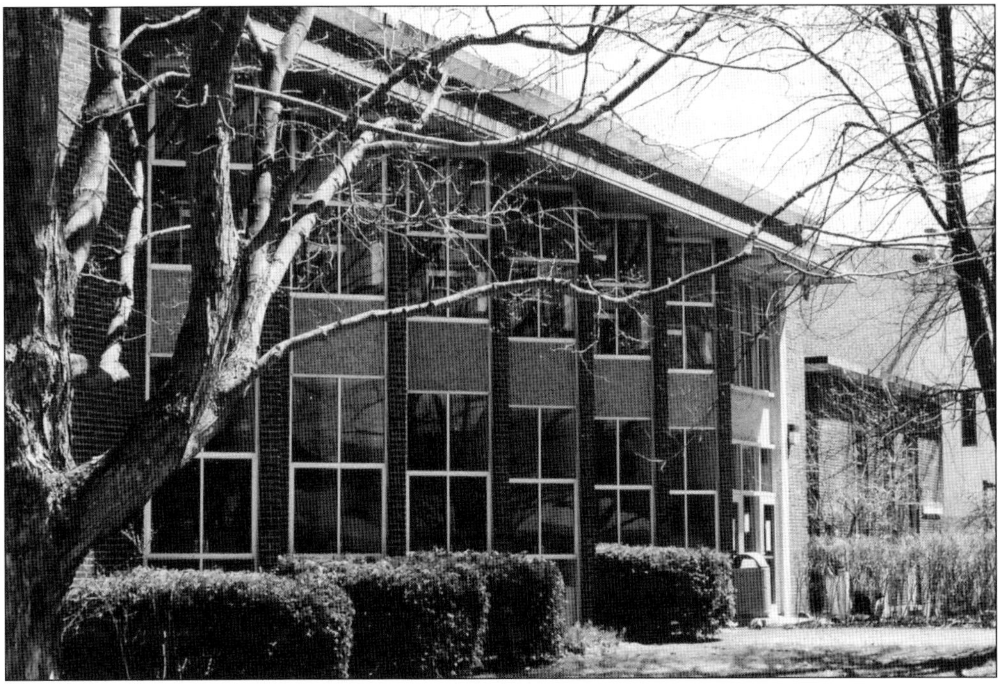

In April 1961, a college spokesperson told a *Pictorial Review* reporter that "Our long range plans . . . are to keep the college small, somewhere between 600 and 700 students. . . . Then, of course, there's that matter of accreditation. For us, that's a long time objective. It'll be the hardest of all to attain. It calls for a well-paid faculty, with advanced degrees as an indication of their competence. It means a library with adequate resources for the courses we offer. There are so many other things involved." It took over a year to raise the final $30,000 for construction of Danforth Library, pictured here. Initial accreditation was achieved in 1967.

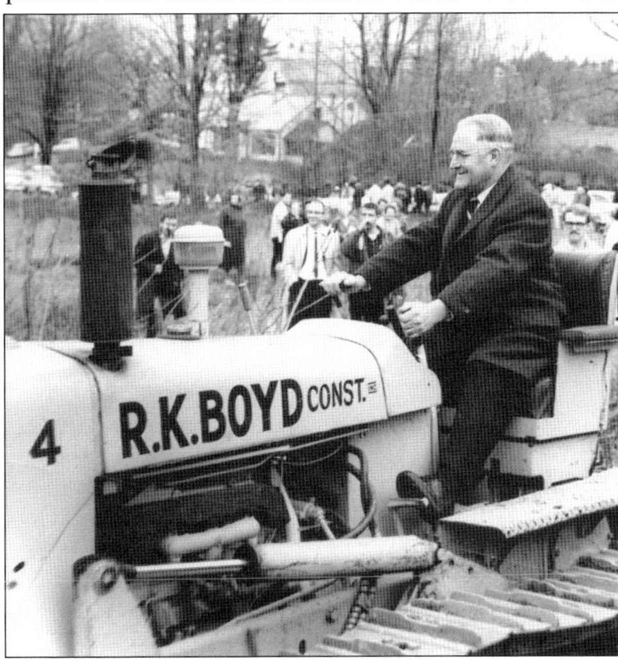

Pres. H. Raymond Danforth broke ground for the library that would bear his name. He later dedicated the building, on October 17, 1976 (Courtesy of Henniker Historical Society.)

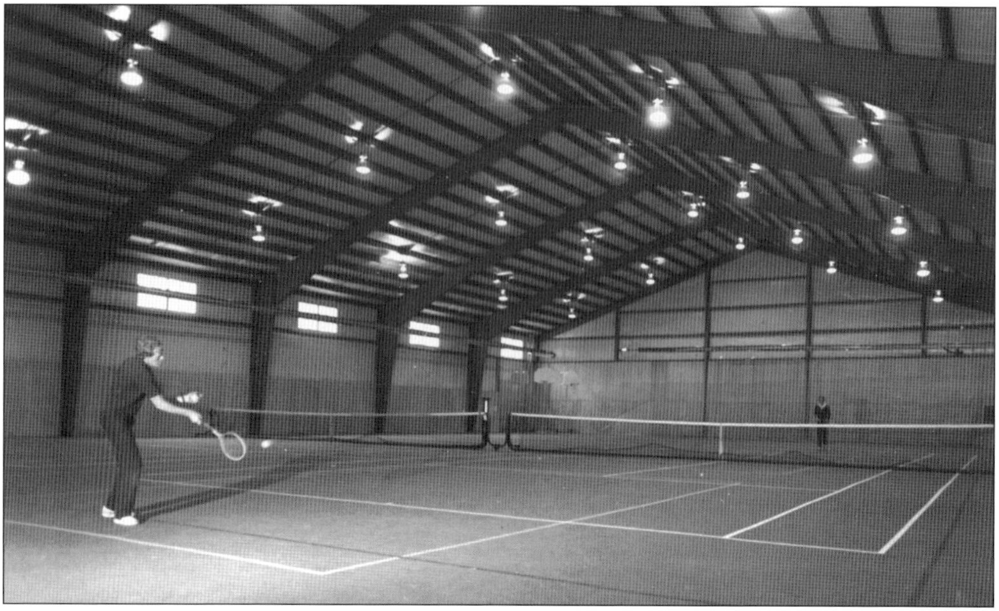

The Field House provides heated indoor space for a variety of sports, including tennis, as shown in this picture of unknown date. In the past, it also was the venue for registration every semester, when hundreds of students waited in long lines to speak with advisors and instructors to enroll for courses for the following semester. Registration is now done online, but students still meet with faculty advisors to discuss course selection prior to registering.

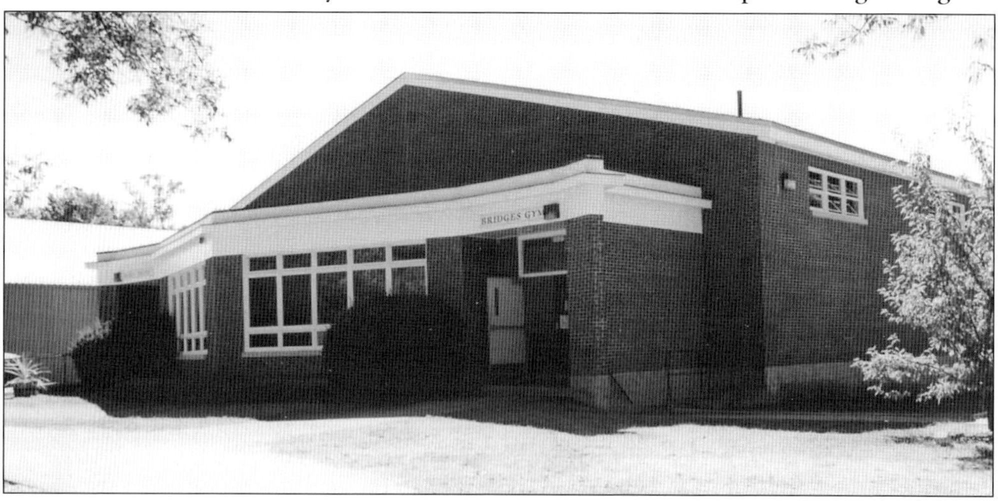

Here is Bridges Gymnasium. The November 18, 1949, *Manchester Union Leader* reports that "through an announcement made by a senior student Robert Dackerman, of Richmond Hill, NY, whose father, Frank L. Dackerman is a trustee, New England College's student body learned today that [the school] will have a new gymnasium and library building. . . . The disclosure, which had been a closely guarded secret, unknown even to many of the members of the Board of Trustees, set off a demonstration which was featured by a mass pledge on the part of the students to see that the gymnasium will be finished not later than 1952 . . . . Immediate support of the 'three year plan' came from Max Israel of Henniker, a trustee . . . . He exhorted the students to 'do the job' and promised that he would make a substantial contribution to the undertaking." The gymnasium is still in active use today.

A bell tower is located on a small hill between the gymnasium and the back of the library. When the Henniker Depot train station closed, the station bell was donated to New England College. According to Martha Taylor, there was once a tradition of ringing the bell after every winning game (in all sports).

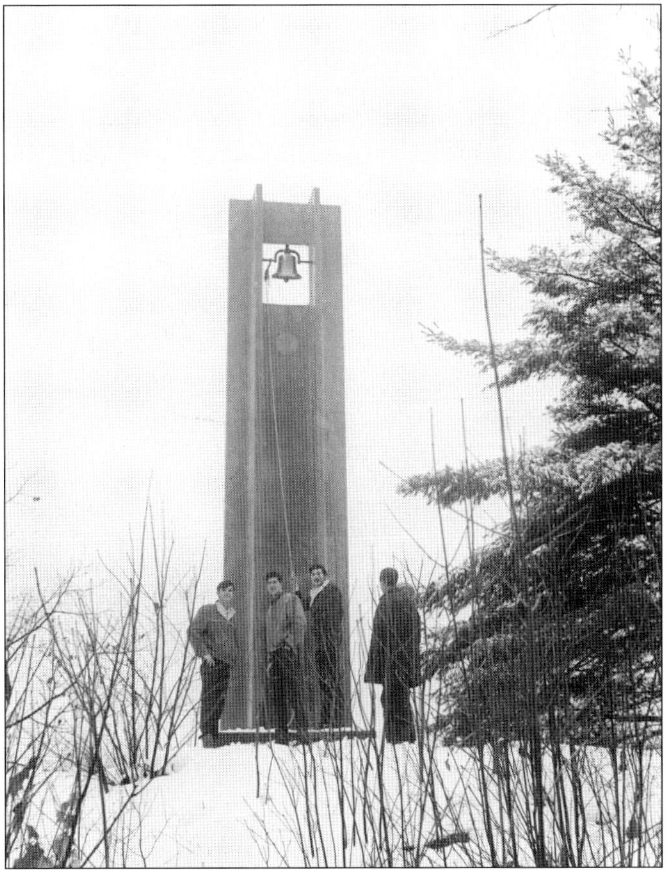

Davis House, adjacent to Danforth Library on Route 114, was formerly the Sigma Alpha Beta fraternity house. This early image was taken before construction of the redbrick dormitories and Gilmore dining hall.

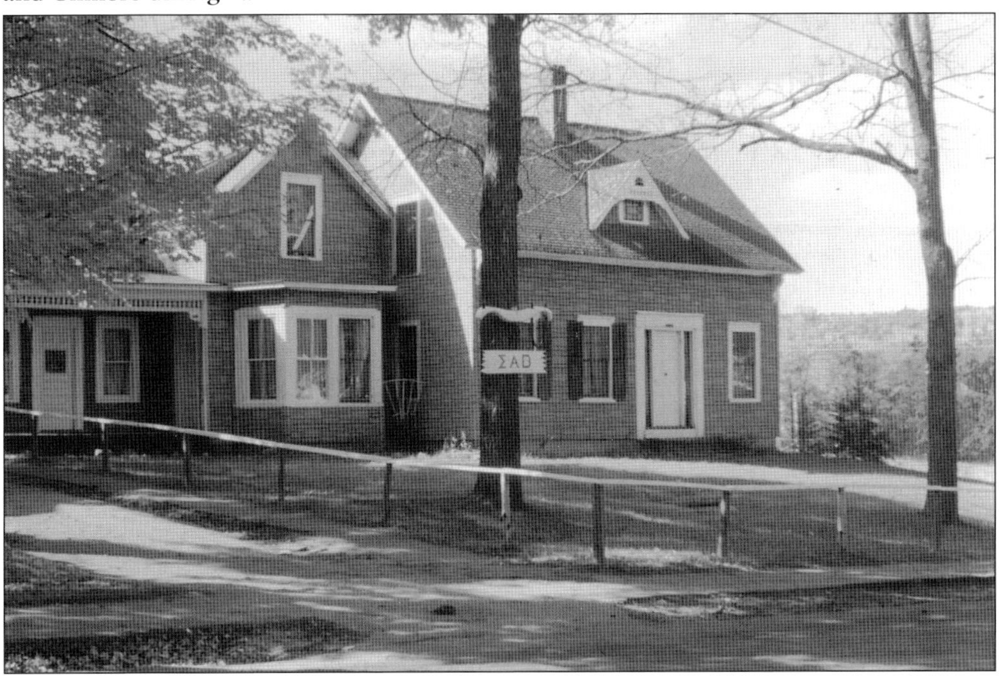

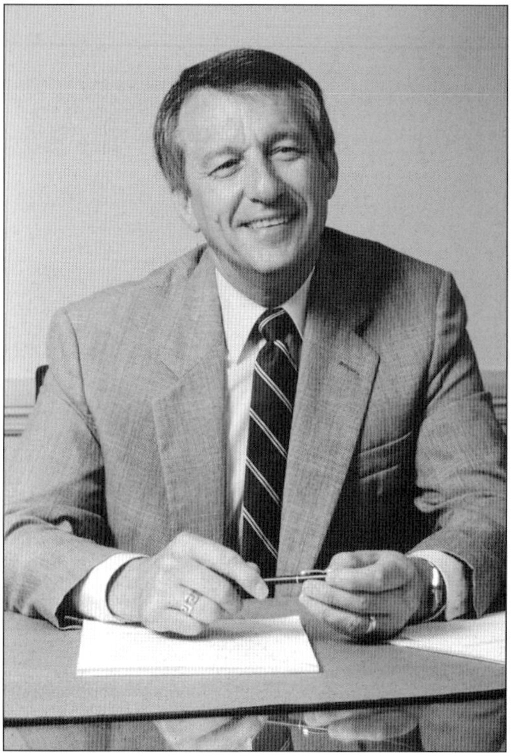

William R. O'Connell Jr. served as president of the college from 1985 to 1995. He was a great believer in the power of international education and loved the Arundel campus, which he visited many times. He led the capital campaign to raise funds for the Simon Center, pictured below. The Simon Center was dedicated in 1994 and serves as the heart of the campus on the west side of the river. It is the central location for student life and student activities.

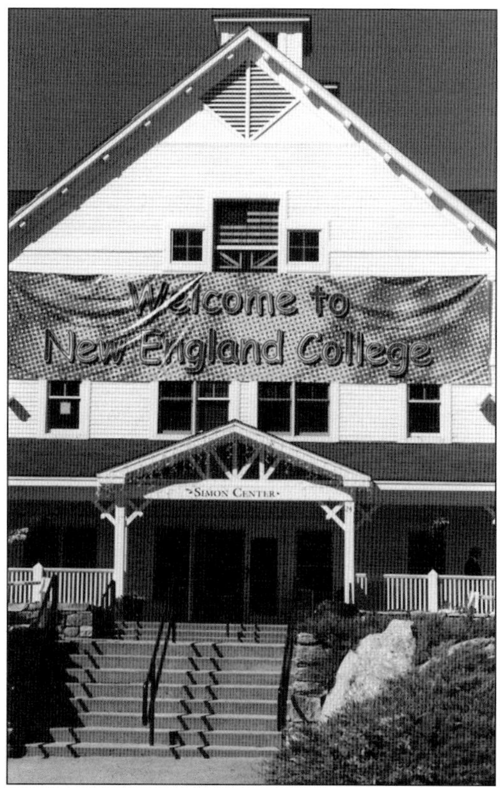

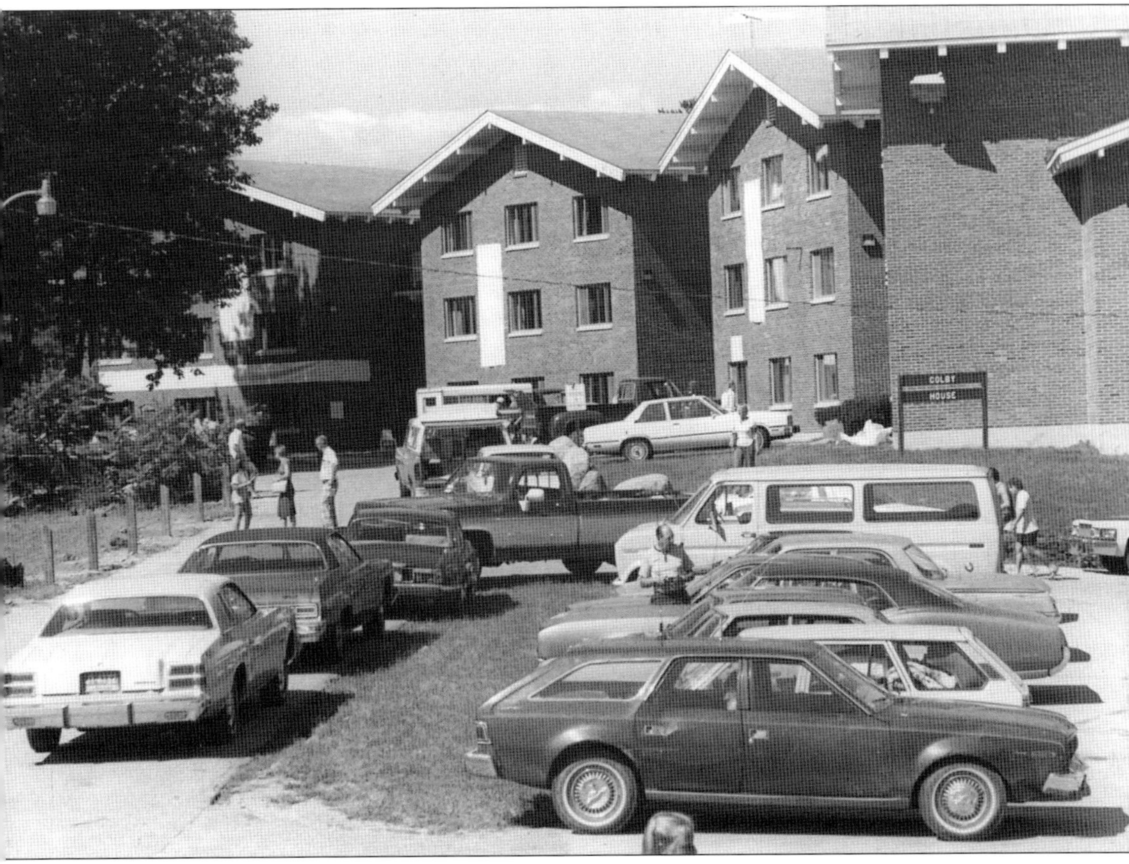

West (left) and Colby (right) are popular residence halls.

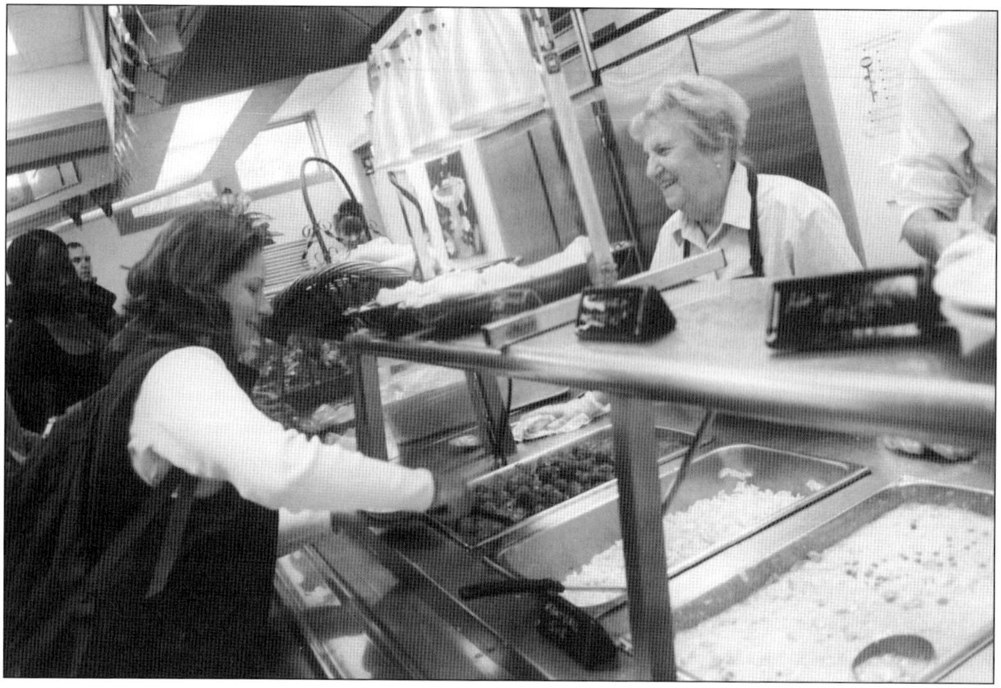

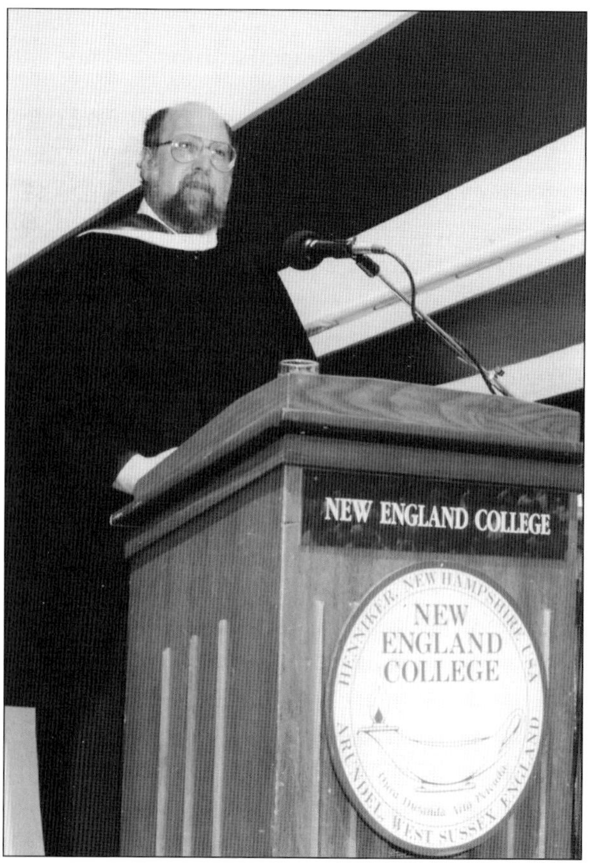

College life is not just what happens in the classroom. A friendly smile and a good hot meal help students striving in pursuit of excellence. The college motto is *Dura duranda, alta petenda* (Endure hard times, strive for the top).

Kenneth E. Smith was a highly respected dean with a great interest in the sociology of Maine fishing villages. A private dining room in Gilmore Dining Hall is named in his honor.

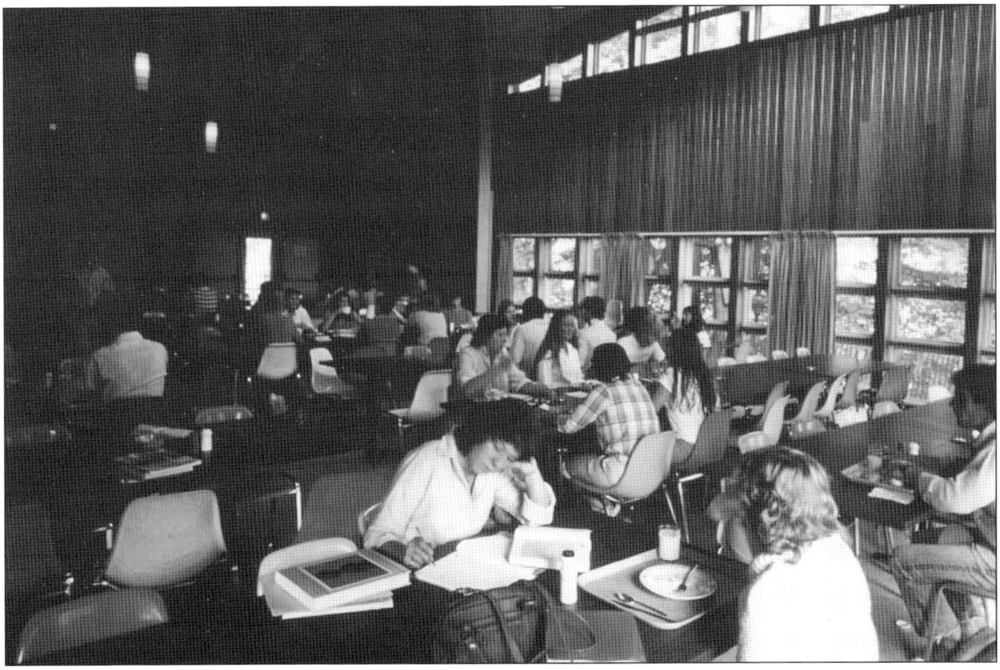

The dining hall is a place for eating, hanging out with friends, and occasionally cramming for exams. This image was taken prior to the closing of the Arundel campus, when the college's collection of flags given by international students was moved from the Arundel Dining Hall to Gilmore Dining Hall at Henniker.

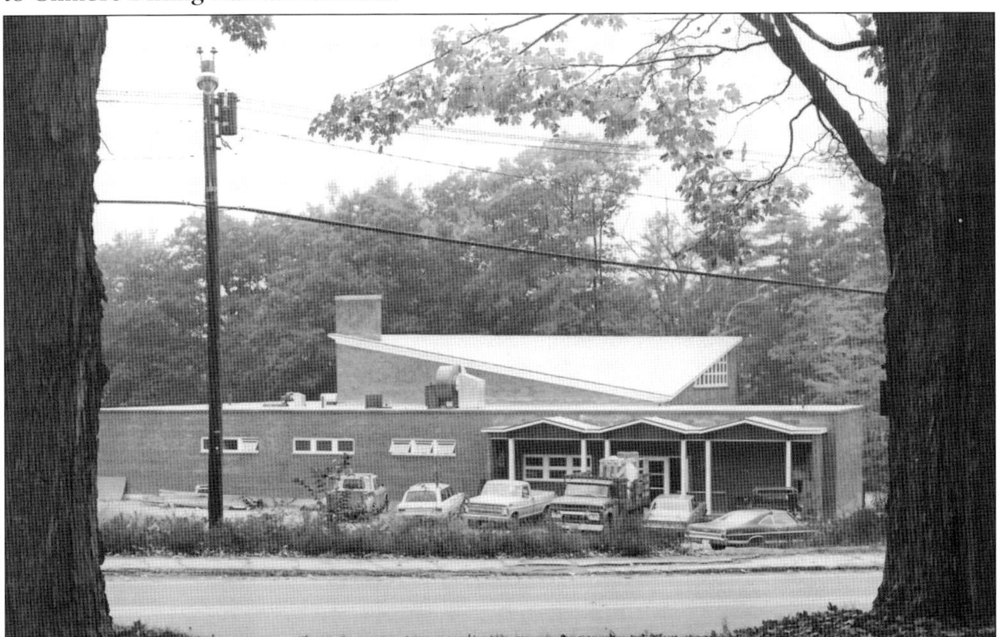

Gilmore Dining Hall was named for Robert Gilmore, the first dean of students. He left a significant bequest to the college in his will allowing construction of this important building in the heart of the campus on the west side of the river.

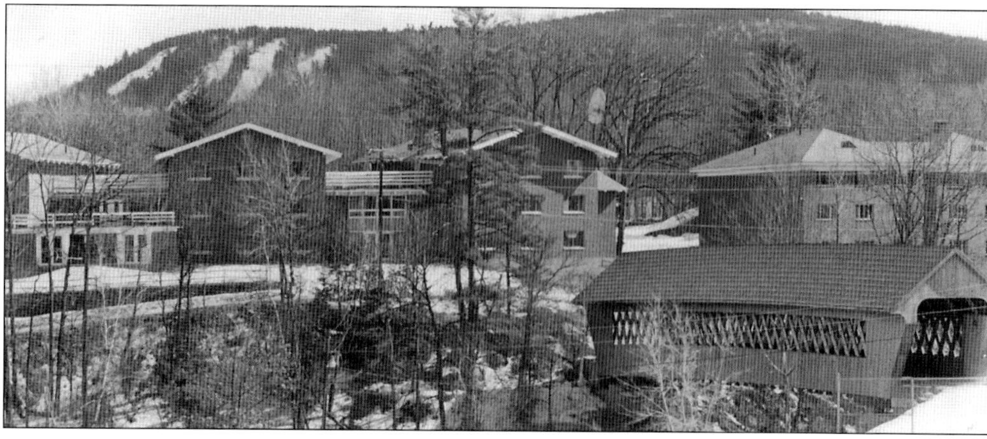

This winter view includes Pats Peak (rear), Colby Hall (left middle), West Hall (right middle), and the covered bridge (front). This image was taken sometime after 1971.

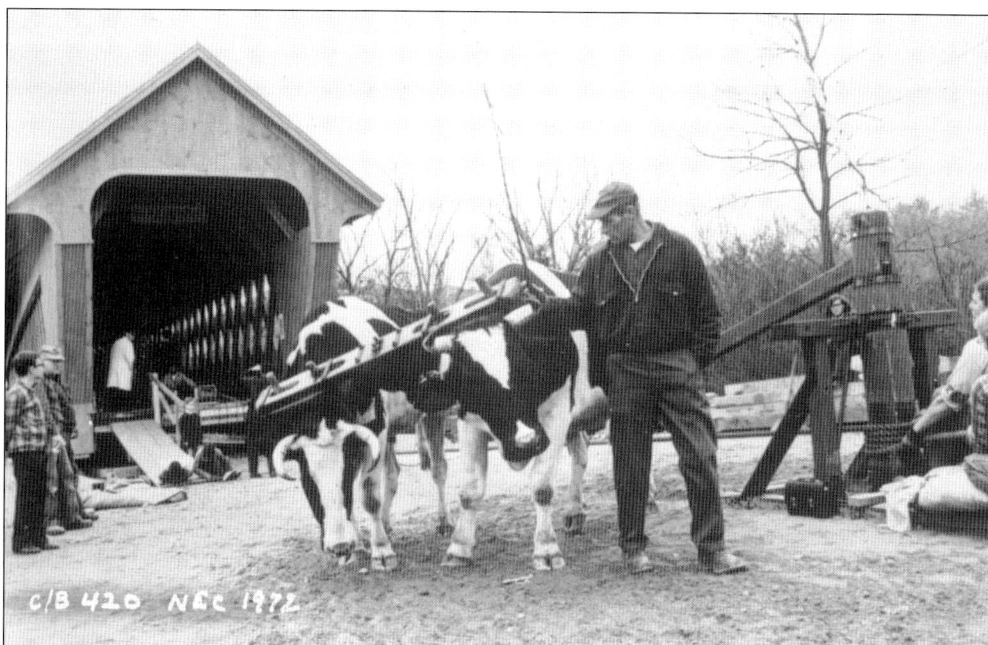

Donald Crane, of Washington, New Hampshire, is pictured with his oxen. On May 8, 1972, the team of oxen began hauling the 90-ton covered bridge inch by inch over the Contoocook River. It took five days to put the bridge in place. The New England College covered bridge is the first authentic covered bridge ever to be constructed by any college and the first one to be built in the state of New Hampshire in over 100 years. (Courtesy of Hillsborough Historical Society.)

Three

We Came to Seek Our Fame

Athletic Teams and Sports

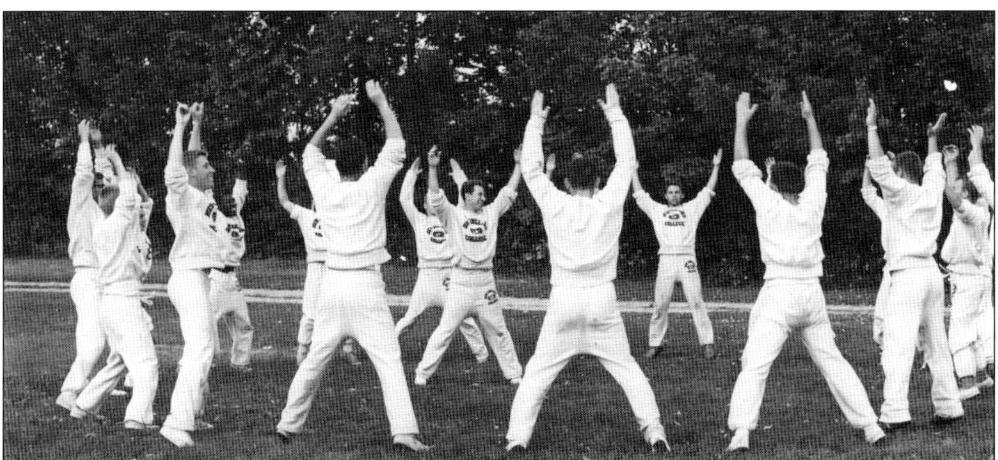

Legendary coach and faculty member Lee Clement coached the 1963 men's soccer team. Ron Nasso (in center), the best all-around player, leads teammates in warm-up calisthenics.

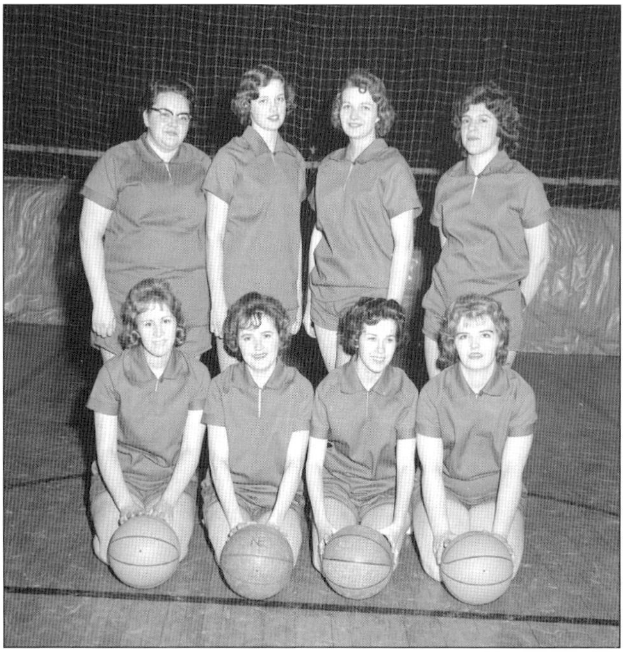

The first women's basketball team at New England College competed during the 1961–1962 season. The team was started by Joanne Whitehead and Lynne Edgerly, both of whom were also cocaptains. The members of the team are, from left to right, (first row) Judy Tiege, Joanne Whitehead, Shirley Drew, and Lynne Edgerly; (second row) Thelma Giroux, Georgia Taggart, unidentified, and R. Fleming. (Courtesy of Hillsborough Historical Society.)

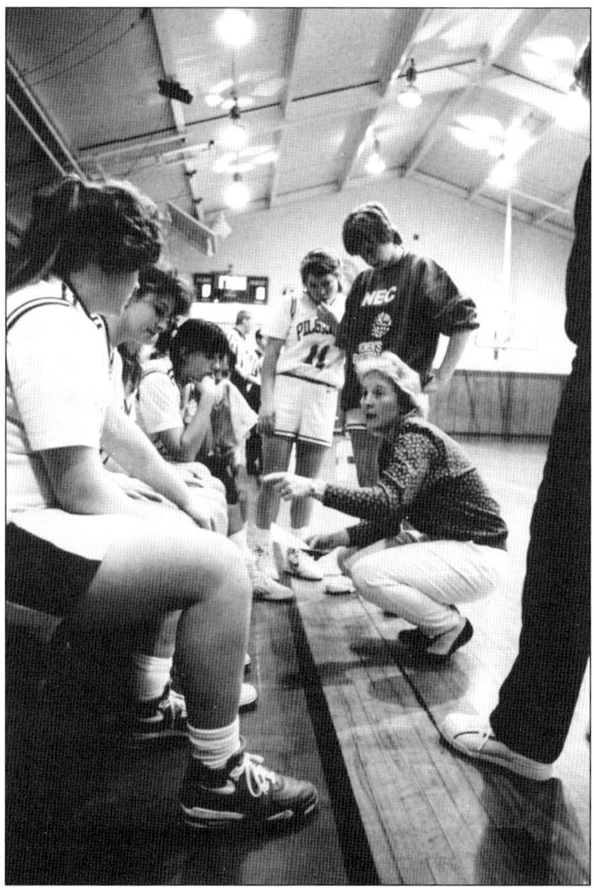

Mary Ellen Alger, shown here coaching the women's basketball team in Bridges gymnasium, joined the college in 1990. She is also a full-time faculty member who teaches sport and recreation management.

The 1947–1948 basketball team is seen huddled around its coach. Kneeling is coach Colby Baker holding a basketball; from left to right are Joe Altott, James O'Sullivan, Milton Knight, Peter Shanelaris, and John McKernan. McKernan was a dominant force on the team; his height allowed him to control the boards. He also possessed a good eye, which helped him get many assists during his time as a Pilgrim.

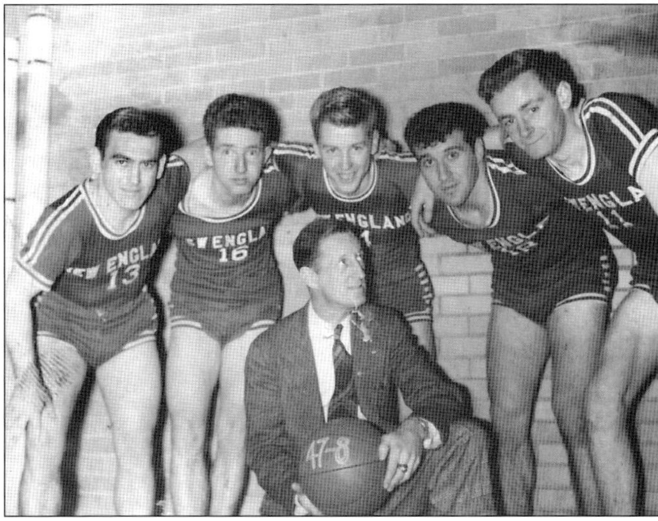

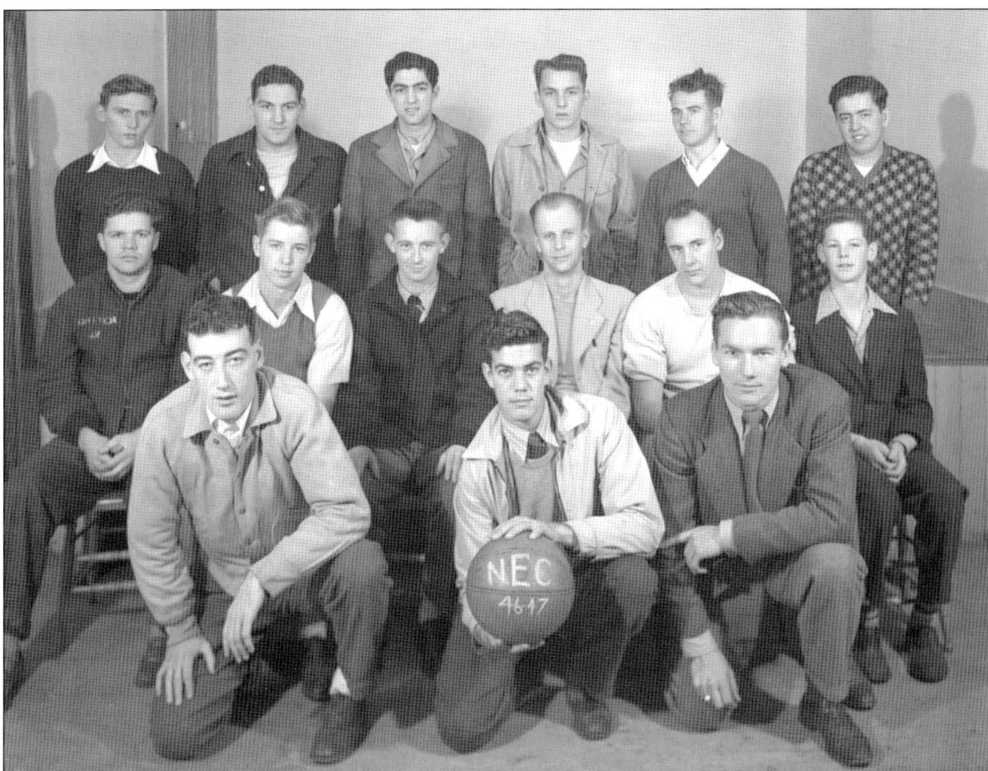

Pictured is the New England College basketball team in the college's first academic year, 1946–1947. Lee Clement is holding the ball. He was a member of the college's first class and a versatile coach for a variety of sports, including basketball, lacrosse, and soccer. (Courtesy of Hillsborough Historical Society.)

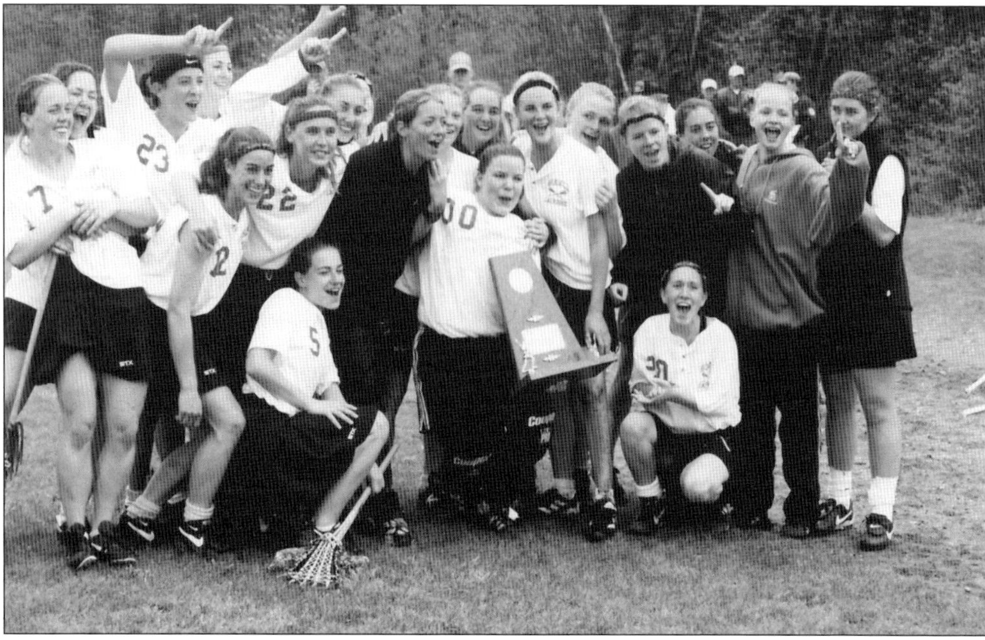

The 1998 women's lacrosse team had a very successful year, winning the Commonwealth Coast Conference Championship. Members of the team include Caitlin Roberts (coach), Louisa Fisher (assistant coach), Moe Brooks, Rachel McKee, Jill Jones, Heather Van Horn, Abby Berman, Alli Reyelt, Amy Swinston, J.B. Kelly, Tilea Warren, Kristin Baldwin, Elizabeth Clark, Amy Terlizzi, Emily Frawley, Liz Cook, Jaimie Jackman, Caddie Knight, Danielle Avicolli, Courtney Lockheat, and Lindsay Drake.

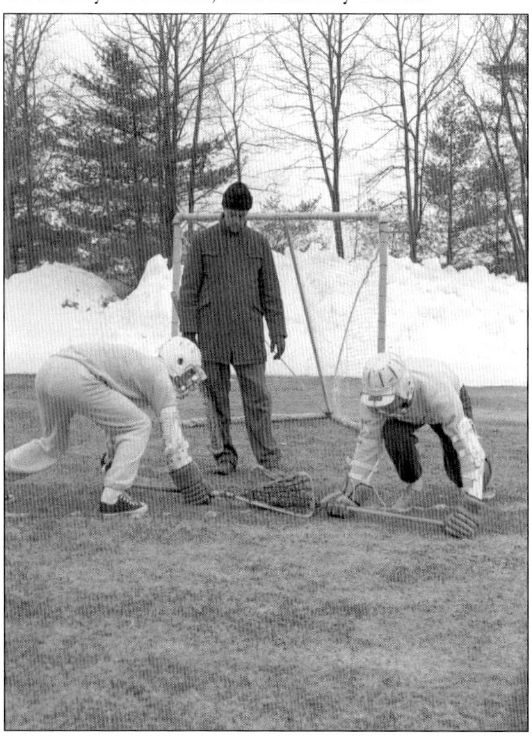

Lacrosse is played in the snow in the late 1960s. The coach is Lee Clement. When Laurie D. Cox assumed the presidency of New England College, he had already earned the title "father of modern lacrosse" at Syracuse University. Cox started the Pilgrims lacrosse team, which has won numerous conference tournaments and appeared in numerous NCAA Division III tournaments.

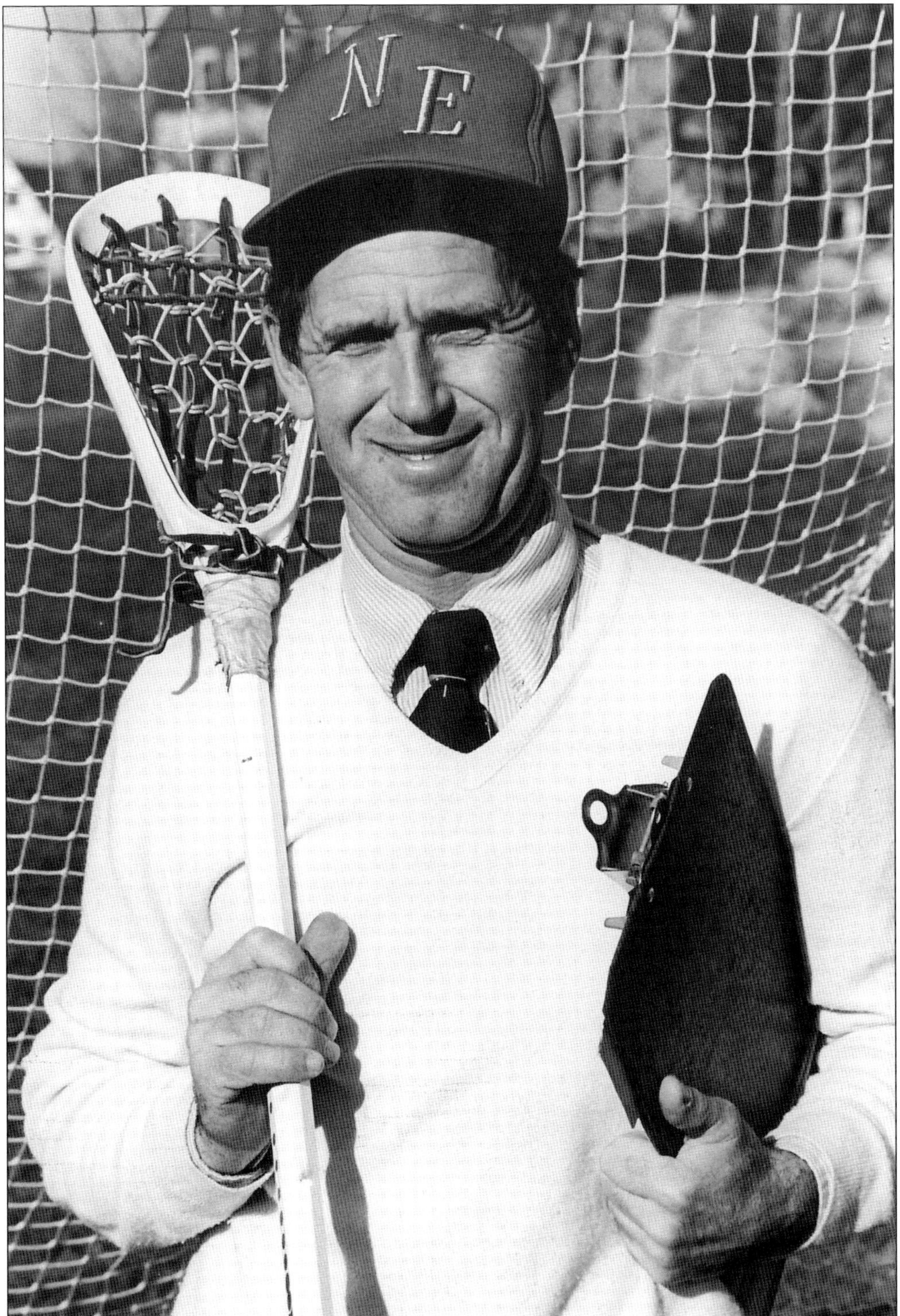

Donal C. Emerson coached the men's lacrosse team for many years and also was a key member of the college's admissions staff.

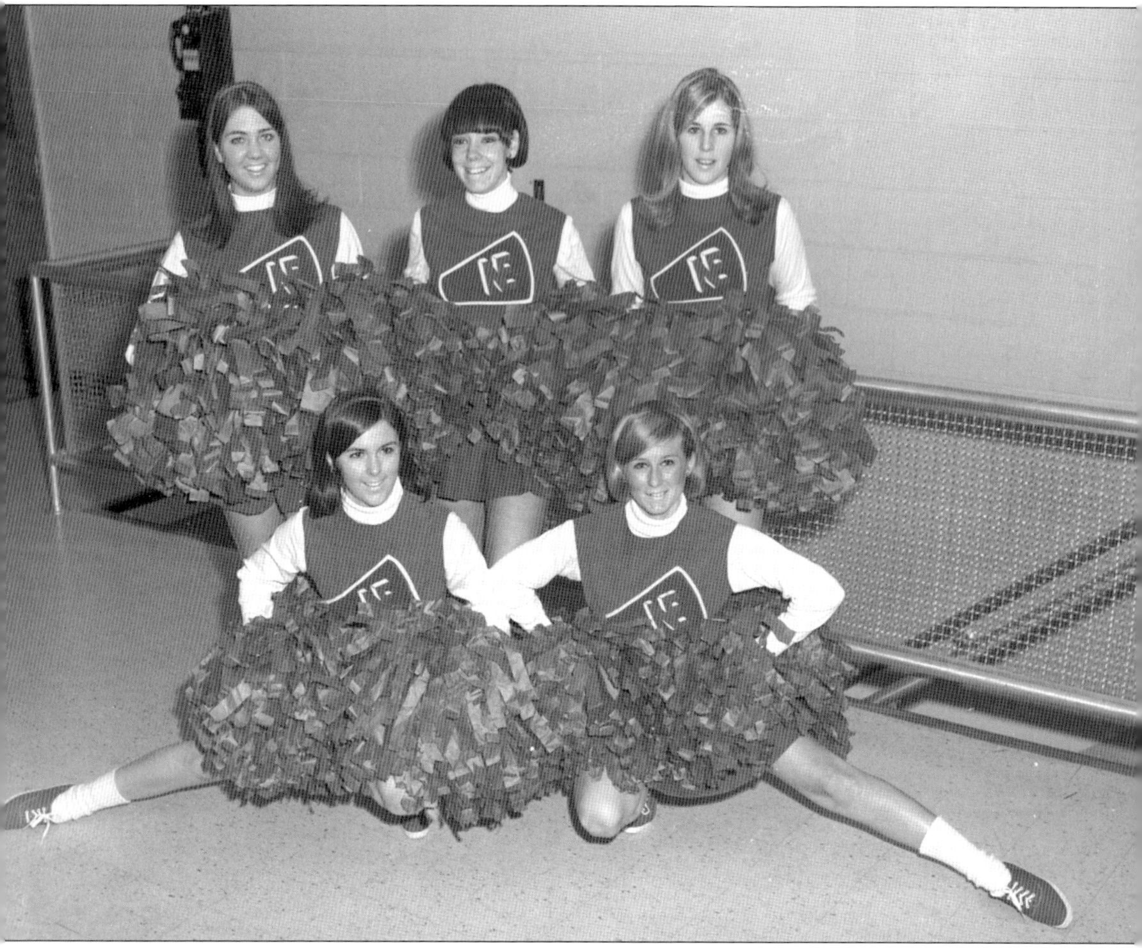

Cheerleaders were an integral part of athletics at New England College. They cheered on the football, soccer, basketball, and lacrosse teams to victory during their time at the college. The cheerleading team was known as the loudest and most passionate fans of all of the sports teams at the college. Pictured are the members of the 1968–1969 cheerleading squad. There are no longer cheerleaders at New England College.

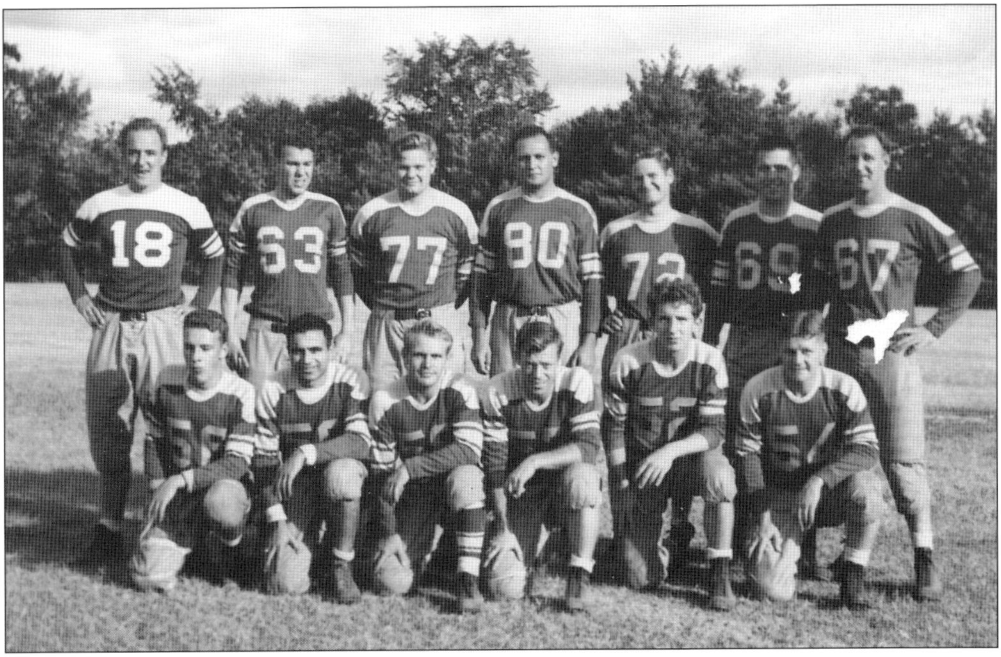

Kickoff was at 2:15 p.m. on Saturday, October 2, 1948, when the Pilgrims football team, wearing red-and-blue uniforms, played its first "home" game on the turf of Concord's Memorial Field against Connecticut State. Despite limited equipment and lack of proper facilities, this team fought hard. Pictured are, from left to right, (front row) Dave Dawson, unidentified, James Morrissey, unidentified, Richard Kurkjian, and Dwight Baker; (second row) two unidentified, Ed Glasson, Charles Quale, Edward Ratcliff, and two unidentified.

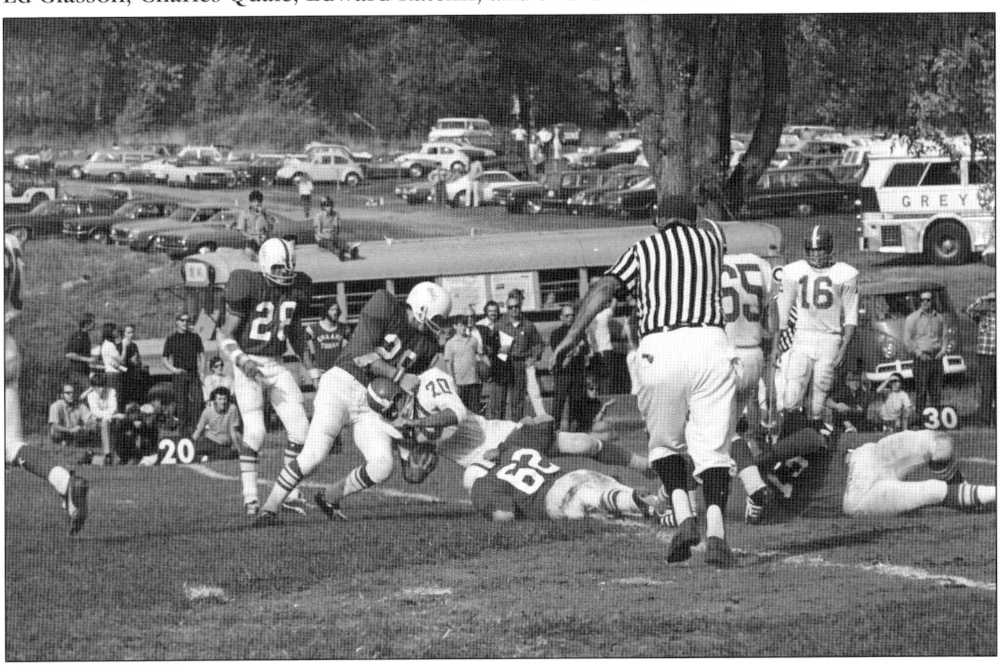

The Pilgrims football team reemerged for a brief comeback in the 1970s. The program was stopped after one year due to a shift in organizational priorities.

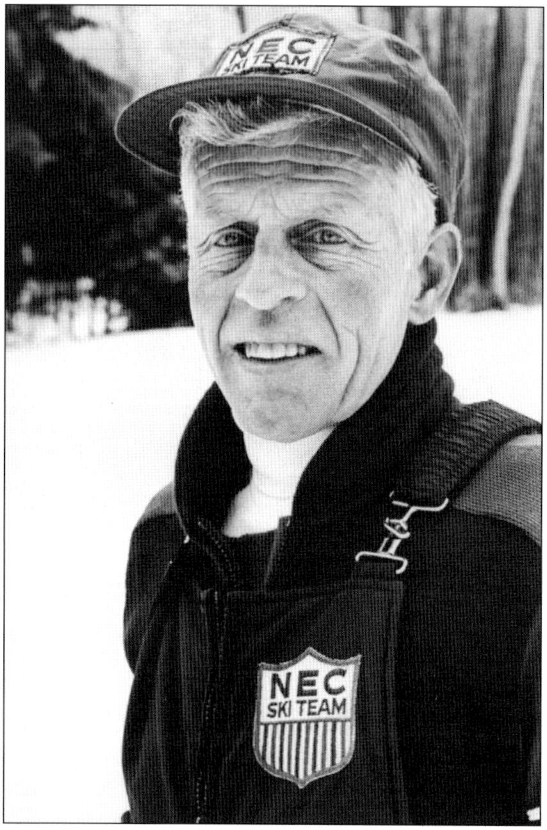

Silas B. Dunklee was a long-term coach of both the ski team and the men's tennis team. He joined the physical education faculty in 1970. An important athletic award is named in his honor.

The 1981 ski team is pictured in front of the lodge at Pats Peak. From left to right are (first row) Barbara Dunn, Noel Miner, Kim Johnson, Kay Durbin, Carolyn Finn, and Julia Lomedico; (second row) "Lex" Scourby, Susanne Amberg, Kathy Grant, Laurene Thayn, Sylvia Szokolay, Joan Henderson, and Charlie Gunn. Scourby later served on the college's board of trustees and wrote the foreword to this book.

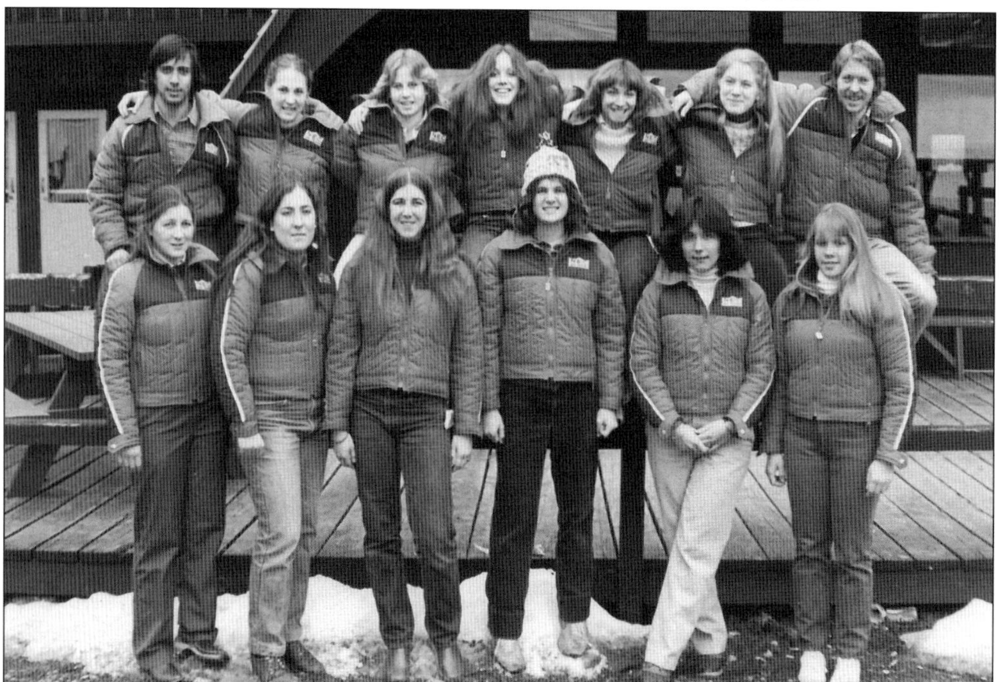

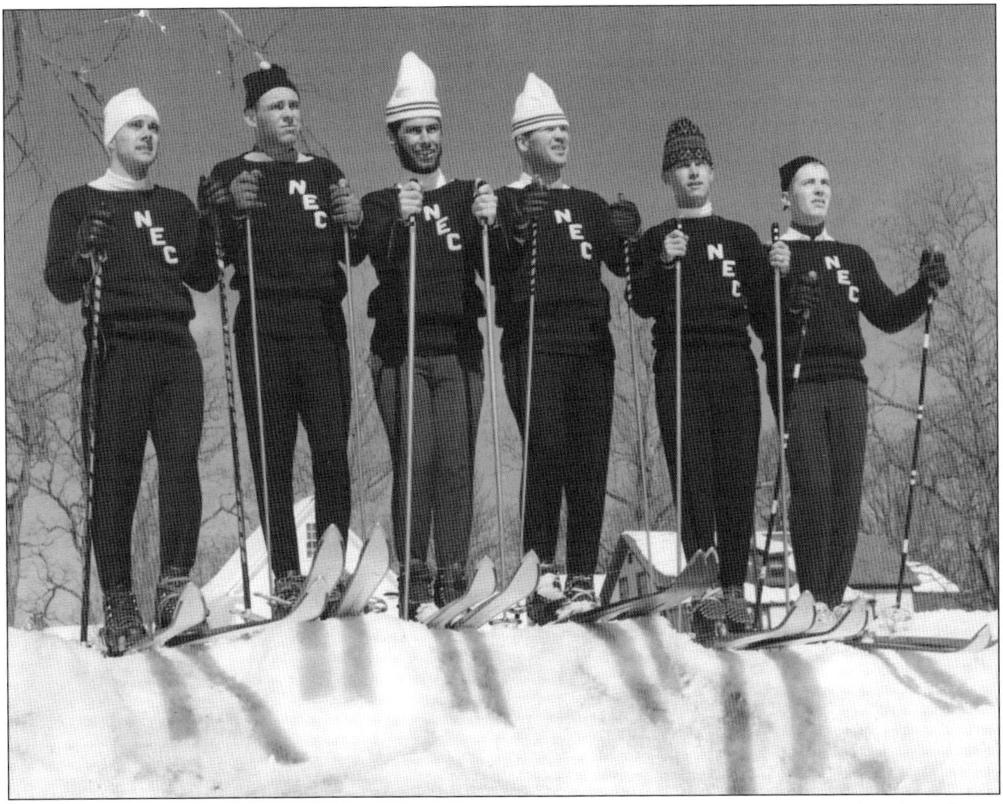

The men's ski team competed at Pats Peak in Henniker, the home of New England College. Skiing is a beloved pastime at New England College, and students get to ski for free at Pats Peak. Pictured are, left to right, cocaptain David Kitteridge, George Hurt, Rick Norton, Arthur Askeland, cocaptain Doug Hastings, and Skip Grant.

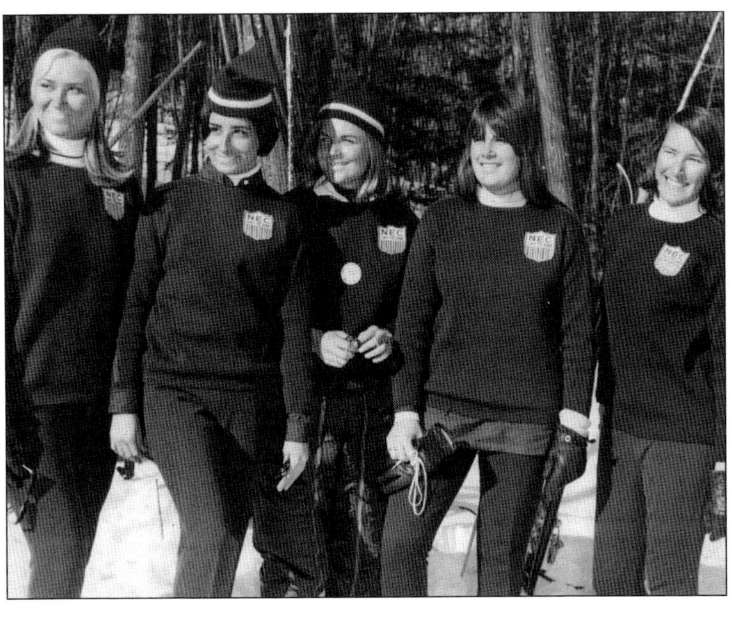

The women's ski team also competed at nearby Pats Peak. The ski club was one of the biggest clubs at the school and included many people who did not make the ski team. The ski team returned to the college in the 2015–2016 school year. On the left is Patricia Deferro; the others are unidentified.

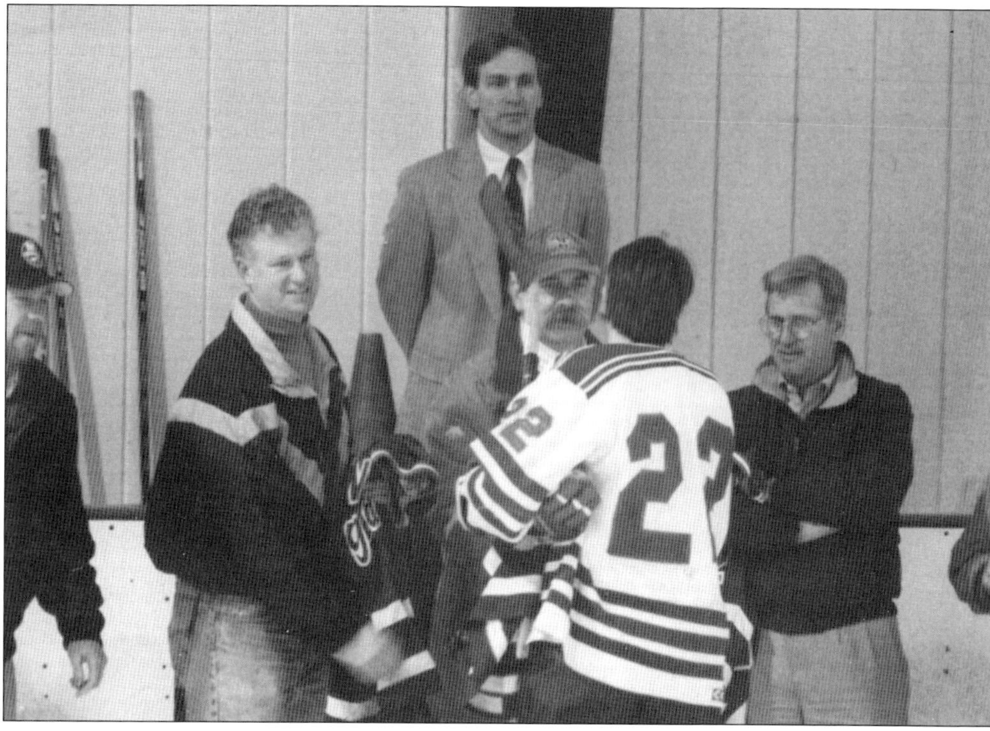

The hockey program at New England College has been one of the most successful sports in the school's history. Teams have advanced as far as the semifinal of the NCAA Division III tournament. No. 22 is Ryan Donohue.

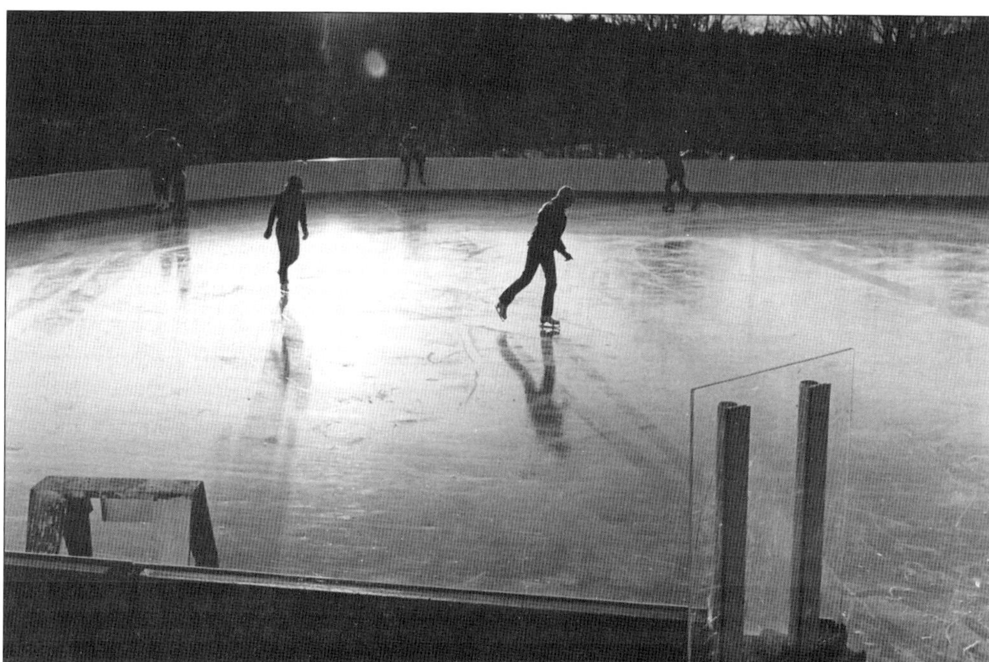

An outdoor rink was eventually replaced by the indoor arena, named for Lee Clement.

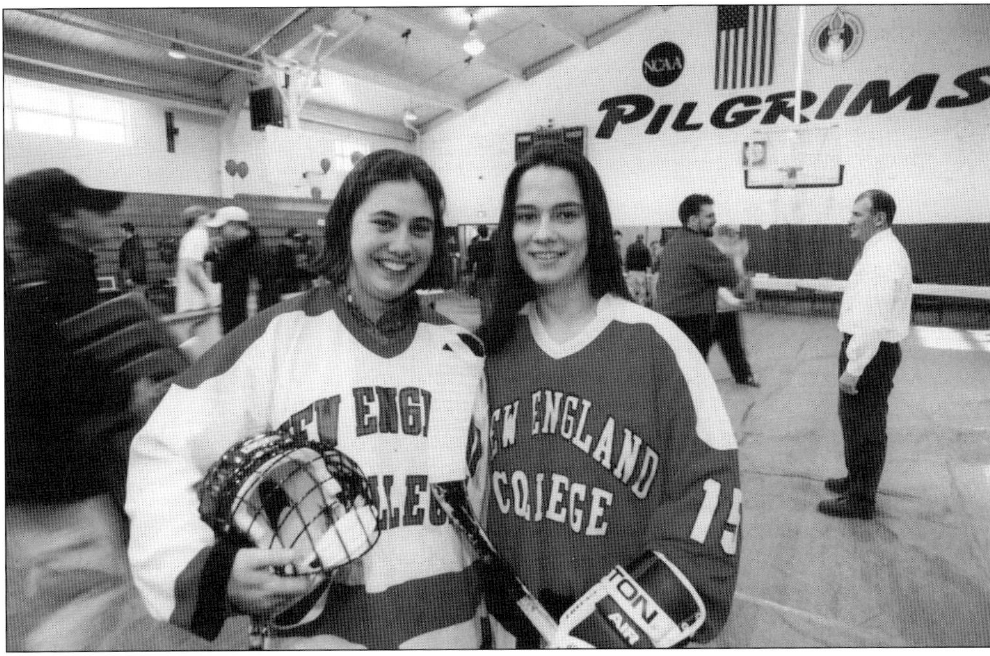

Two members of the class of 2000, Sara Webb (left) and Traci Hayes (right), founded women's club hockey, which quickly became the varsity women's hockey team. They are pictured here at an athletic event in Bridges Gym. Women's hockey faculty advisors were professors Phillip Huckins and John O'Connor.

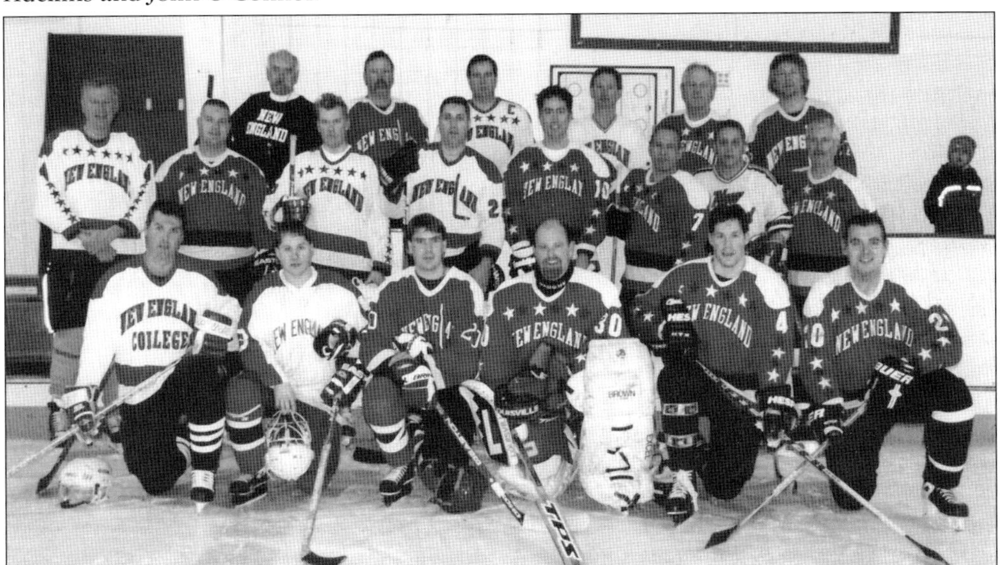

The hockey alumni are very involved in the program, forming a booster club called Friends of NEC Hockey. Hockey alumni after a game are, from left to right, (first row) William Engel, Brian Stone, Todd Sharp, James Doremus, Tom Guidi, and Jeff Dandretta; (second row) Robert Tappan, Jeff Cain, U.K. Flygh, James Ingraham, David Campagna, Paul Centauro, Jon Brawn, and John Lineberry; (third row) Jay Jones, James Douglass, Ray Desmarais, Brian Brown, Duncan Matthews, and James Hayes.

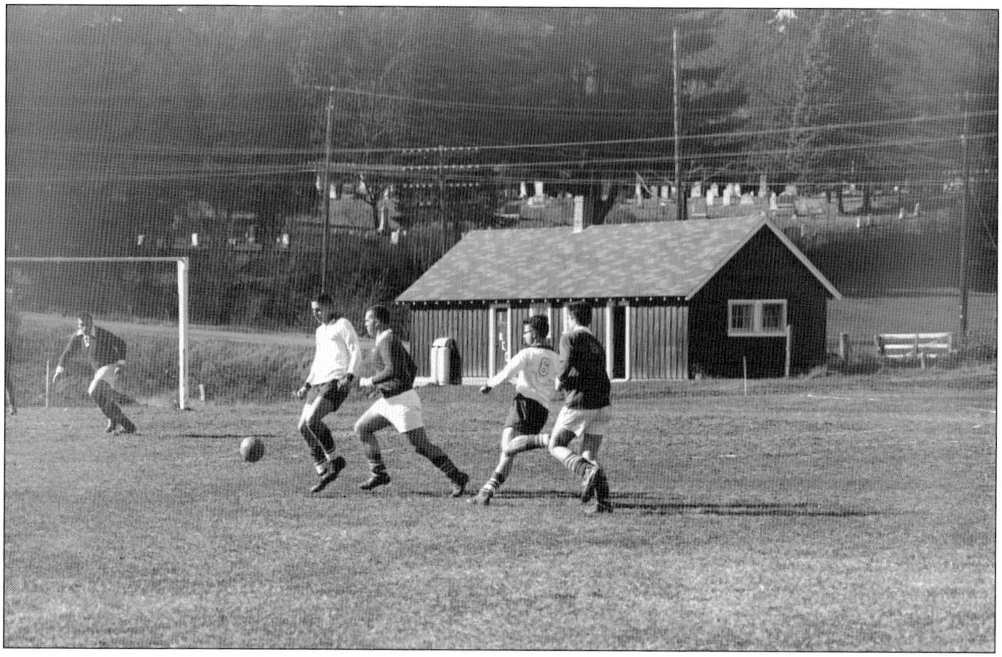

In September 1947, the college rented a large athletic field from the local cemetery association to be used as a combined football, soccer, and lacrosse field. This soccer game took place there at homecoming in 1958. (Courtesy of Hillsborough Historical Society.)

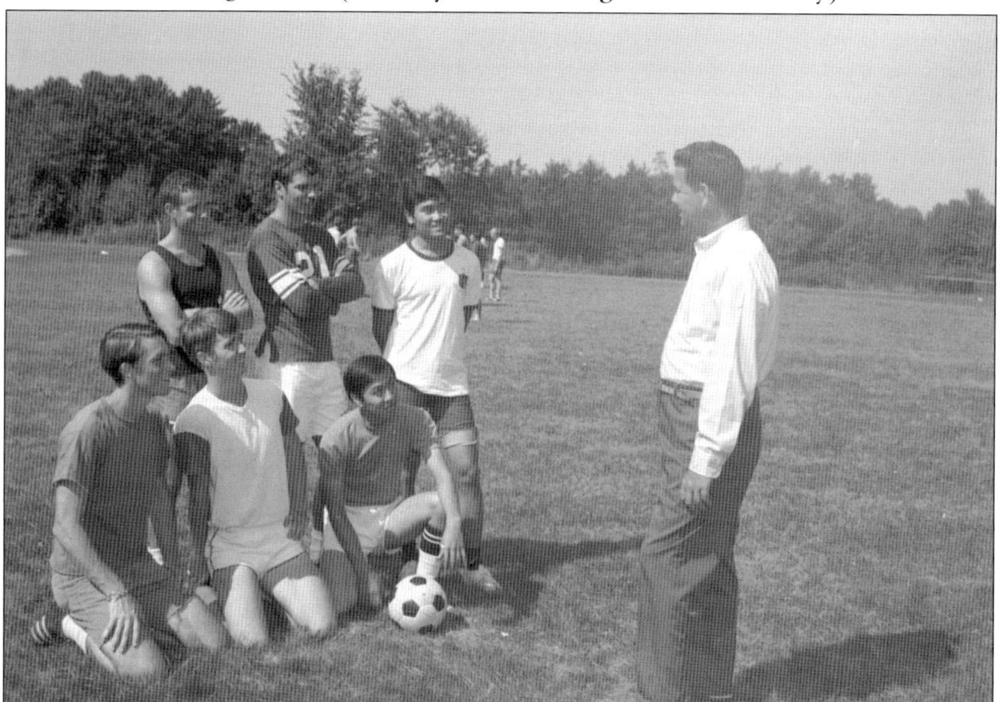

Men's soccer was coached by the legendary Lee Clement, who was a member of the first graduating class. He was an outstanding athlete and athletic director who stayed with the college for 34 years and was instrumental in establishing the college's athletic programs.

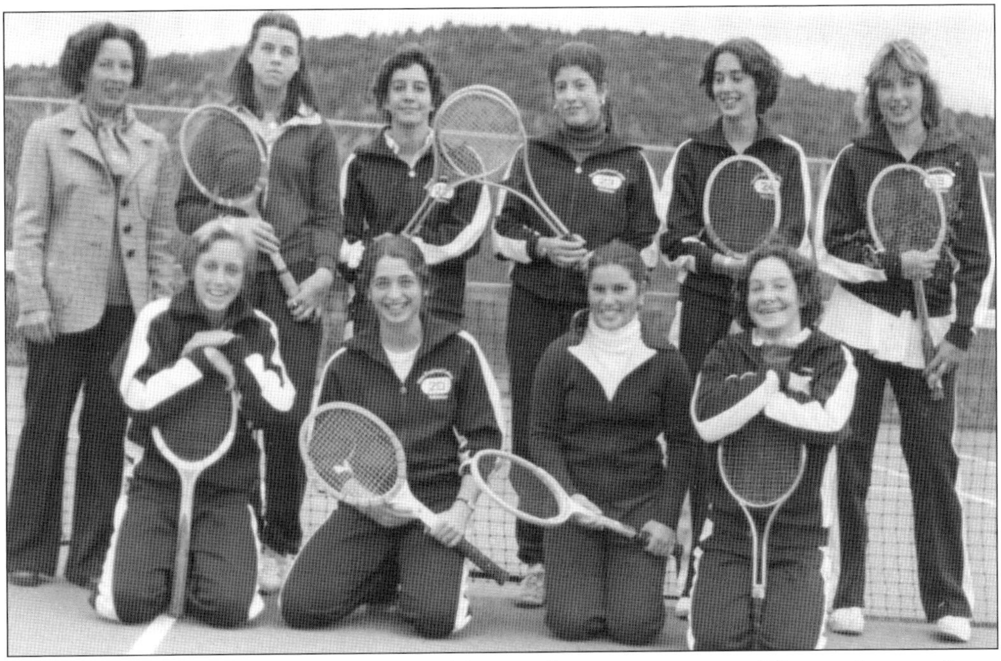

The 1977 women's tennis team is pictured here at the tennis courts on Western Avenue. From left to right are (first row) Chris Jenkins, Robin Gordon, Judy Weir, and Kate MacMillan; (second row) Charlotte Dunklee (coach), Jean Kelly, Robin Butcher, Linda Kaplan, Suzanne Miner, and Astrid Williams.

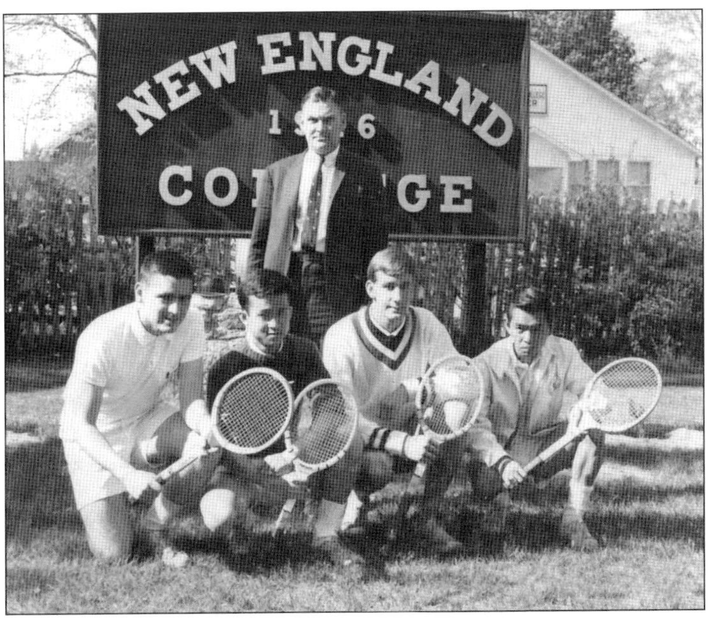

The 1963 men's tennis team is pictured in front of the college sign. From left to right are (first row) Charles Conole, Werapong Saeparn, David Baumhart, and Voravitya Joonnasuphya; (second row) Richard Hatton (faculty advisor).

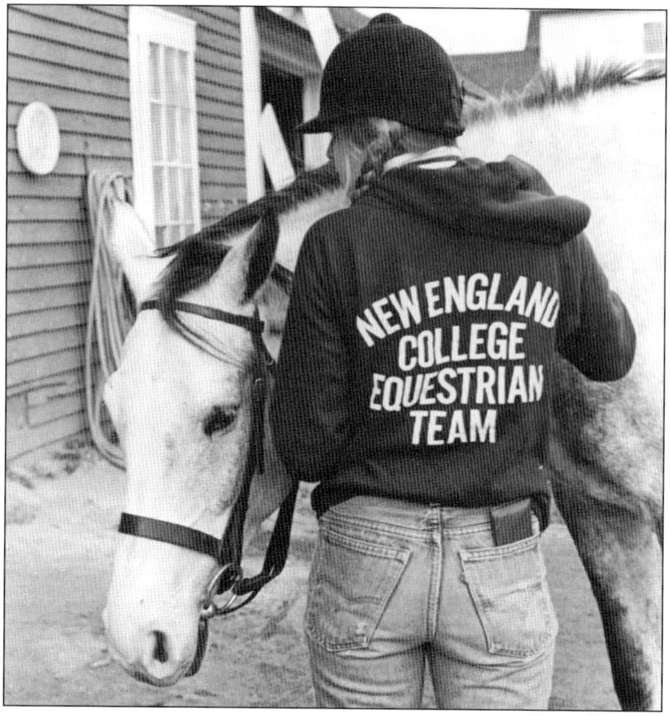

New England College's equestrian team competed regionally against teams from other institutions. There were numerous farms in rural Henniker willing to board horses for New England College students.

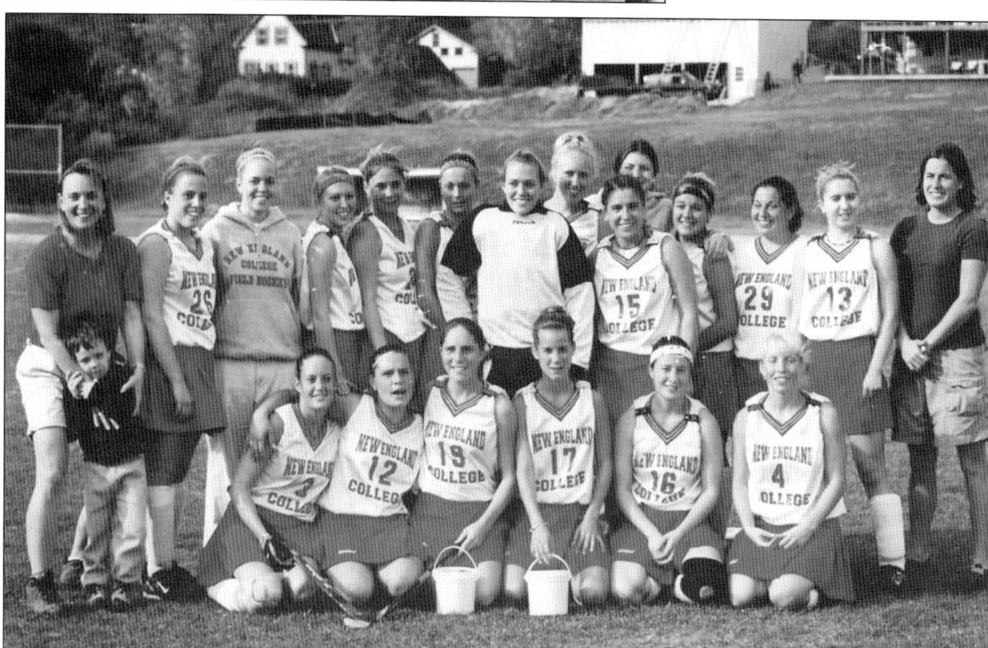

Coach Susan Murray led the field hockey team to numerous conference championships. Pictured is Murray with the 2001 team, including Erica Rabe, Heather Chevarie, Johanna Richardson, Nicole Richardson, Kristy Saunders, Laura Buffa, Kelly Perrow, Kristen Coffin, Erica Neila, Erin McFarland, Carrie Bergman, Amanda Guzzi, Taylor Pape, Ashley Day, Julia Whalen, Keri Apt, Lindsey Inman, Gina DePerry, and Kristen Milroy. Murray joined the college in 1992 and is a member of the sport and recreation management faculty.

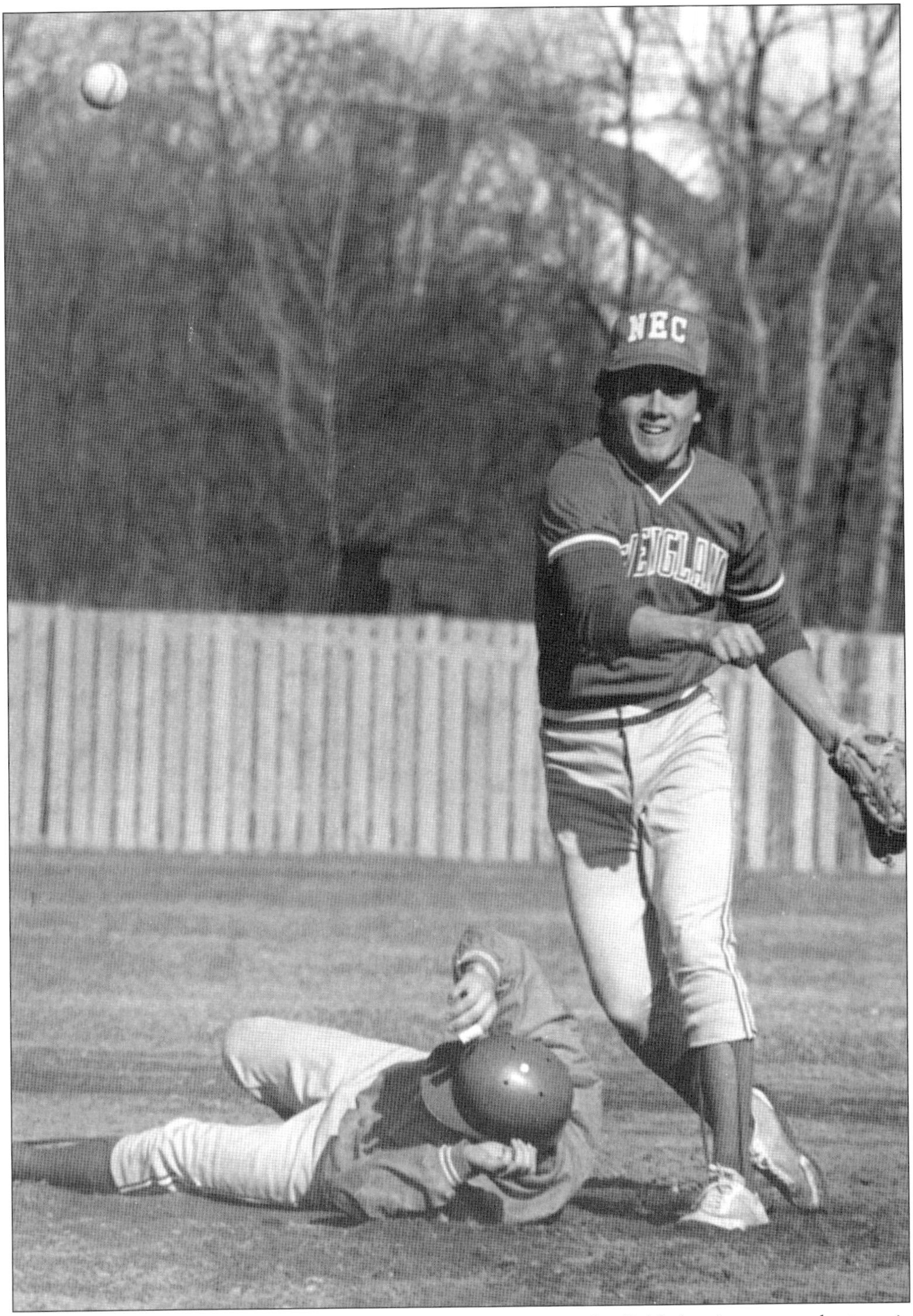

Today's New England College baseball teams compete on the field that is next to the tennis courts on Western Avenue. Pictured is a member of the 1985 baseball team working hard to avoid a slide and complete a double play. The captain of the 1985 baseball team was William McNeil.

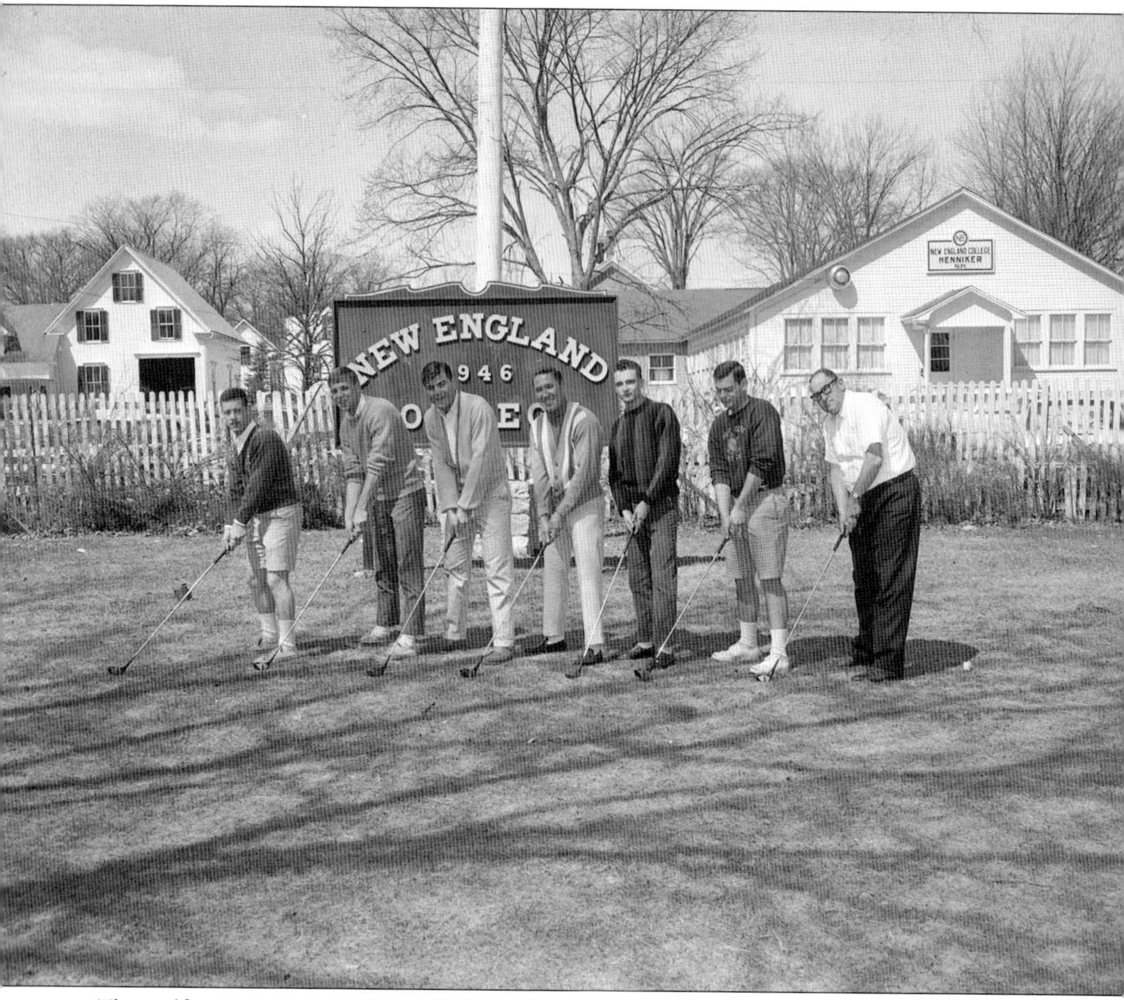

The golf team is seen in front of the college sign in 1963. On the right is coach Ken Beres, who was a professor of business administration for many decades. (Courtesy of Hillsborough Historical Society.)

Four

Pride in Thy Name
Traditions, Clubs, and Activities

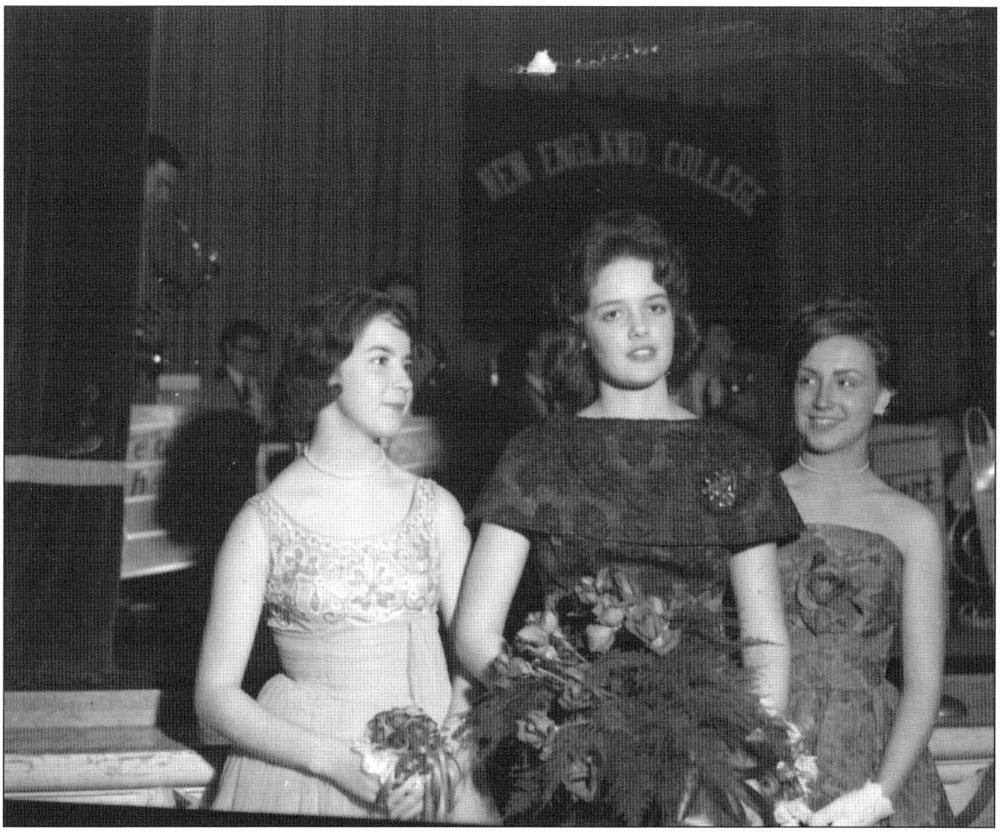

In the early years of the college, when the majority of students were male veterans, they recruited sisters and friends from home to compete for the honor of being crowned Winter Carnival Queen. One alumna remembered, "Miss America had nothing over the girls crowned in the queen's chair at the Saturday night ball. Friday night was the sock hop where all the girls paraded around the room. Saturday, the Queen would be announced and Saturday night at the ball, crowned and presented with many gifts from the local merchants." This queen of the Winter Carnival, at center, is Georgia Taggart, who went on to become Miss New Hampshire and modeled as a Breck girl in the company's print ads.

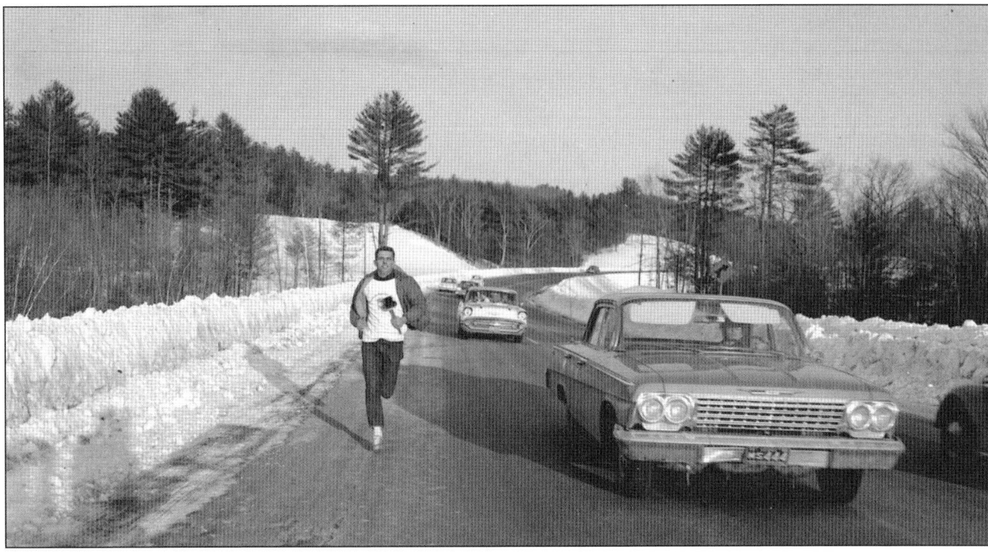

The annual torch run started at New England College and ended in Concord at the state house with a presentation to the governor of New Hampshire. (Courtesy of Hillsborough Historical Society.)

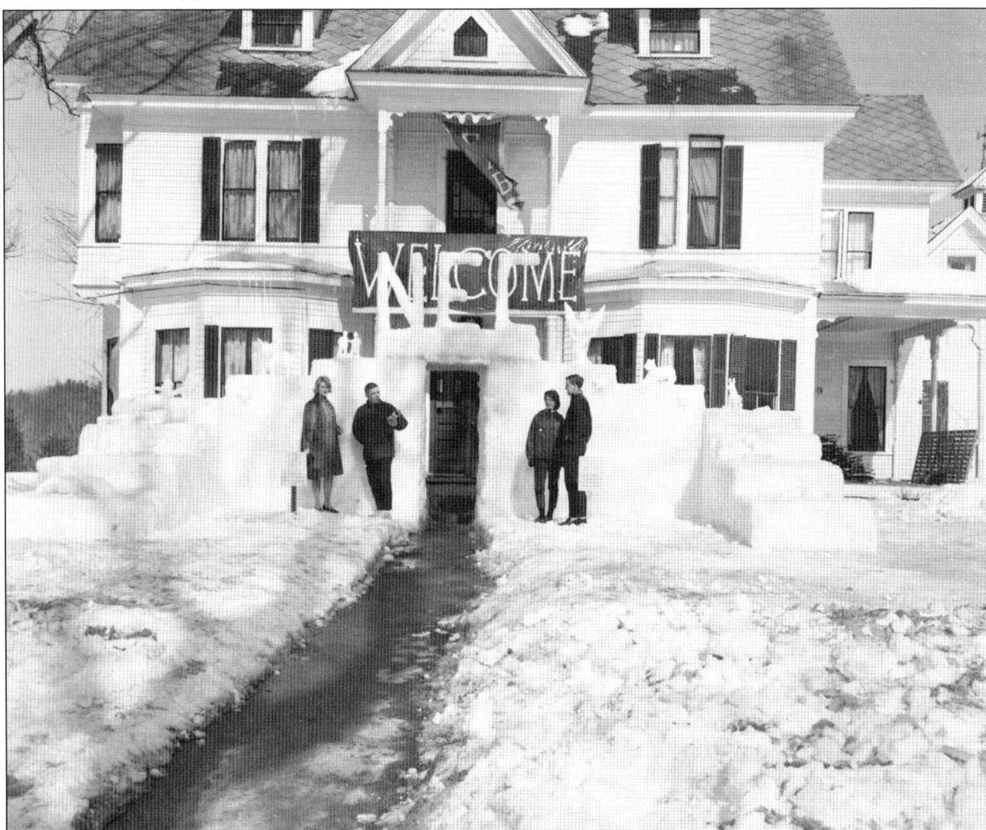

This snow sculpture was created for Winter Carnival in 1963. (Courtesy of Hillsborough Historical Society.)

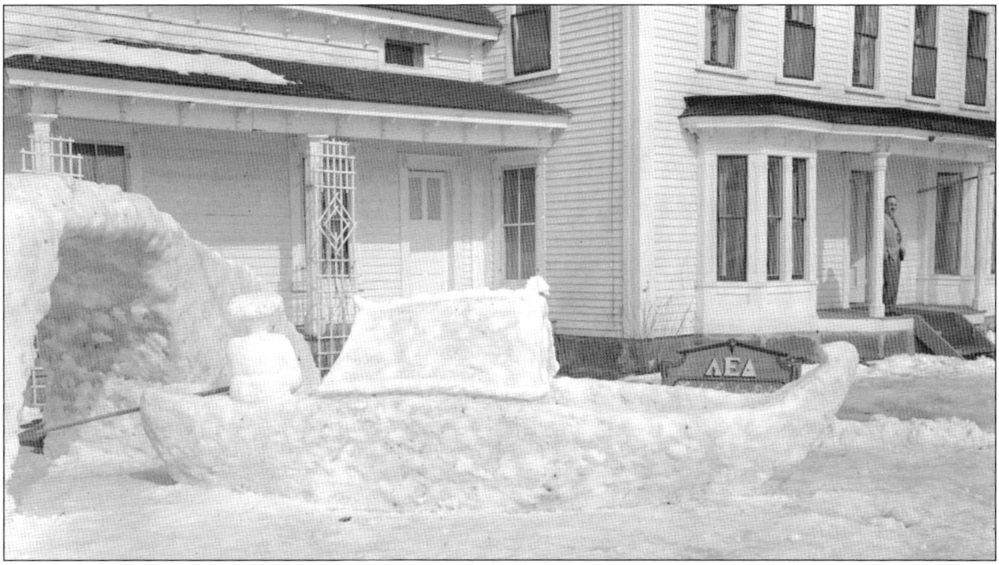

An alumna from Henniker recalled, "The Winter Carnival week-end began with the Town Crier. We would be sound asleep in bed when suddenly there would be loud clatter and banging outside and someone would open the front door and go running upstairs to get everyone up to begin the festivities. There would be a truck full of college boys—usually a trumpet and a drum—whose job it was to go to every house in town where the boys lived and get them up." This snow sculpture was also built during Winter Carnival in 1963. (Courtesy of Hillsborough Historical Society.)

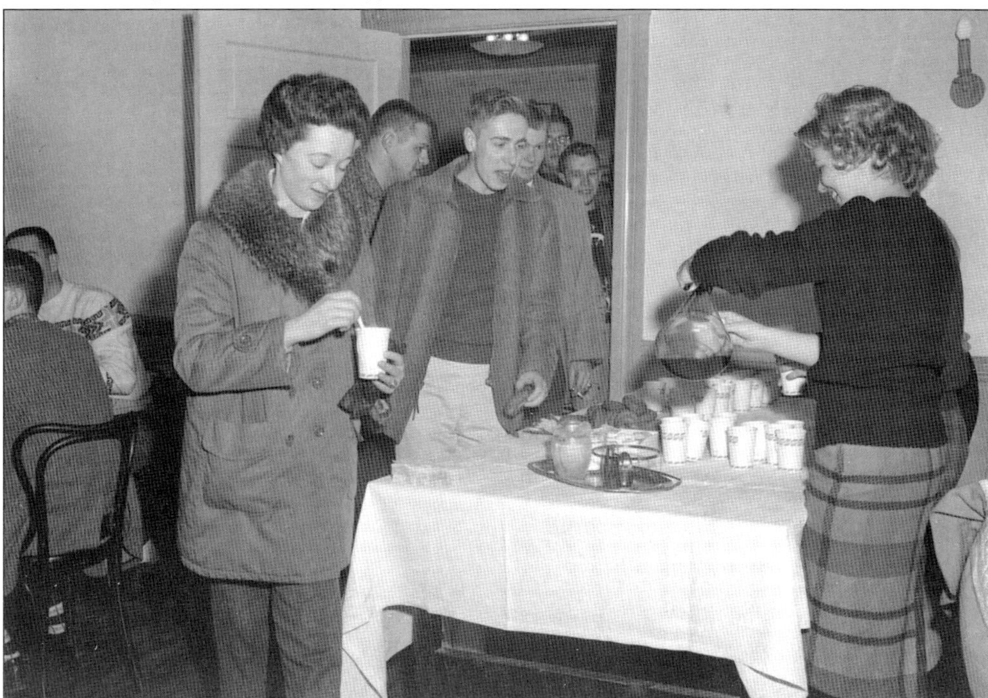

During the college's annual Winter Carnival, hospitality was extended not just to fellow students but also to faculty, staff, and townspeople. (Courtesy of Hillsborough Historical Society.)

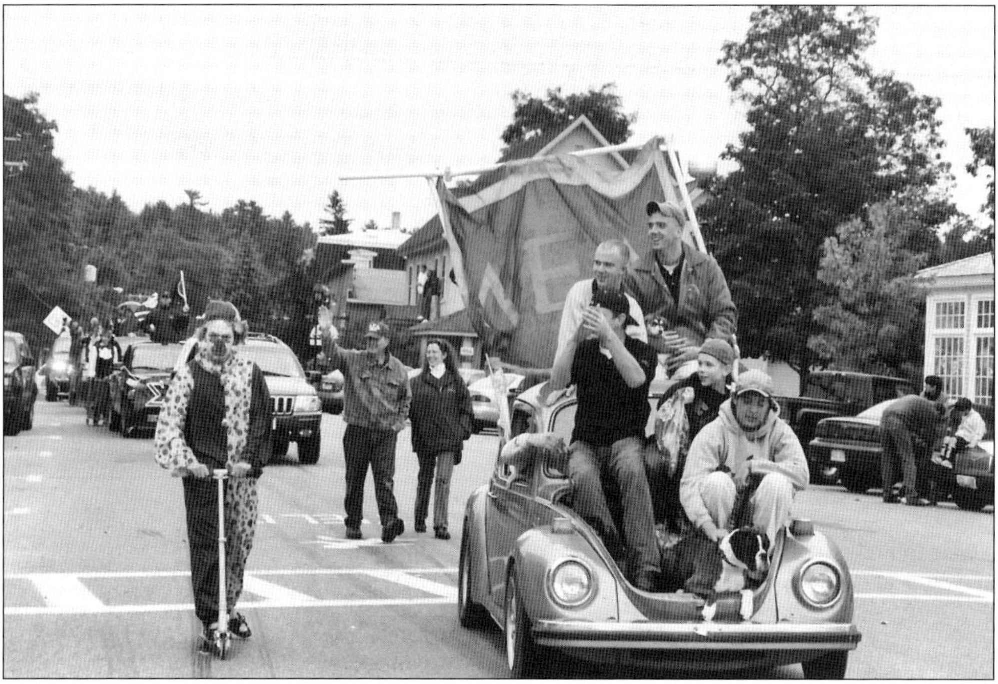

The annual homecoming weekend, when New England College alumni return to campus for parties and a parade through campus, began the year after the first class graduated and continues to this day. Lambda Epsilon Delta brothers created this float for the annual homecoming parade down Henniker's Main Street.

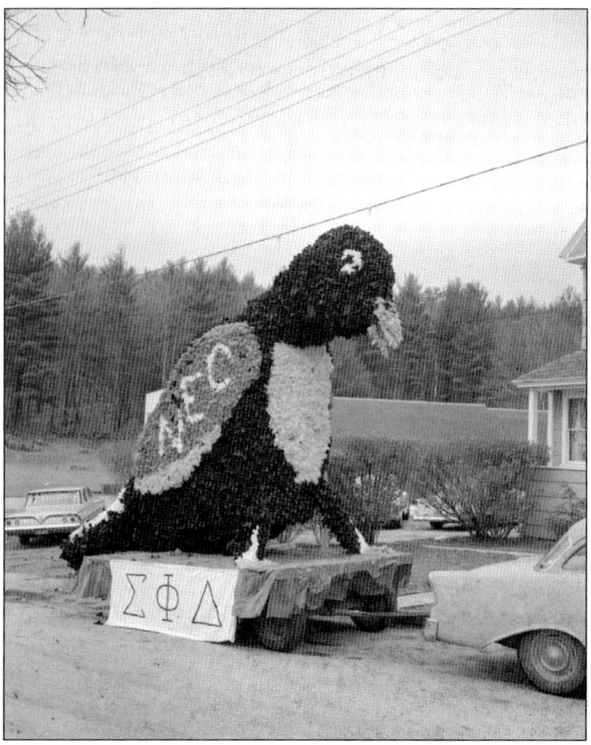

Sigma Phi Delta's 1962 homecoming float is shown here in front of the fraternity house, located on the site later occupied by the Science Building. (Courtesy of Hillsborough Historical Society.)

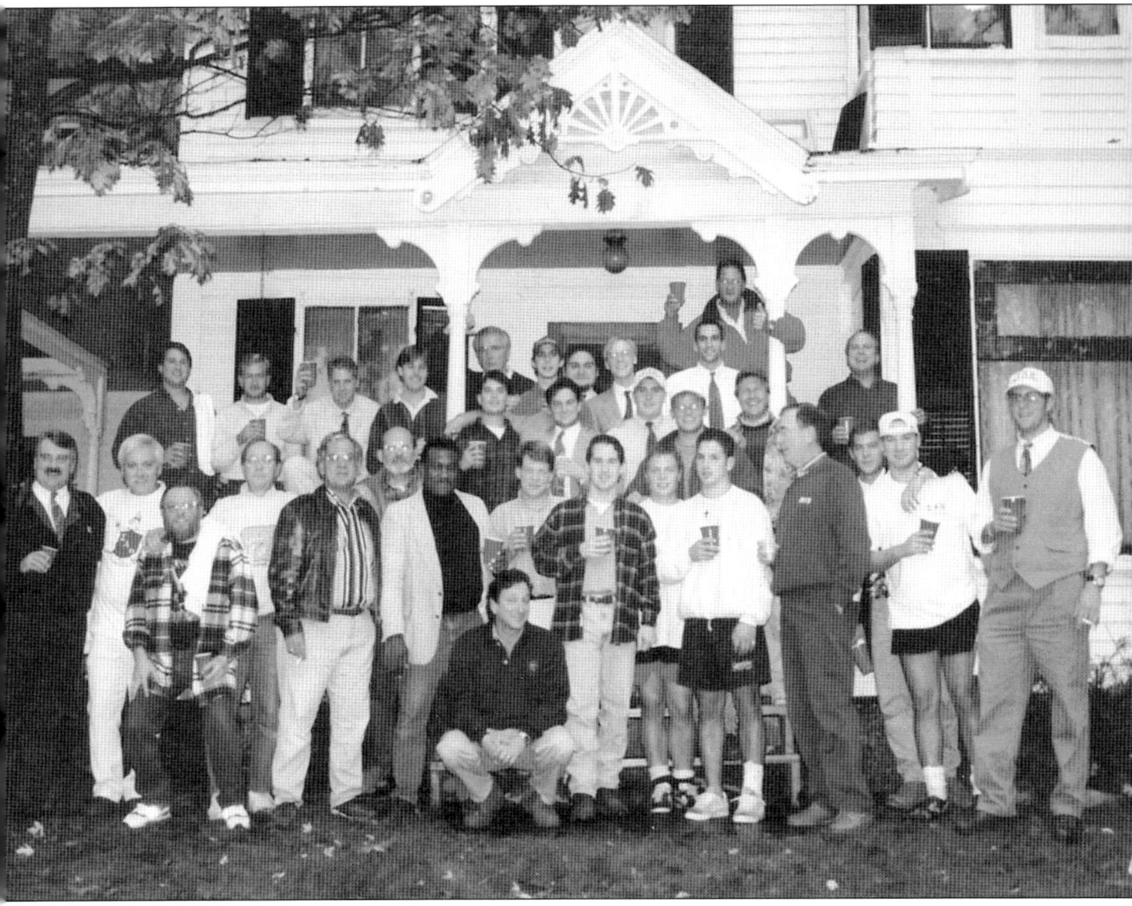

Many large Victorian houses in Henniker served as residences for fraternities and sororities at one time or another. This house at 177 Maple Street was built in 1893 and was the Sigma Alpha Beta fraternity house at the time of this reunion party in November 1995. Later, it was purchased and renovated by Gary McGrath, former director of the Arundel campus. (Courtesy of Henniker Historical Society.)

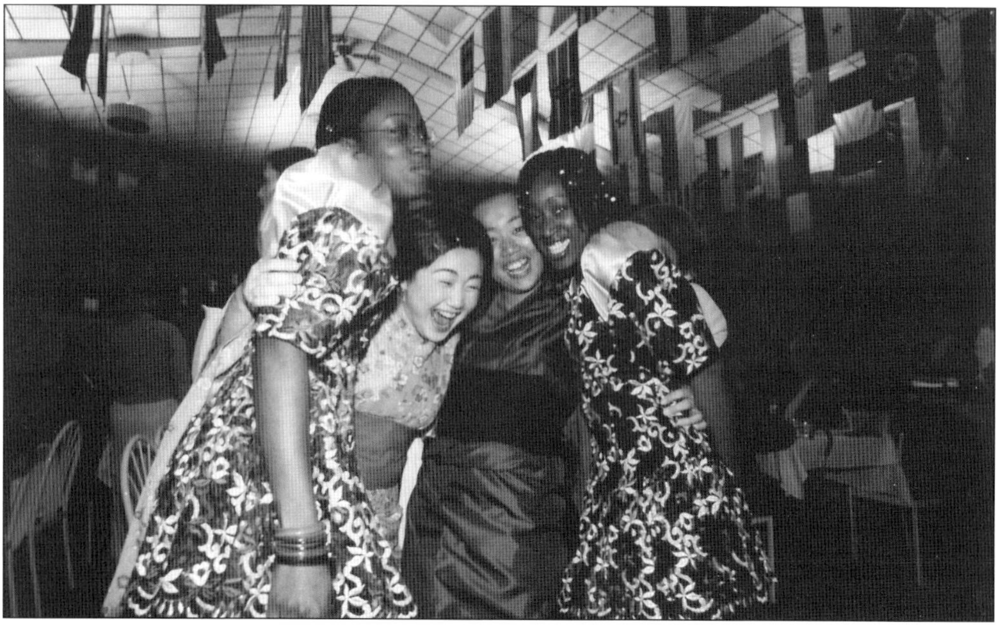

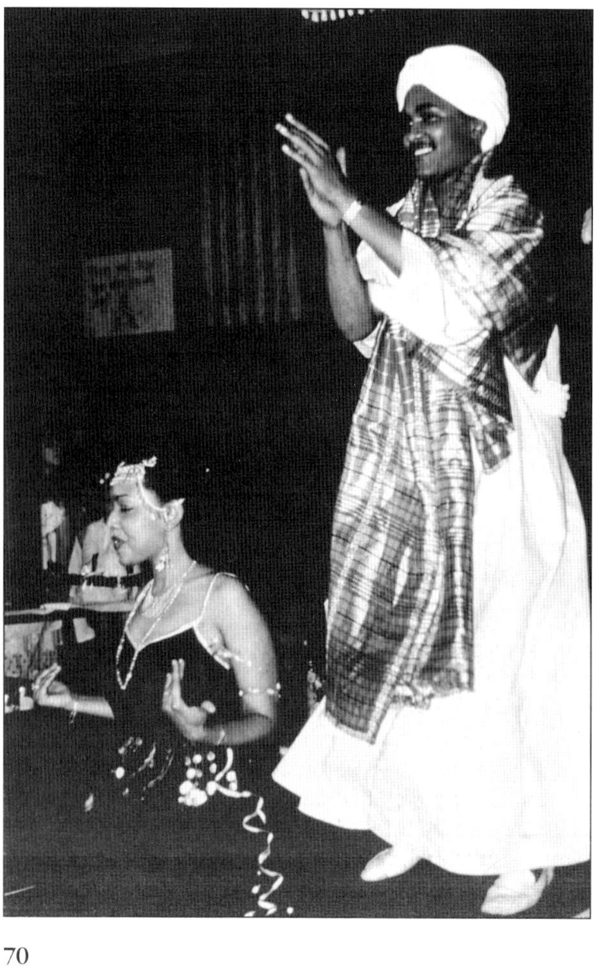

International Night is a New England College tradition that celebrates diversity. Students prepare and share food from their home cultures.

Students also provide after-dinner entertainment at annual International Night festivities.

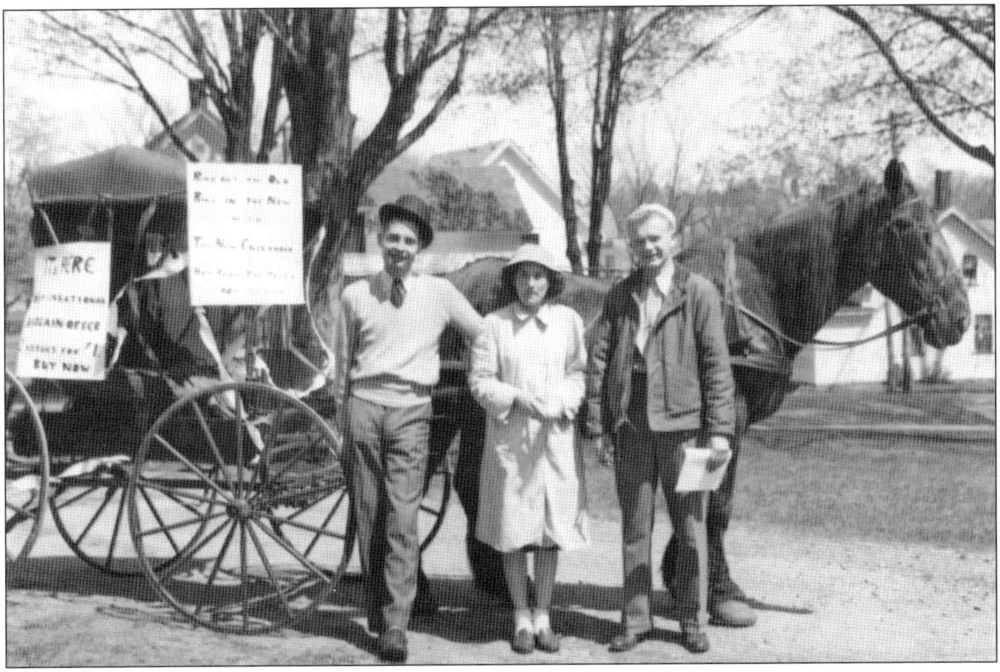

The *New Englander* newspaper staff once sold annual subscriptions using a buggy to draw attention and signs that read, "It's here. A sensational bargain offer. 10 issues for $1. Buy now" and "Ring out the old, ring in the new, with the *New Englander*. Hot from the press. 10¢ per copy."

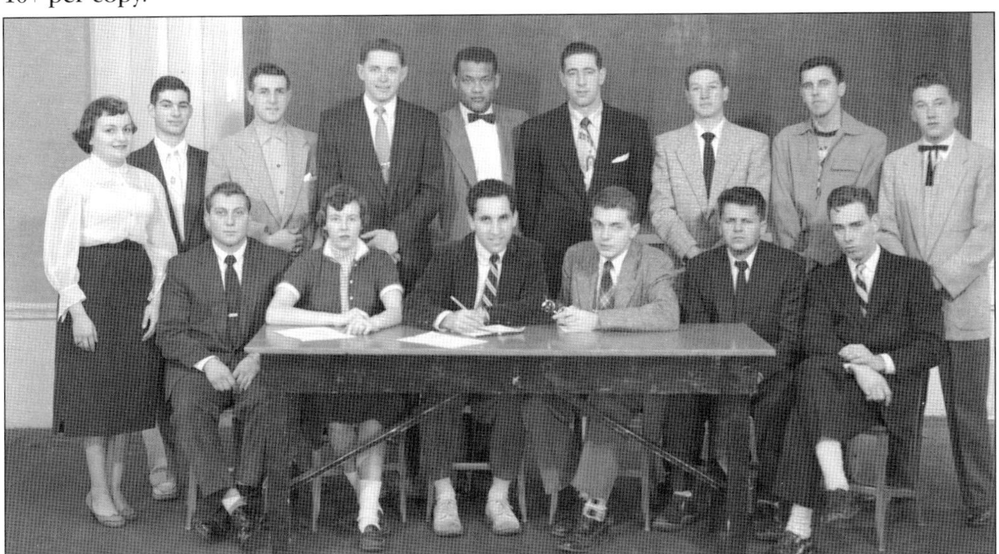

The *New Englander* newspaper has been published continuously since the college's early years. The 1954 staff, from left to right, are (first row) Nicholas Borrello, Barbara Hunter, Oscar Donati, Andler Alexander, Matthew Petarys, and James Flynn; (second row) Frances Tedesco, Leonard Pomerantz, Raymond Samodovitz, William Sylvester, Guy Denizard, Robert Bonazzoli, Richard Bergeron, Thomas Bushlow, and Arthur Hayward. (Courtesy of Hillsborough Historical Society.)

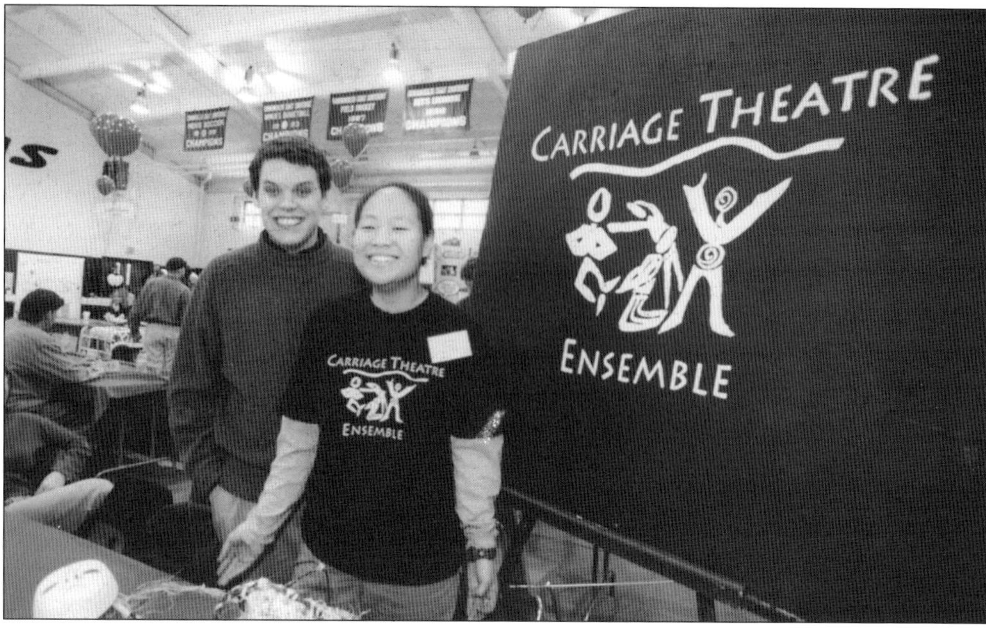

Theatre has long been a strong major at New England College, and students are enthusiastic about opportunities, including the Carriage Theatre Ensemble.

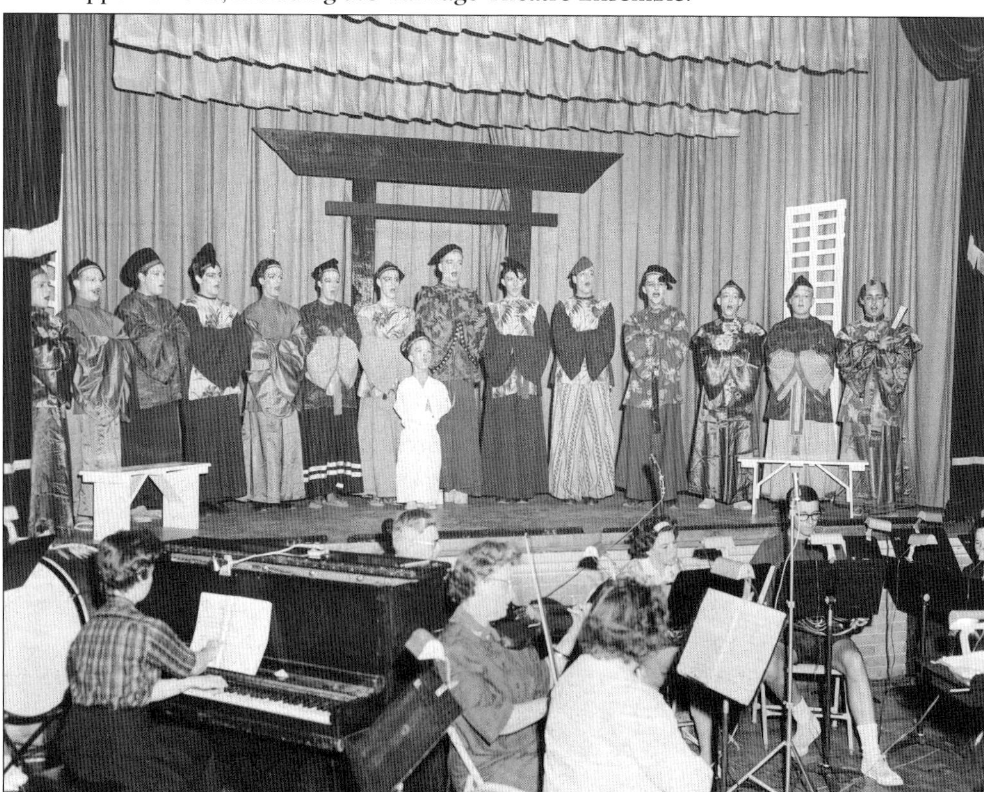

The Mikado was performed by New England College students in 1963. (Courtesy of Hillsborough Historical Society.)

"The shows were held upstairs in the town hall and it would be packed. The lights would dim and a three piece combo would play 'There's No Business Like Show Business' and Broadway could not have been more exciting," recalled a member of the class of 1960. This picture shows students onstage in 1962, the year that the New England College Players presented *You Can't Take It With You* under the direction of Dean Paul Eisler. (Courtesy of Hillsborough Historical Society.)

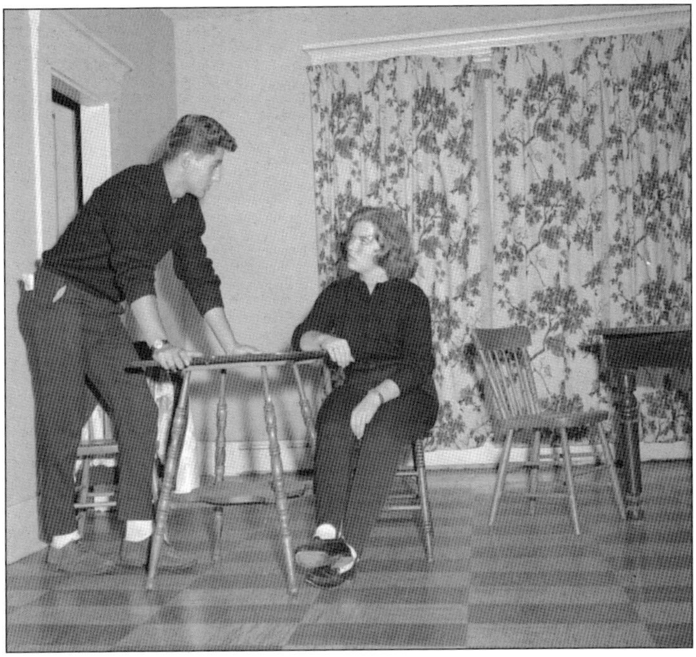

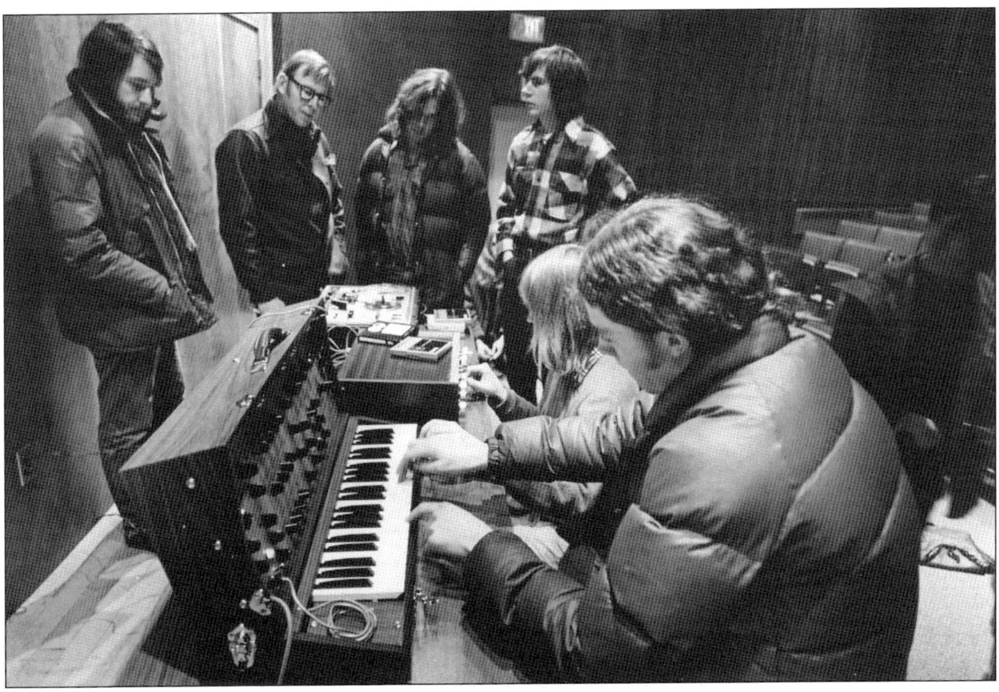

The stage and auditorium in the Science Building provided a place for live theater on campus as well as opportunities for students interested in lighting, sound, and stage management.

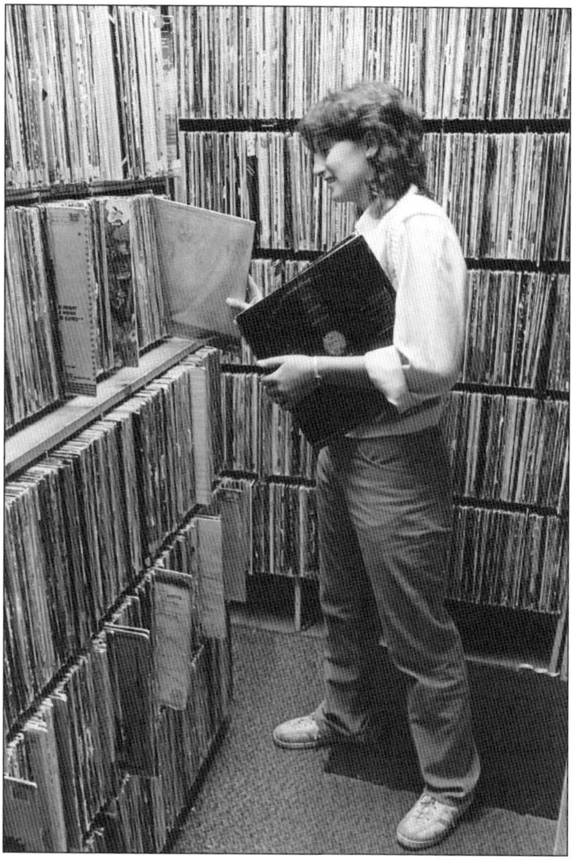

Danforth Library had a large collection of records in the days of vinyl recordings. Students could borrow records. They were also used by the college radio station.

The WNEC radio studio looked like this in the early 1980s.

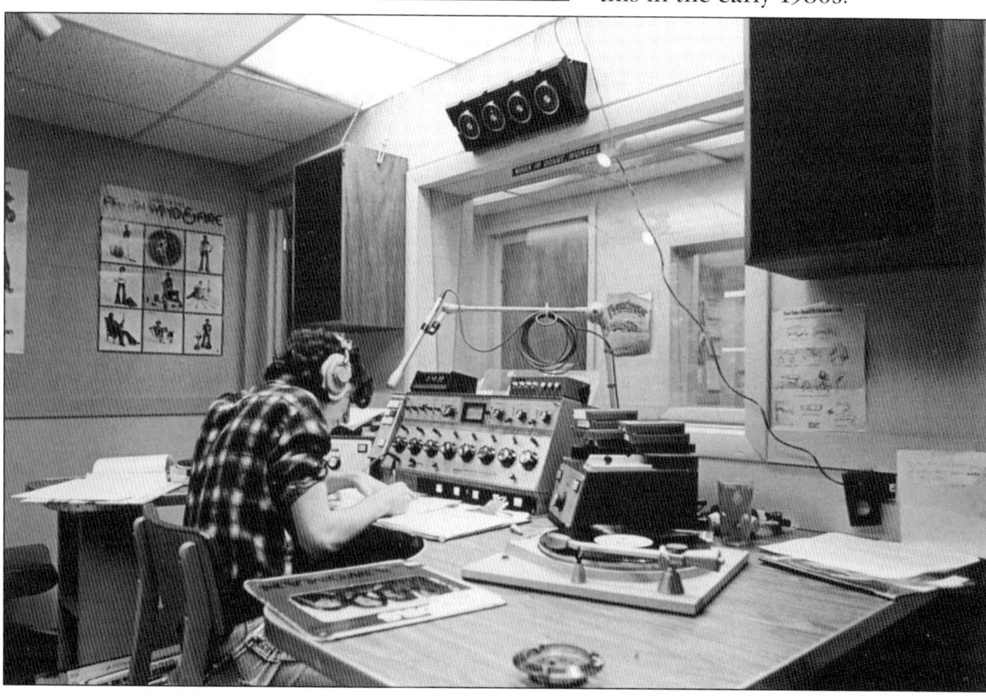

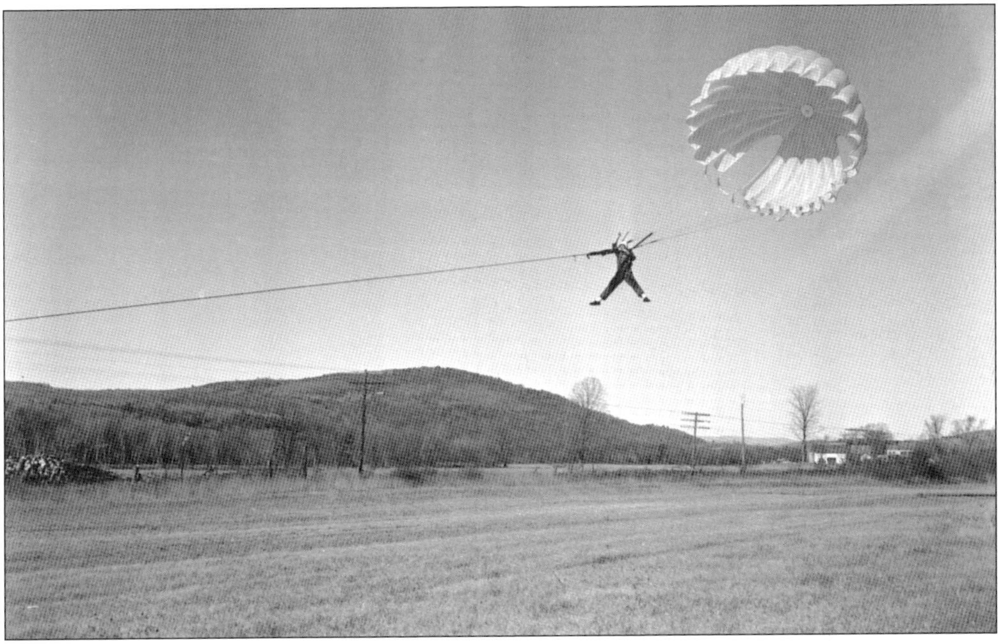

Car chuting was a sport invented at New England College by Sigma Alpha Beta member Dave Arnold. Arnold, a former Navy skydiver, said that car chuting was "an easy sport, just as safe as snow or water skiing." The sport had a big following within the Sigma Alpha Beta fraternity. (Courtesy of Hillsborough Historical Society.)

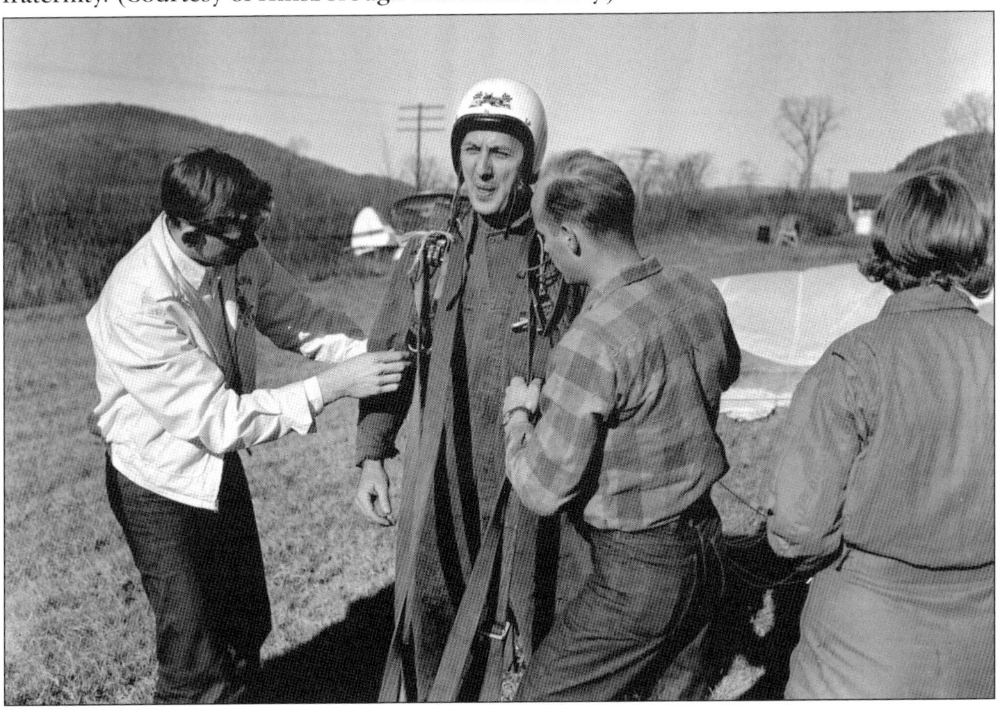

From left to right are student Dave Arnold, dean Don Woodrow, and student Joe Giardina. Woodrow was strapped into the harness for a modified 28-foot parachute to go airborne, towed by a cut-down 1951 Ford truck. (Courtesy of Hillsborough Historical Society.)

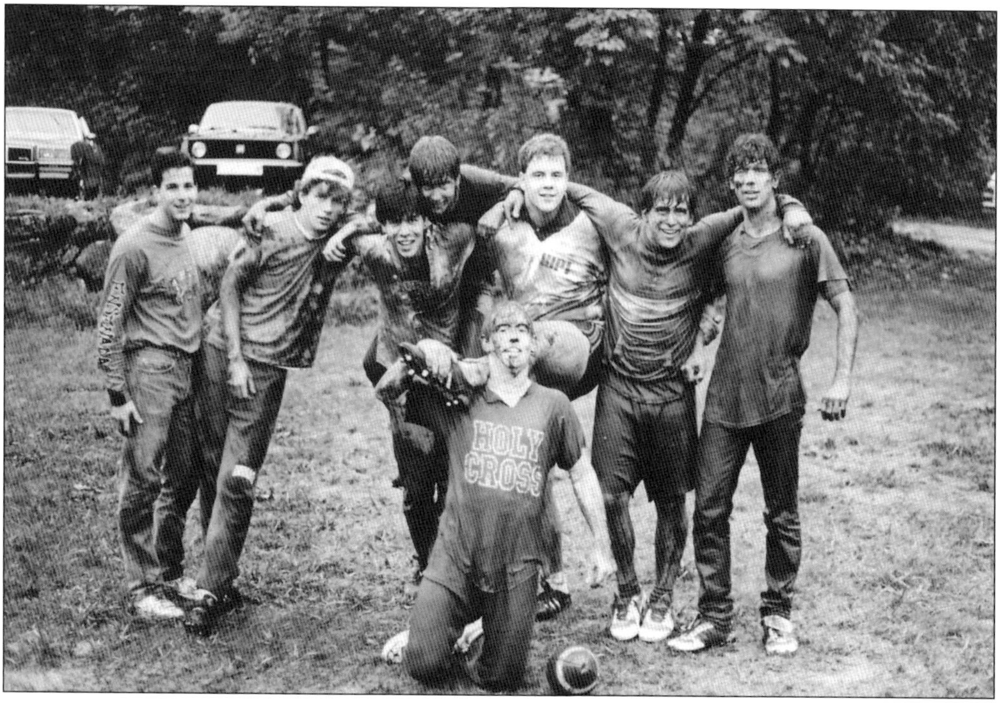

"Mud season" does not deter hardy New England College students from having fun outdoors. "Work hard, play hard" is the motto for many students at the college.

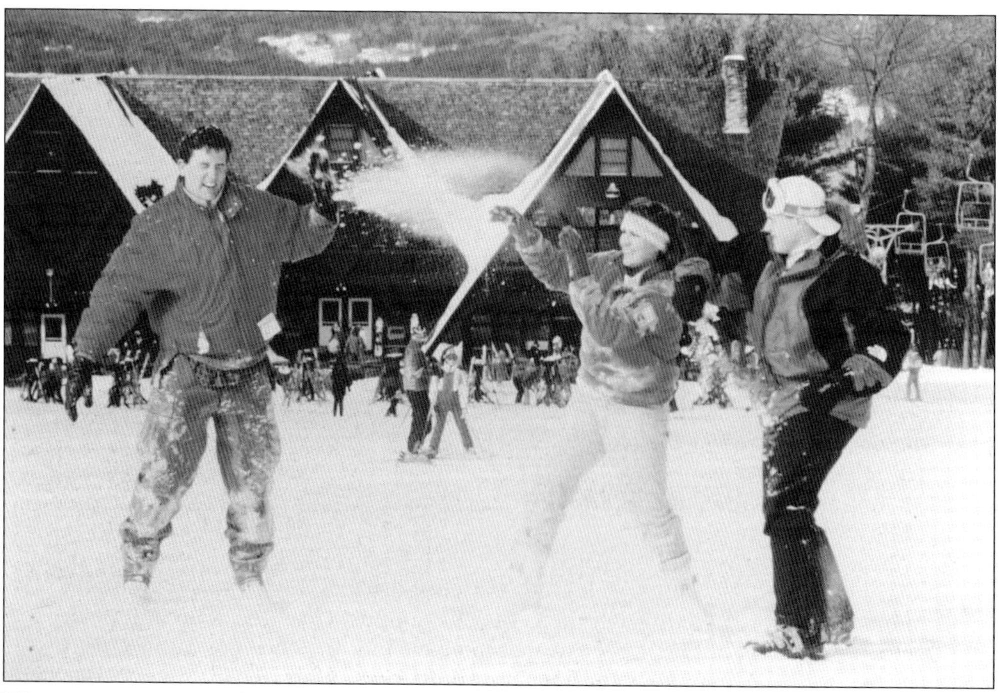

Winter gives New England College students lots of healthy outdoor activities like alpine and Nordic skiing, snowboarding, and just playing in the snow at nearby Pats Peak..

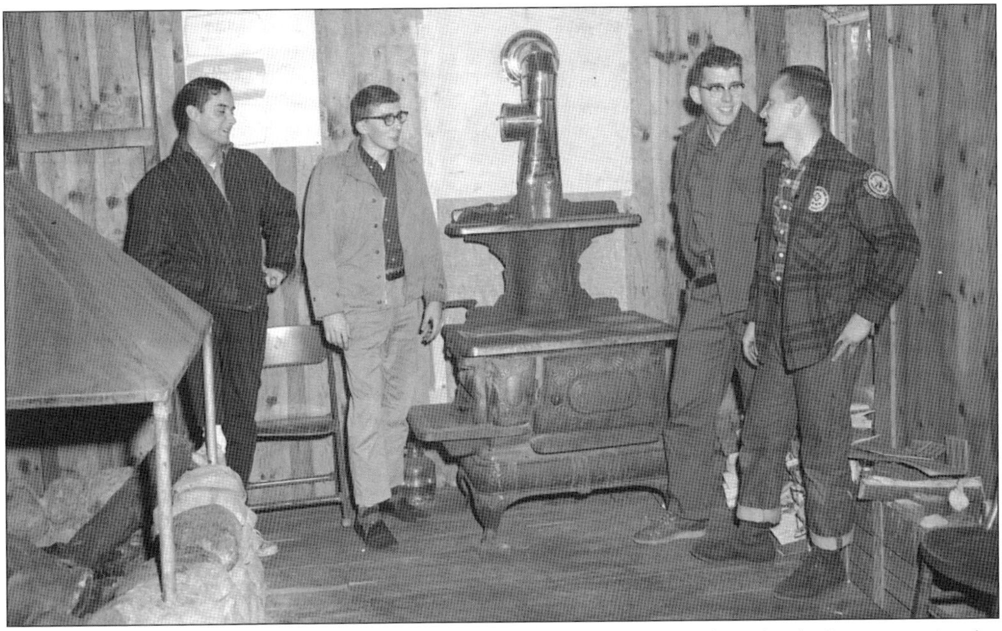

The May 2, 1947, *Kearsarge Independent* reports that "the student body has organized a Sportsman's Club and already submitted an application for membership to the National Rifle Association. Meeting every Wednesday at the local inn, the twenty-five members heartily enjoy swapping tales and discussing the many outdoor activities which they have planned for the summer." Pictured here are members of the Sportsmen's Club in 1962. (Courtesy of Hillsborough Historical Society.)

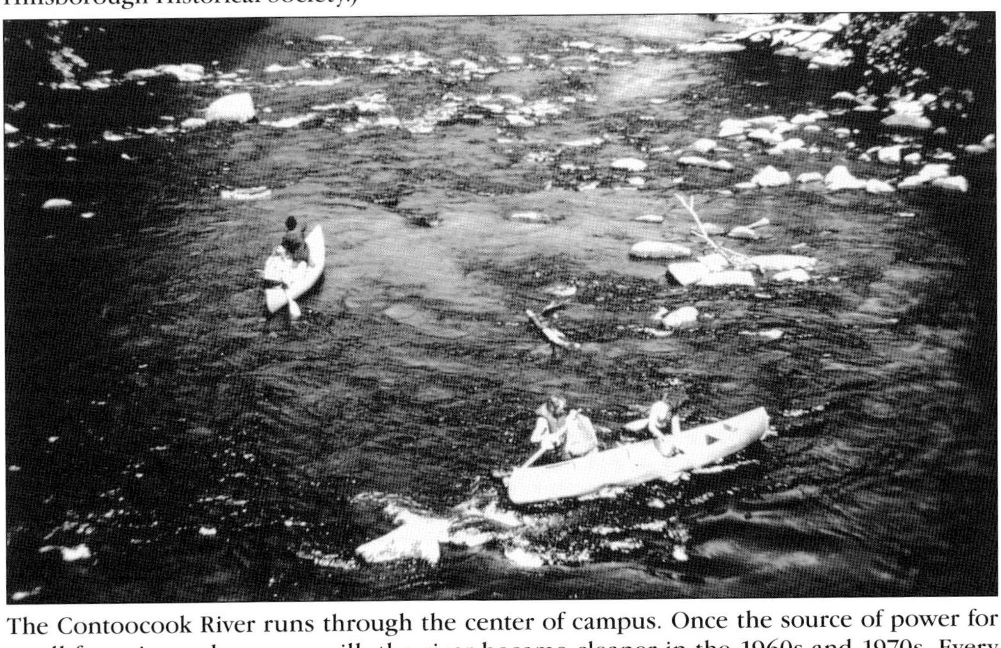

The Contoocook River runs through the center of campus. Once the source of power for small factories and a paper mill, the river became cleaner in the 1960s and 1970s. Every spring, the winter ice thaws and giant floes float downriver. When the ice is gone, kayakers come from near and far to enjoy white water a little upstream from the covered bridge. In the summer and fall, calm waters attract canoeists and trout fishermen.

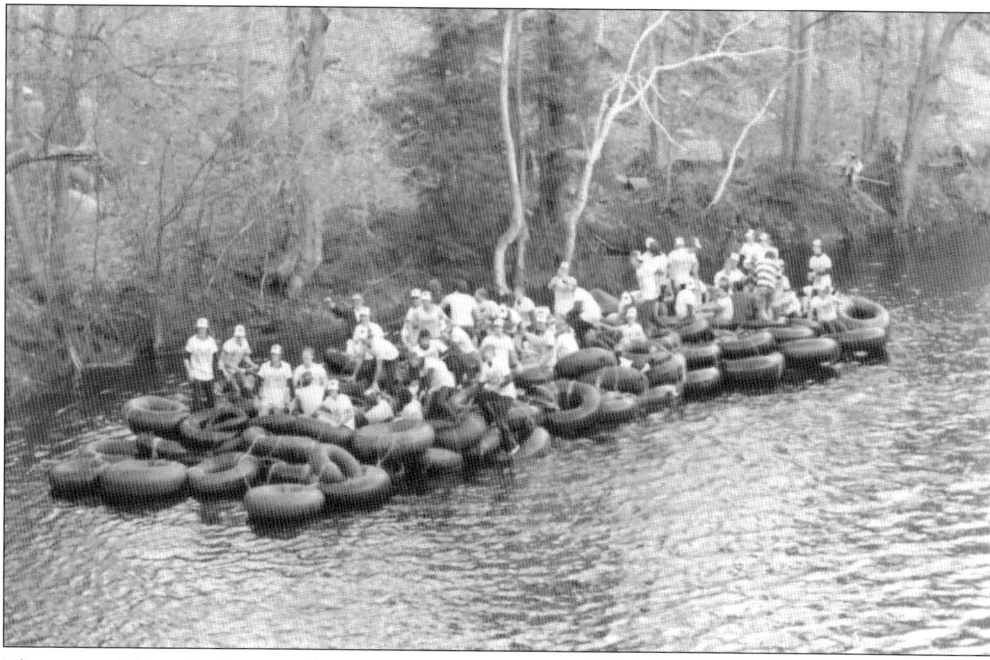

The annual River Raft Race (shown here in May 1979) was a rowdy student-driven celebration during an era when students became environmentally active. It has evolved into the annual college-sponsored spring River Day celebration, which is not announced until the morning of that event, when classes are cancelled and the entire community enjoys outdoor events on or near campus. (Courtesy of Henniker Historical Society.)

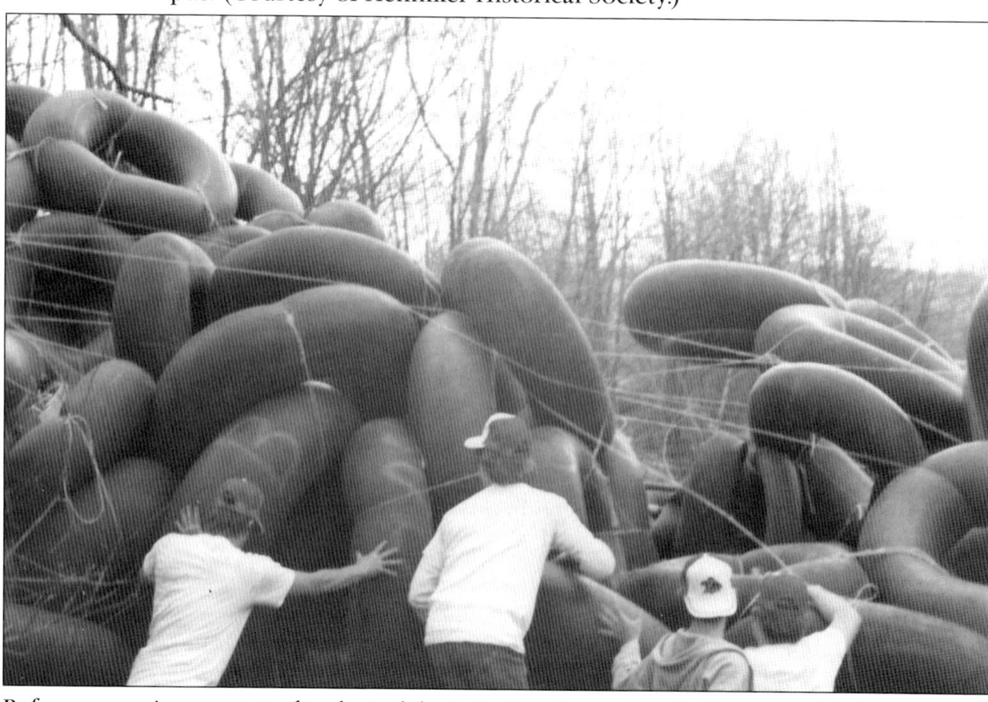

Raft construction presented technical, logistical, and creative challenges tackled by students from many different majors. (Courtesy of Henniker Historical Society.)

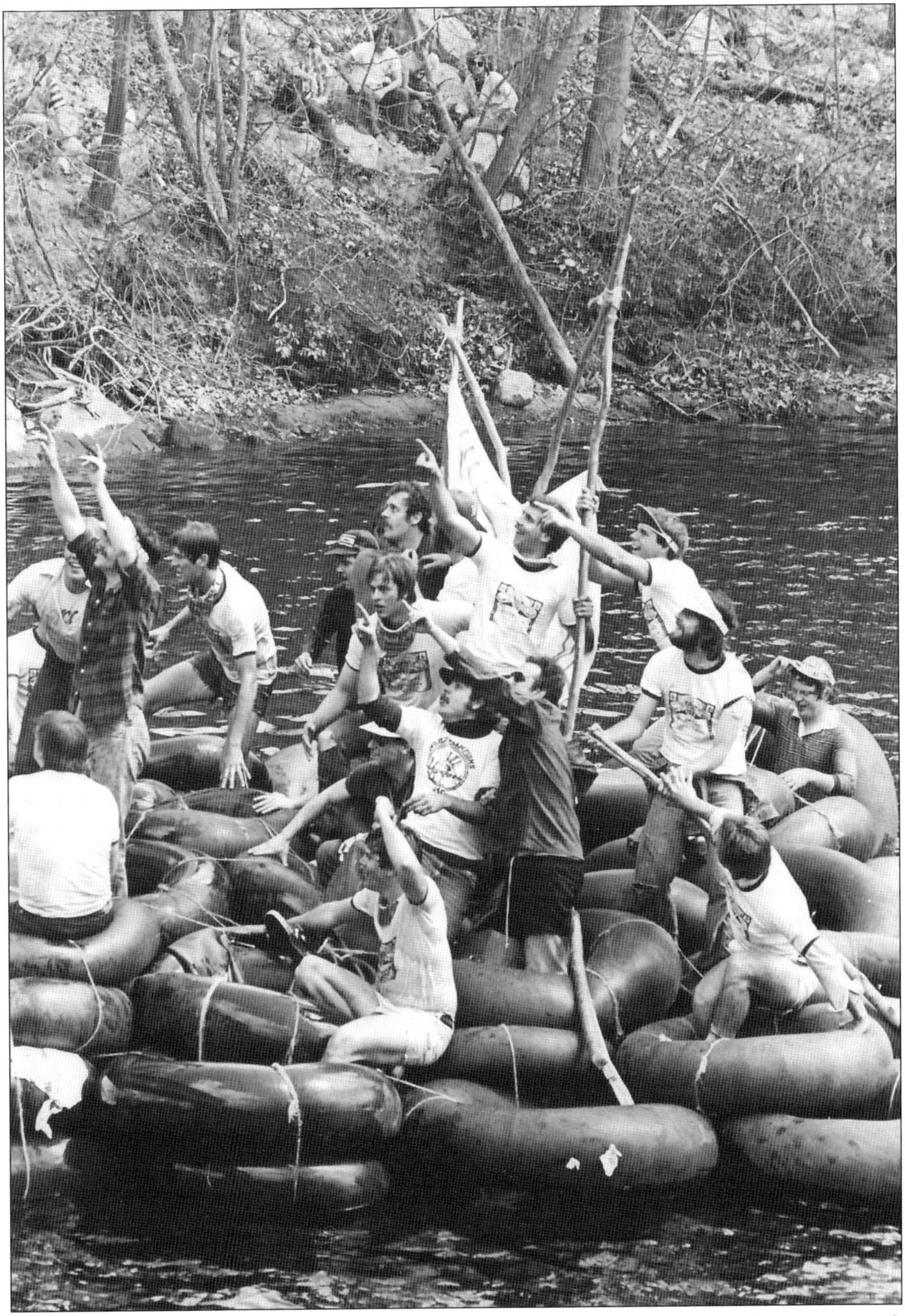

Students inflated and roped together hundreds of inner tubes to float down the Contoocook River, which runs through the center of the campus, for the River Raft Race. Enthusiastic revelers occasionally needed poles to free rafts stranded in shallows or on rocks.

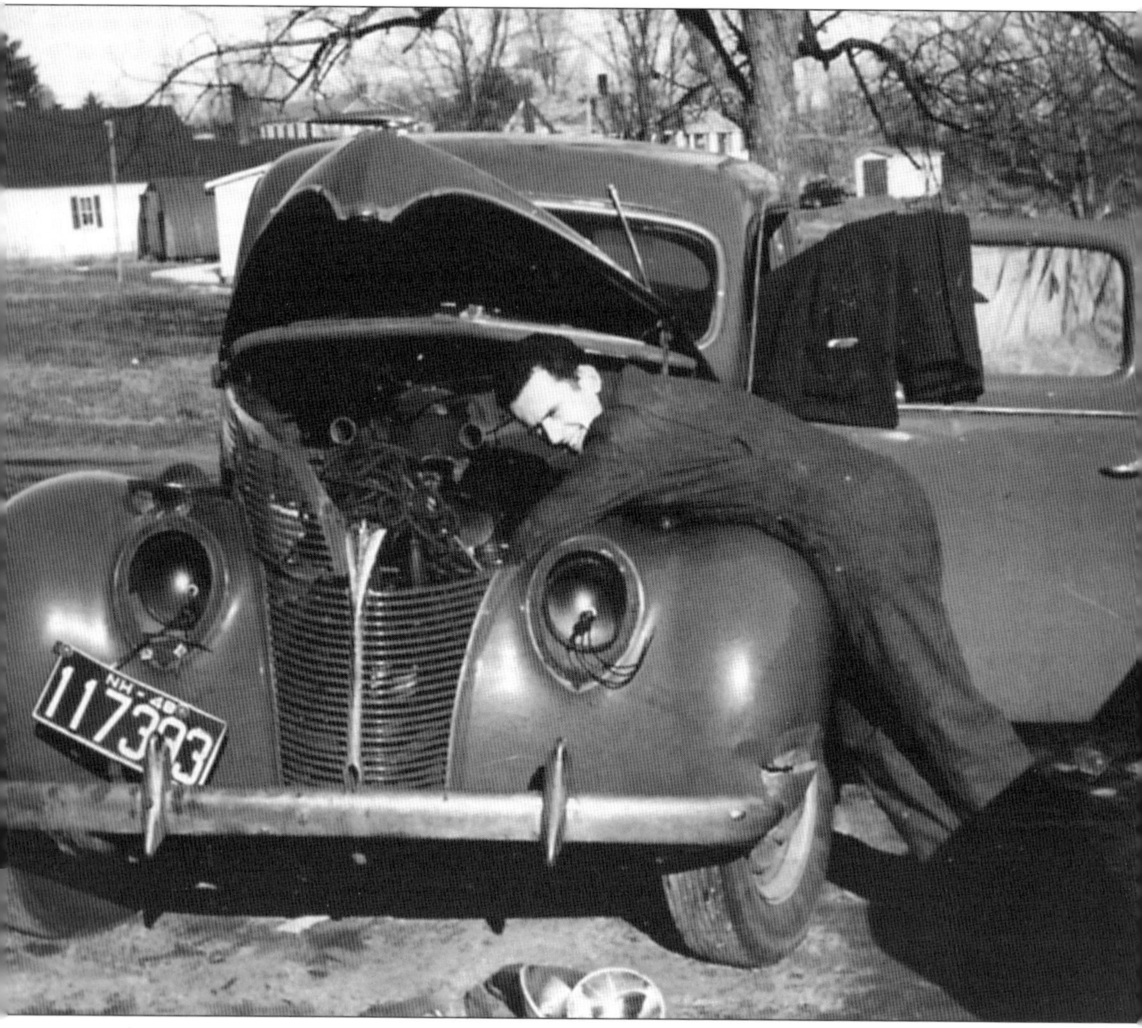

Jack Lannon had to take time out of sophomore activities to do much-needed repairs on a car. Sophomore activities included a competition between the freshman and sophomore classes, which started with a softball game, followed by numerous other athletic events and ended with a freshman-sophomore dance party. Lannon graduated in 1950.

Five

The Happy Days Are O'er

British Campus at Arundel

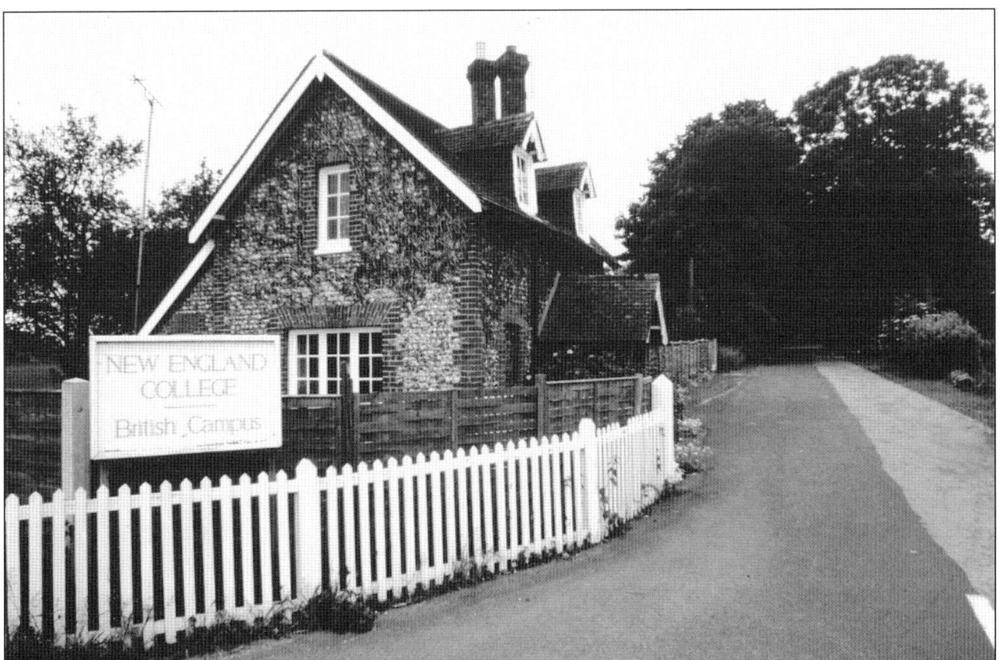

The Gatehouse welcomed visitors to the British campus of New England College, at Arundel, West Sussex, United Kingdom. The campus was surrounded by fields, and cattle sometimes grazed right outside the Gatehouse windows.

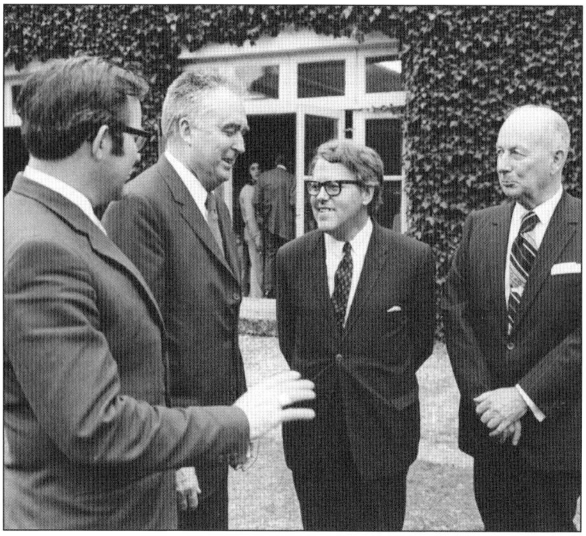

At the reception following dedication of the Arundel campus on October 22, 1971, on the lawn outside the Oak Room are, from left to right, Gordon Bennett, director of the Arundel campus (1971–1976); Jere Chase, president (1969–1973); Asa Briggs, vice-chancellor of the University of Sussex [1967–1976]; Life Peer [1976]); and William C. King, chair of the board of trustees. Bennett was the visionary who proposed purchase of the Arundel campus to facilitate travel-based cross-cultural experiential programs. Briggs was awarded an honorary doctorate of laws on that day

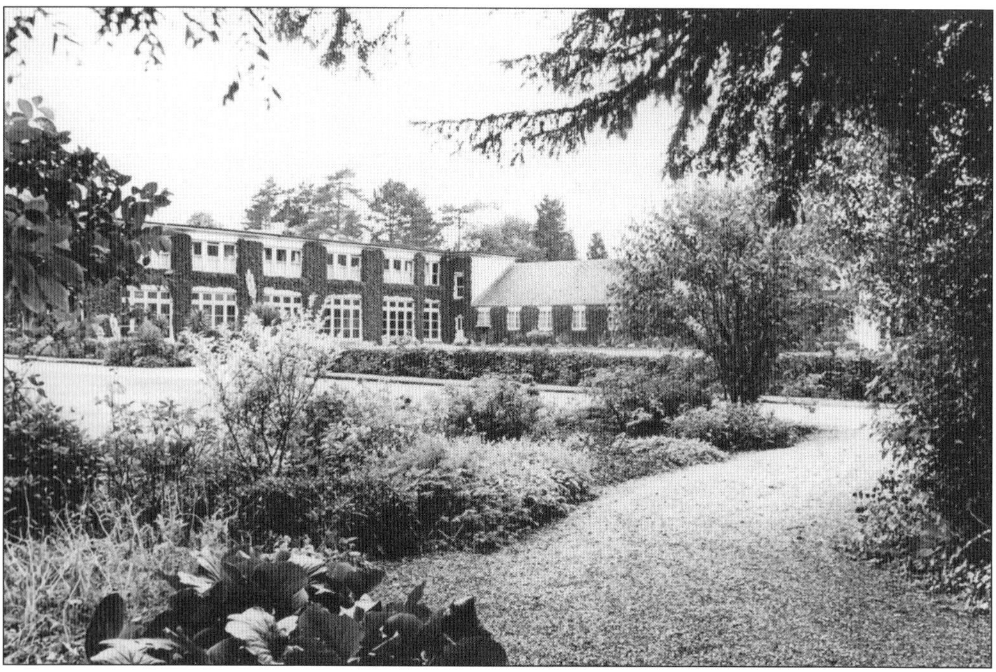

In September 1971, after two years of planning, New England College announced the opening of a branch in West Sussex, England, in a campus that formerly housed Tortington Park, an English boarding school for girls. For the dedication ceremony, Pres. Jere A. Chase chartered a 150-passenger DC-8 from Air Canada. Invited guests each paid $200 for their tickets. The dedication on October 22–24, 1971, included an academic procession, awarding of an honorary degree, and a grand ball. This image accompanied the invitations.

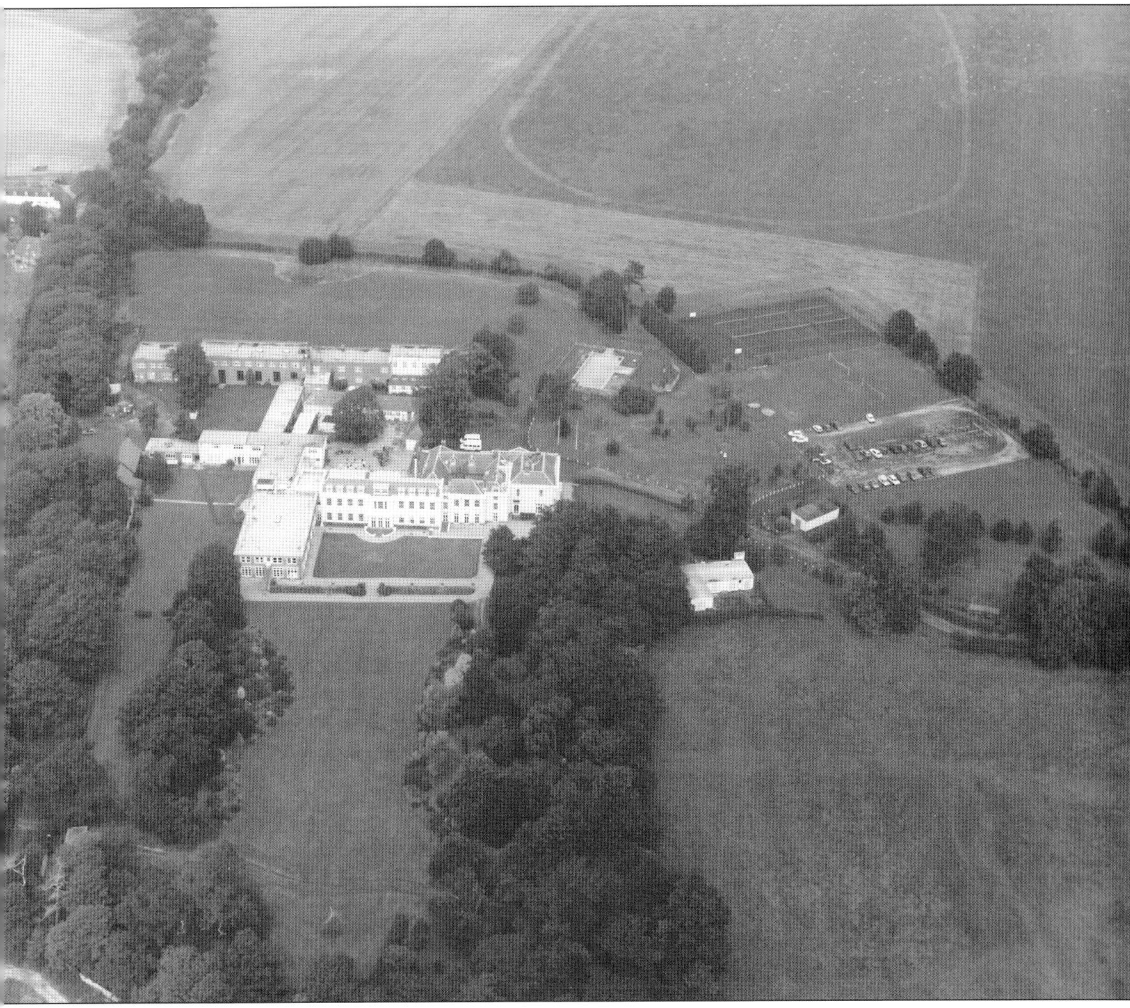

This aerial view shows the Arundel campus surrounded by fields. Trees (left) at the edge of the fields mark back roads where students could walk for miles. Just out of view, past the car parks (right) is the main road to town, which followed the meandering Arun River.

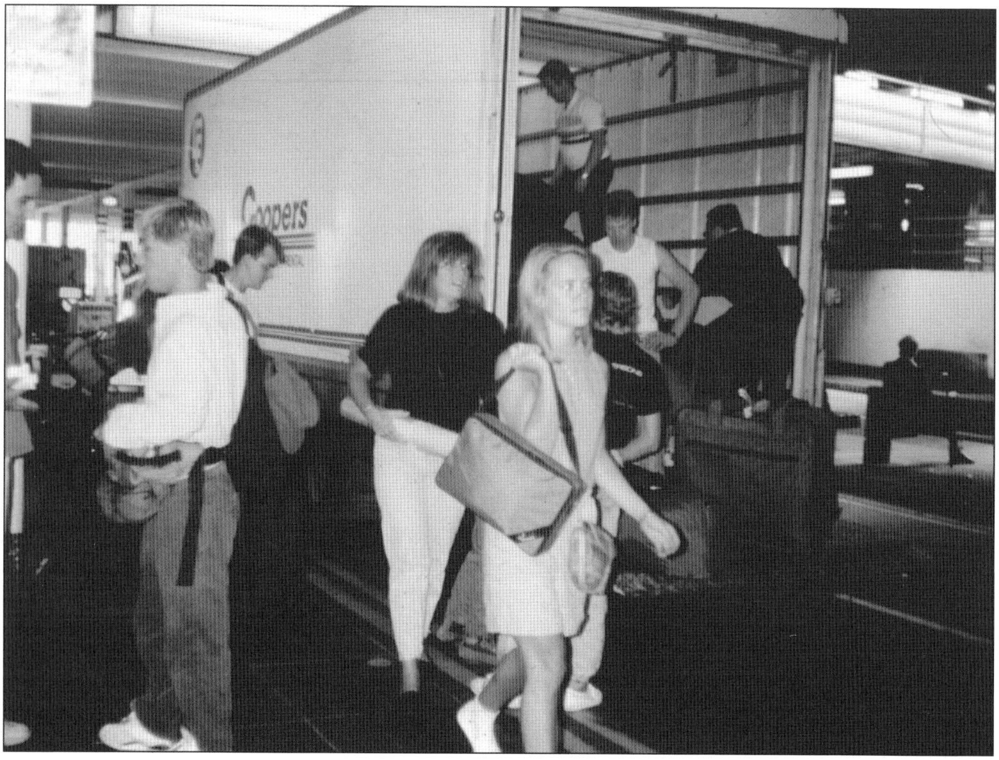

Hired vans transported luggage between the Arundel campus and the London airports of Heathrow and Gatwick.

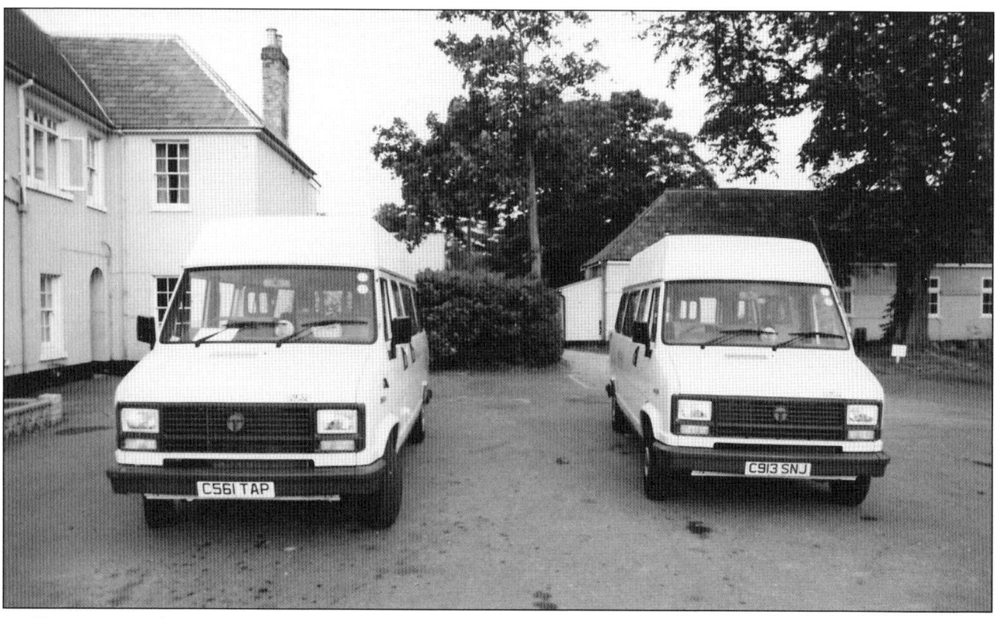

College-owned vans ran to and from Arundel on weekdays. They were used for field trips for travel courses related to British art, ecology, archaeology, history, and theater. In the late 1980s, the college driver, Ken Scutt, maintained the vehicles and regaled passengers with stories about life in England.

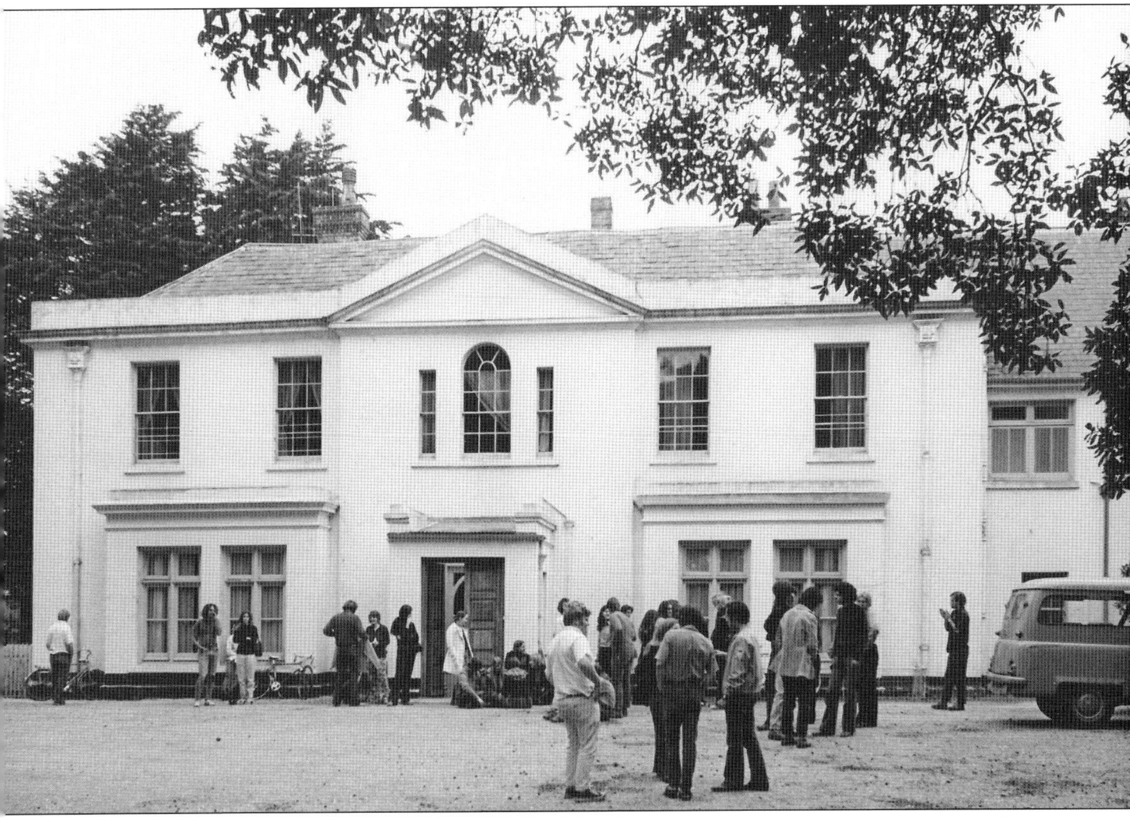

Manor House, pictured here, was reportedly constructed as a hunting lodge for the dukes of Norfolk, hereditary owners of nearby Arundel Castle.

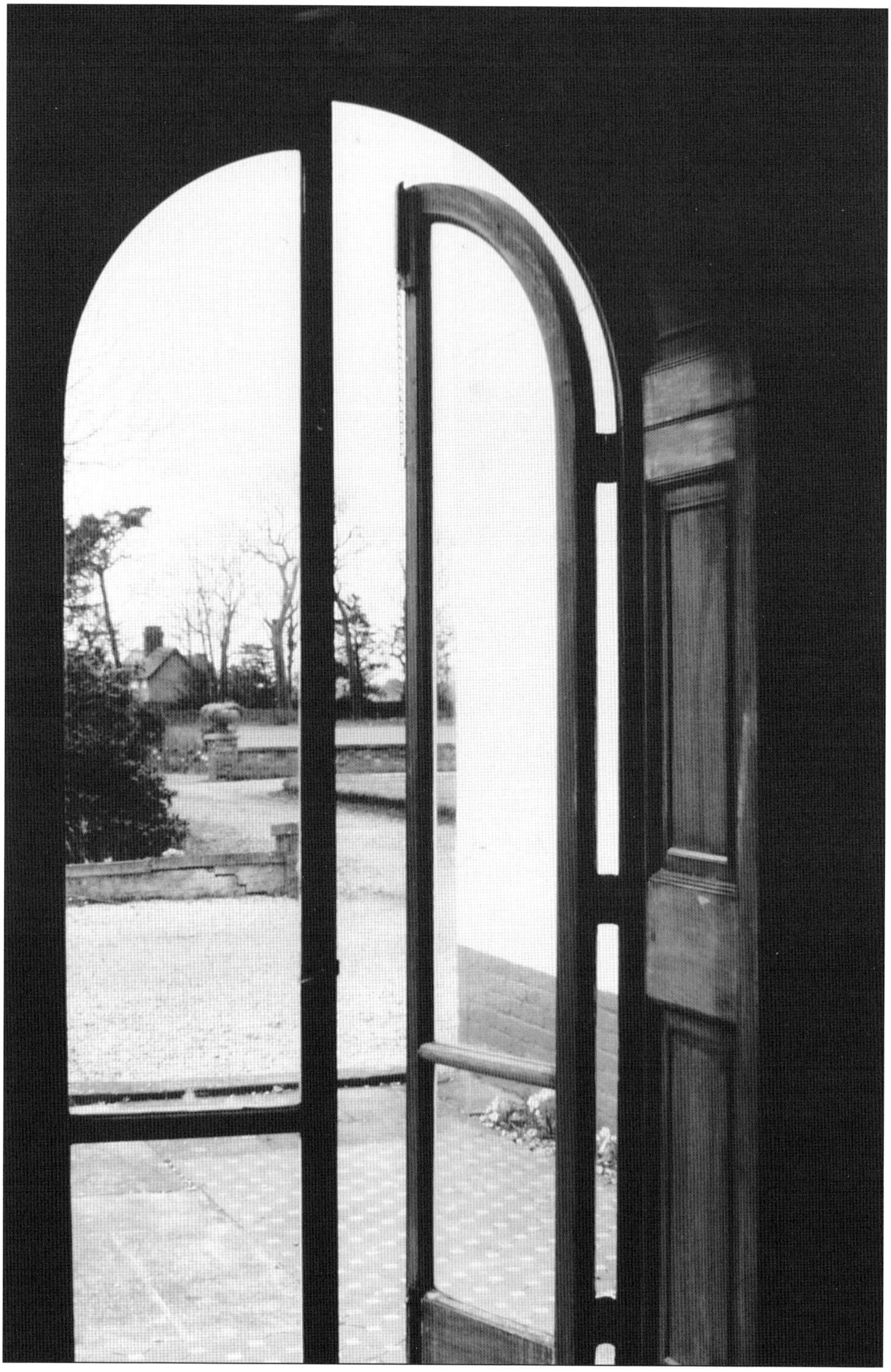

Here, someone could slide back the worn metal bolt and push open the heavy wooden door to let in the breeze when it finally stops raining. Jill Robertson McDonald tended a small hedge of lavender outside the front door of Manor House.

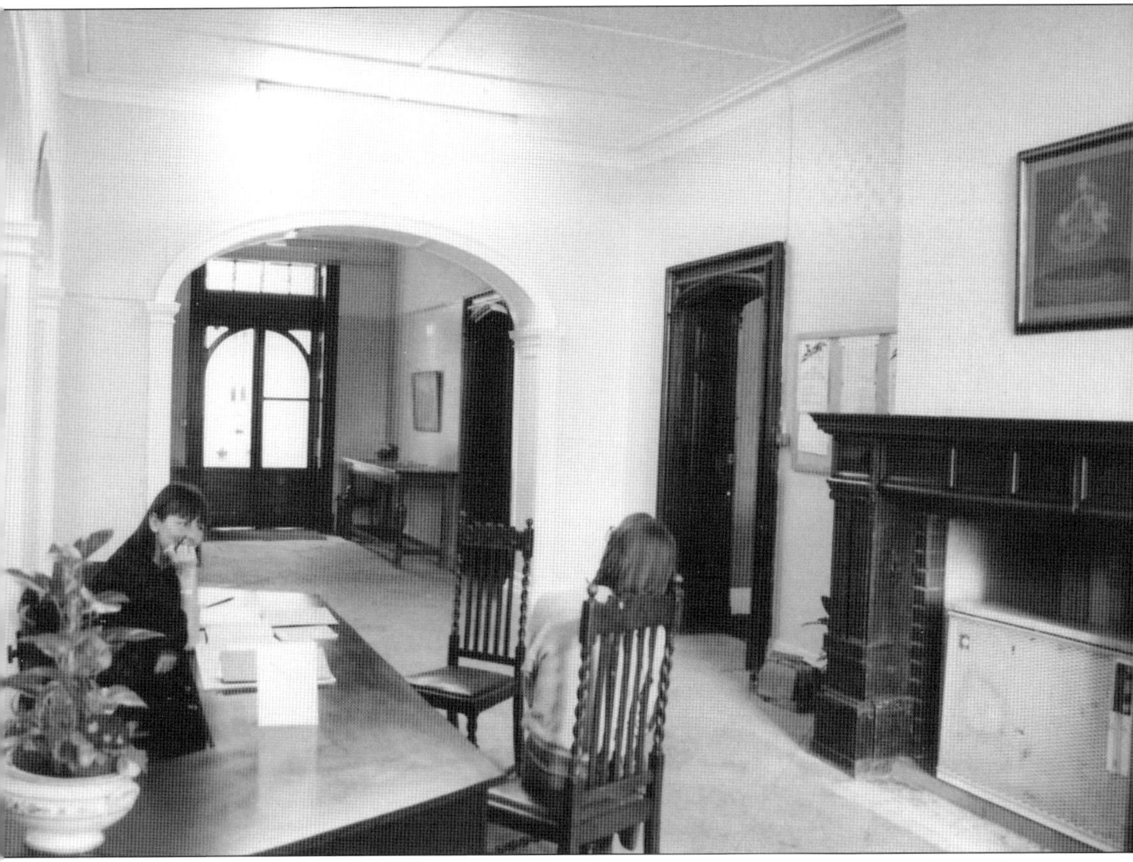

In the main lobby of Manor House were many reminders of bygone days: graceful arches overhead, smooth flagstone underfoot, embossed wallpaper punctuated by heavy wooden doors, fireplaces lined with green ceramic tiles, and posture-improving barley-twist chairs.

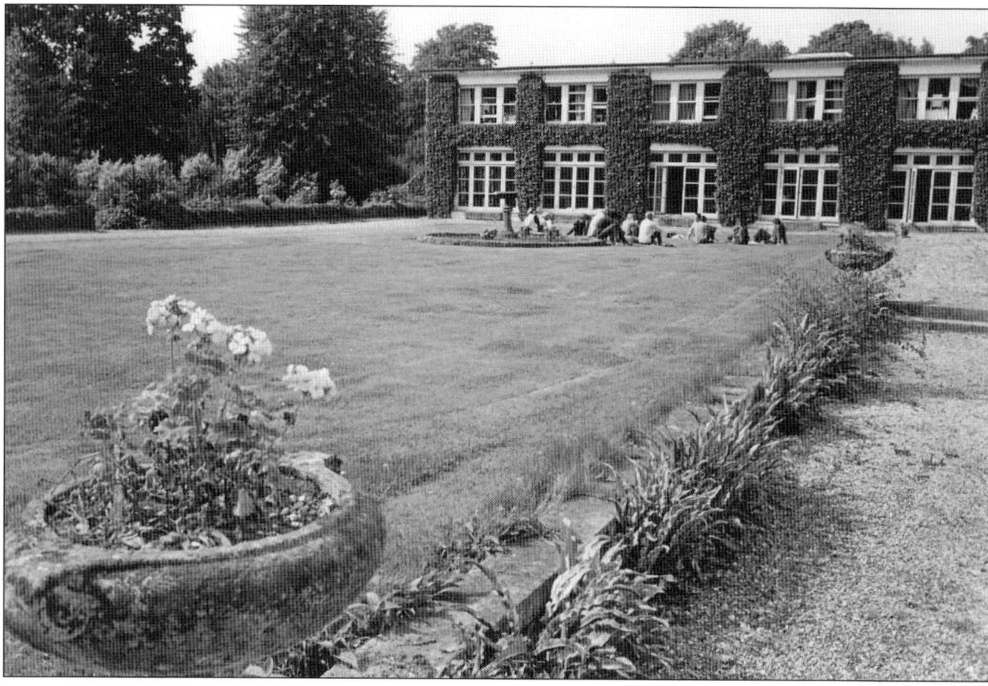

Arundel summer-session students gathered on the lawn. International Wing classrooms had double French doors that could be opened to gardens outside. The second floor of this wing was a student residence hall.

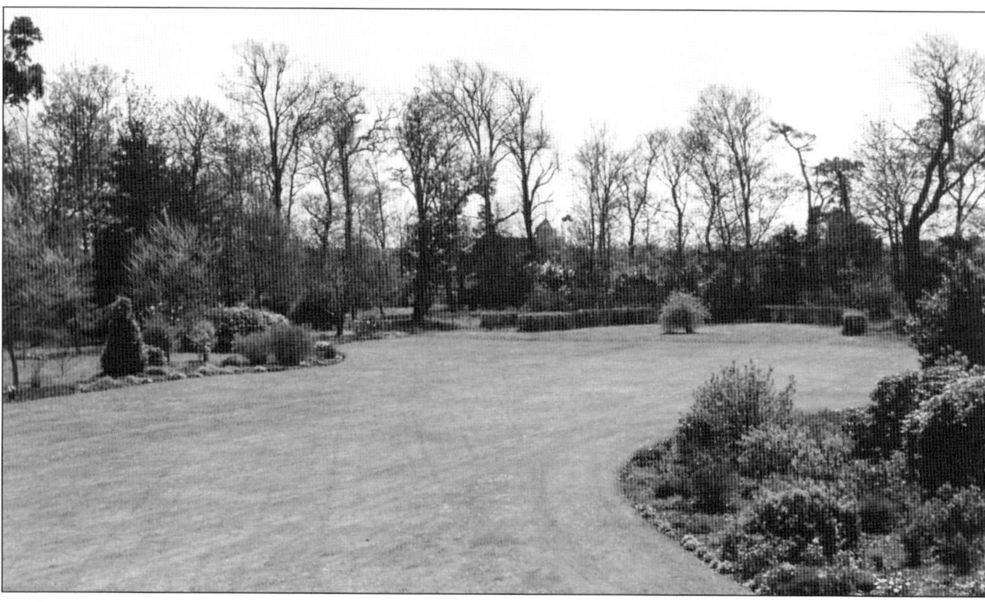

At dawn in midsummer, rabbits and hedgehogs came out from hiding in nearby hedgerows and wandered the garden lawn. At the end of the garden (left) was a moss-covered wooden gate that led to the tiny church at Tortington Park (roofline just visible at center). There was also a small duck pond with water lilies until the great hurricane of November 15–16, 1987, uprooted an ancient tree, believed to be 300 years old. The enormous tree fell into the pond and cracked the clay liner, draining the pond.

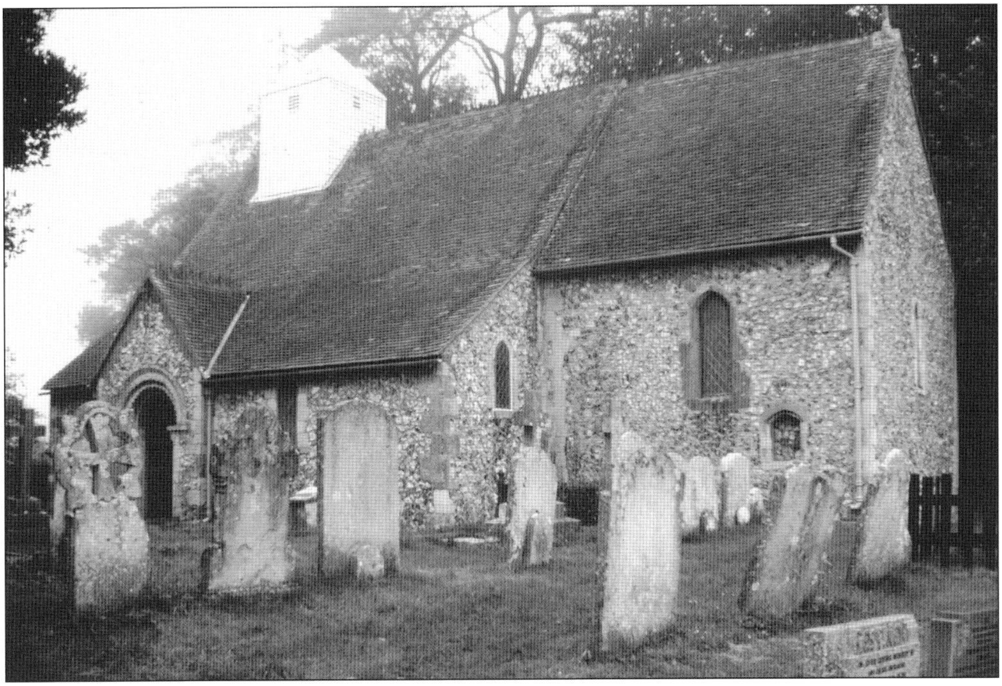

Adjacent to campus, the ancient Ste. Mary Magdalene's Church at Tortington Park was a quiet retreat for members of the college community. A neighborhood farmer occasionally allowed a couple of sheep to graze among the tilting headstones in the cemetery, keeping the grass short.

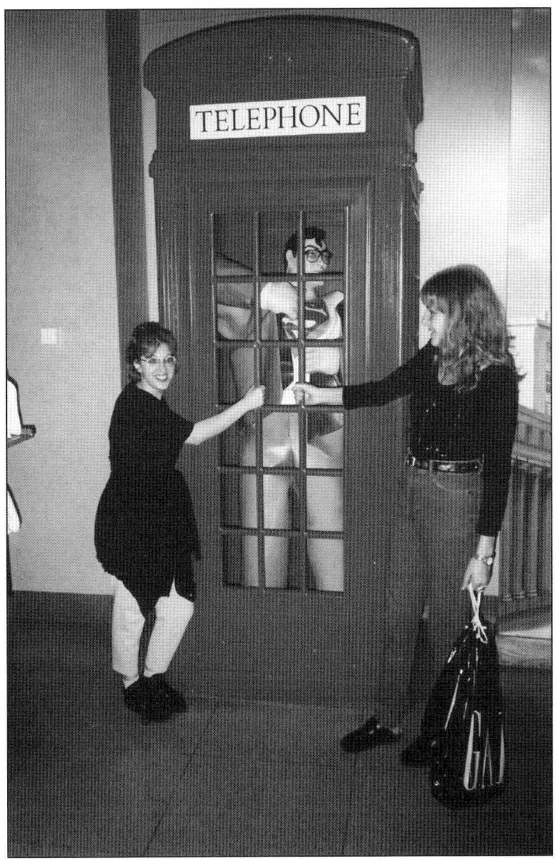

On weekends and evenings, a queue of students waited for incoming international calls at the red pay phone in the mailroom on the ground floor of Manor House. Apparently even superheroes used this phone.

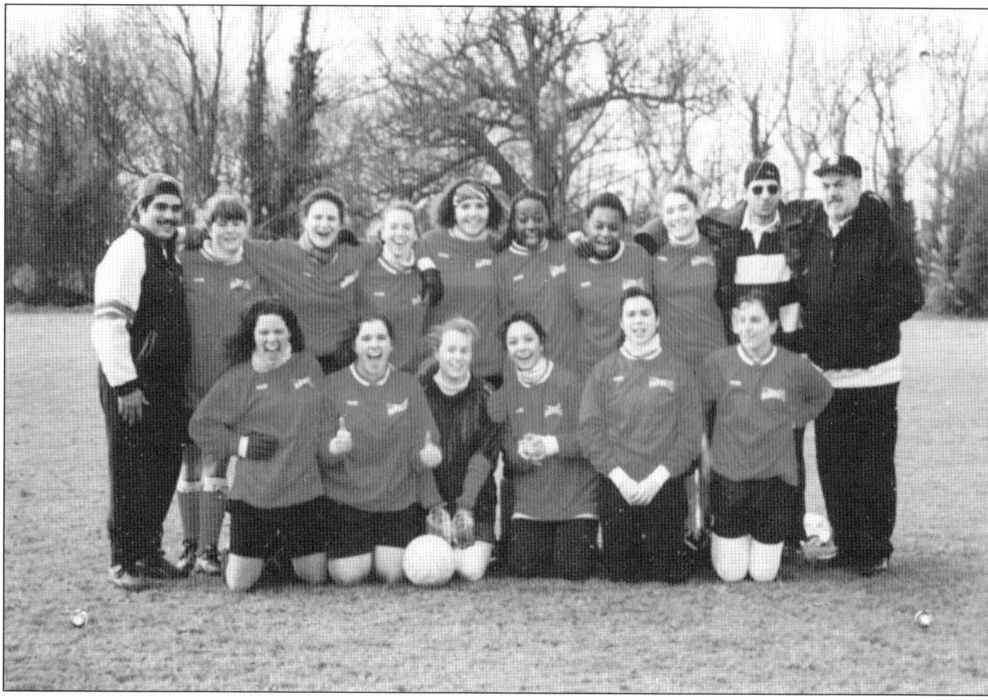

The first women's football (soccer) team at the Arundel campus, pictured here with Bill Eckford (on right), was formed in the spring of 1993.

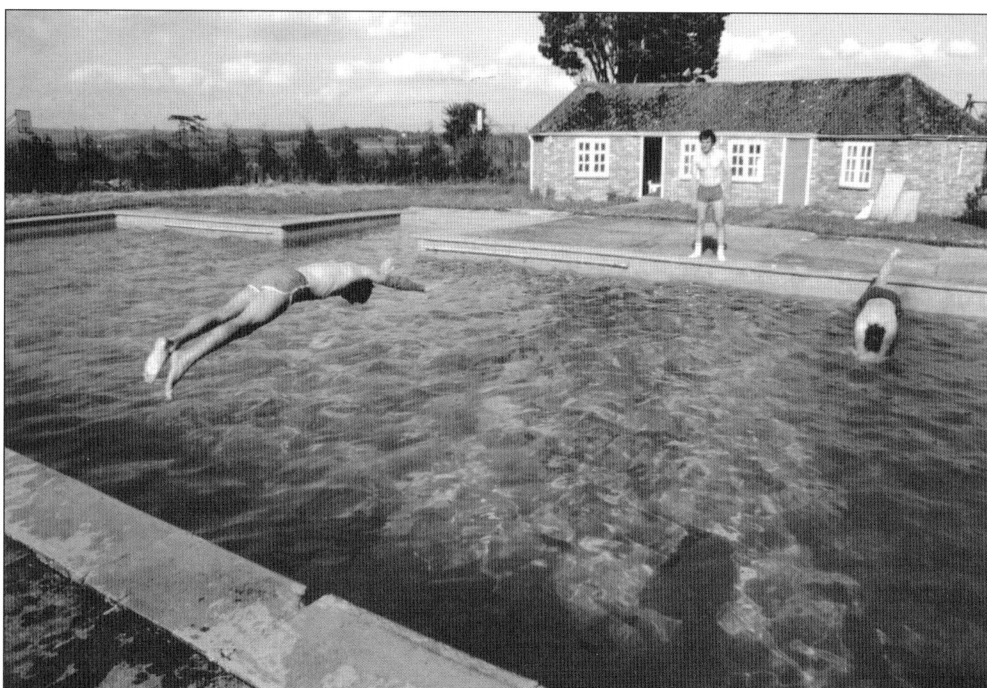

The cement-lined pool was spring-fed, and the water was bone-chillingly cold at all times of year. Intrepid students would dive in on a dare, but most did not linger long in the water.

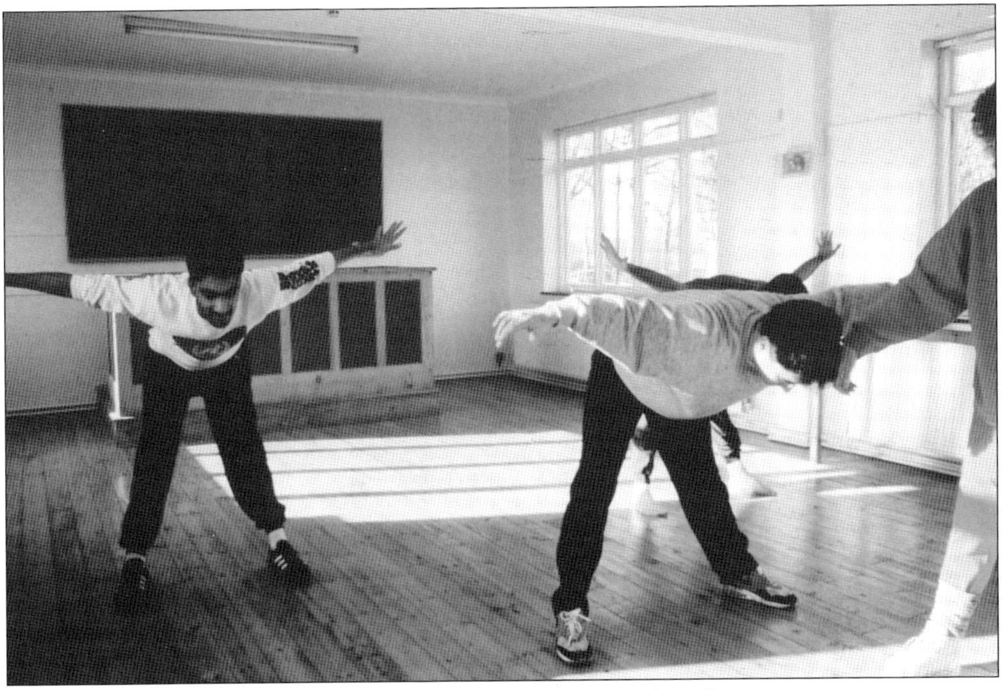

Yoga and dance classes were offered in the gymnasium and studio space.

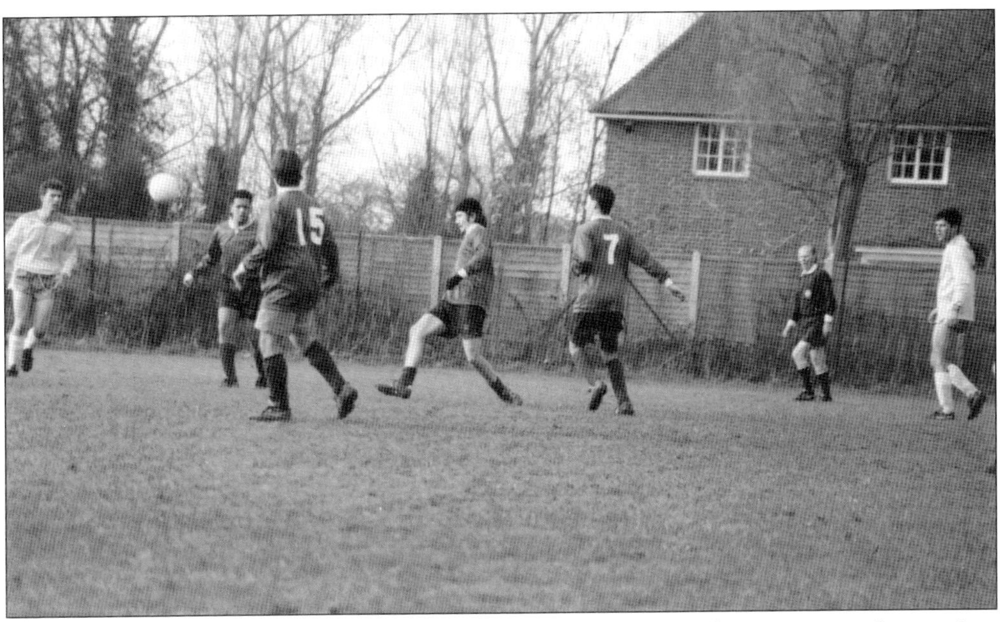

International students from the Arundel campus played football (soccer) matches against local teams in West Sussex.

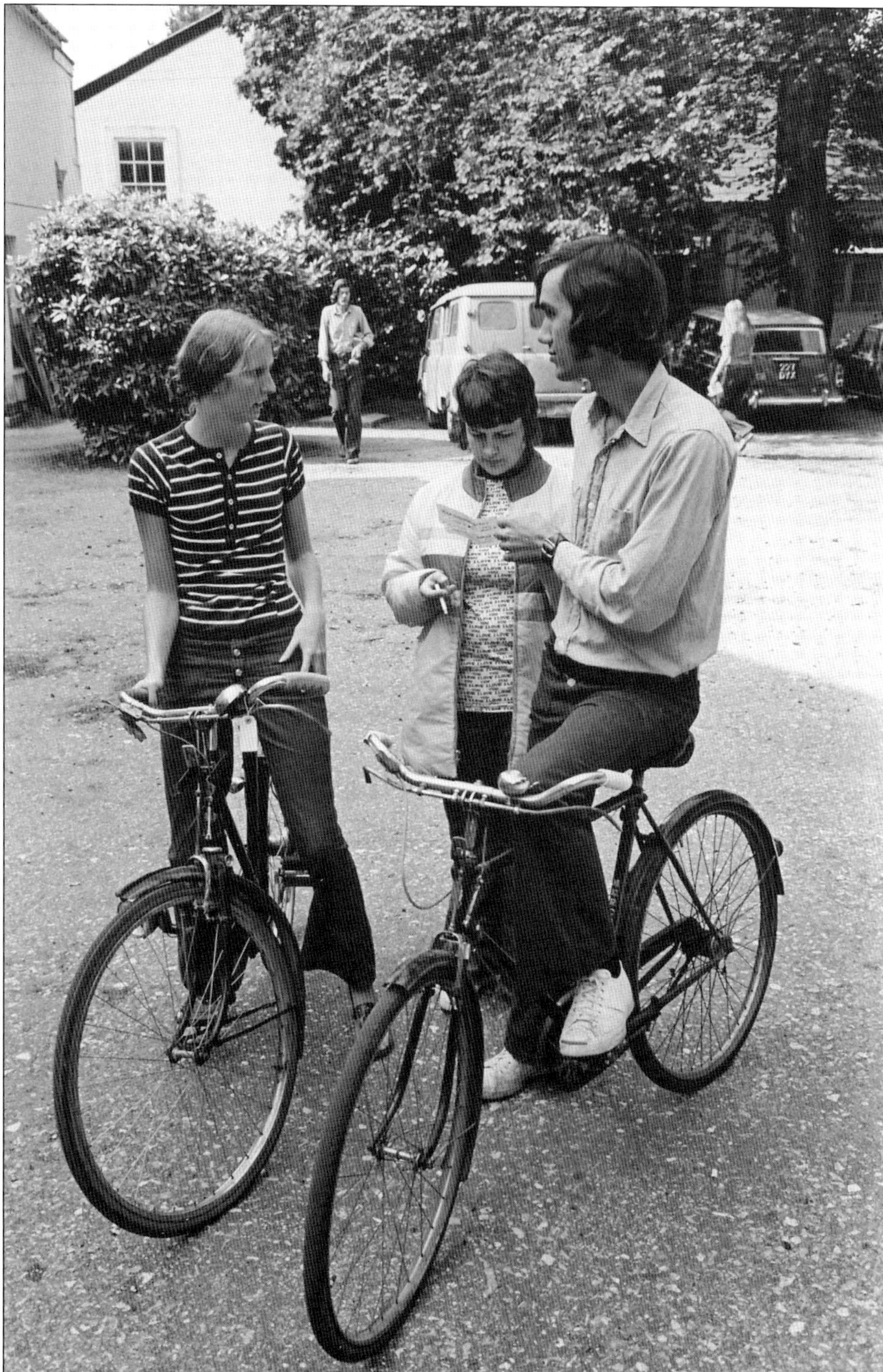

Bicycles were a convenient way to head north along the A7 to the town of Arundel or south along the motorway to the Ford train station or as far as Littlehampton. Many American students were surprised by the popularity of cigarettes in England in the early 1980s.

Six

We Have the Memories
A Quarter Century at Arundel

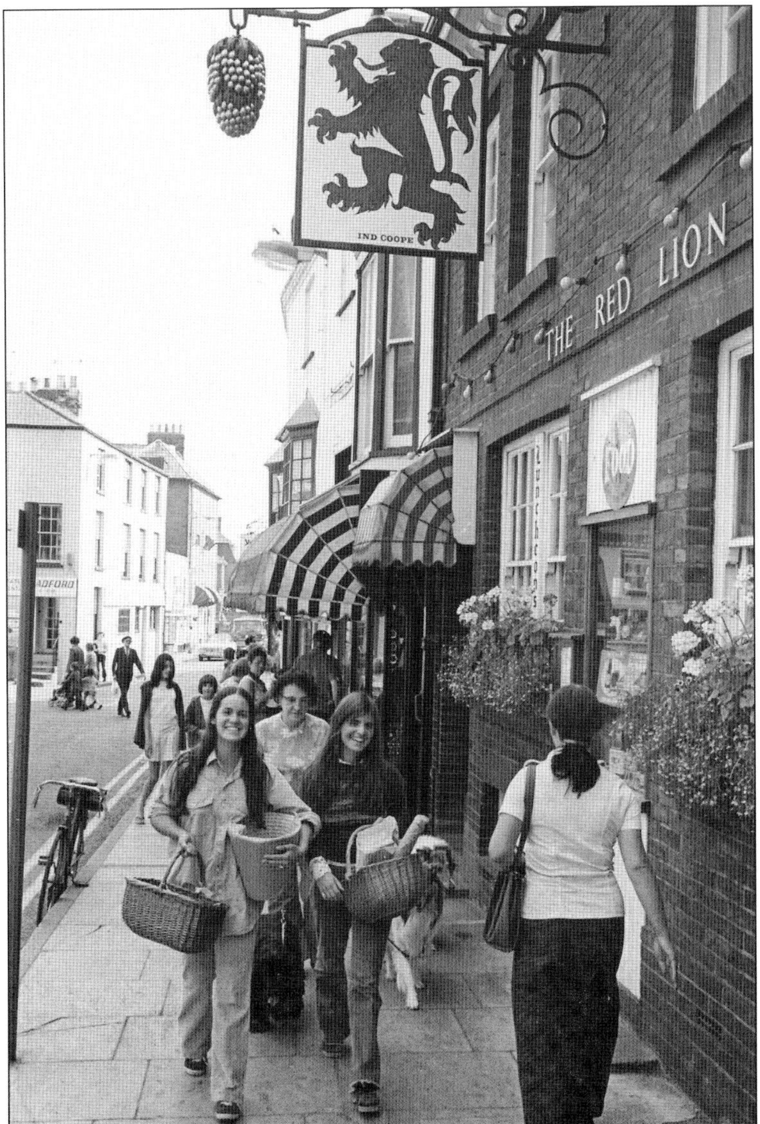

The Red Lion attracted tourists visiting the castle and occasionally attracted New England College students as well. Wicker shopping baskets avoided a 5-pence charge for bags when shopping in the High Street.

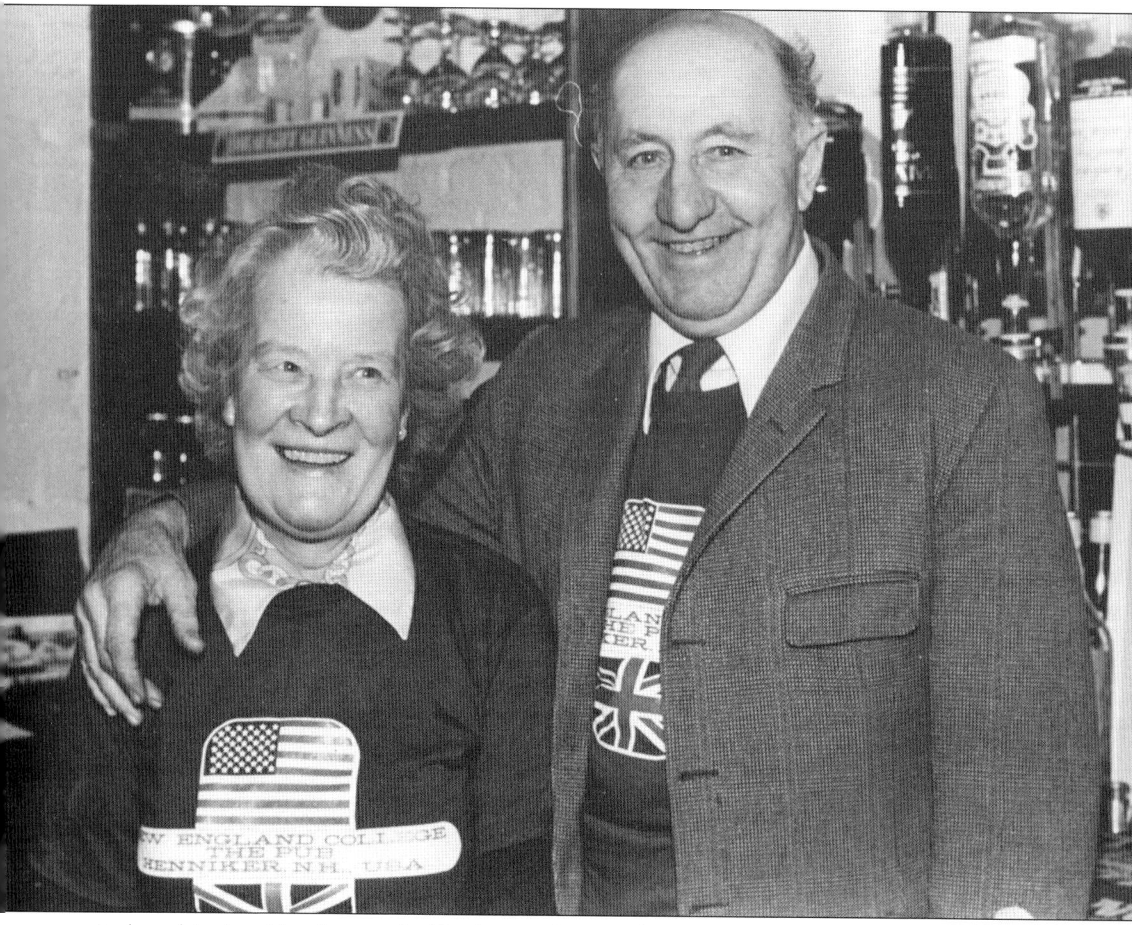

Jack and Audrey Brazier ran the Tortington Arms Pub in 1978. (Courtesy of Nancy Weinheimer Rowlatt Wilson.)

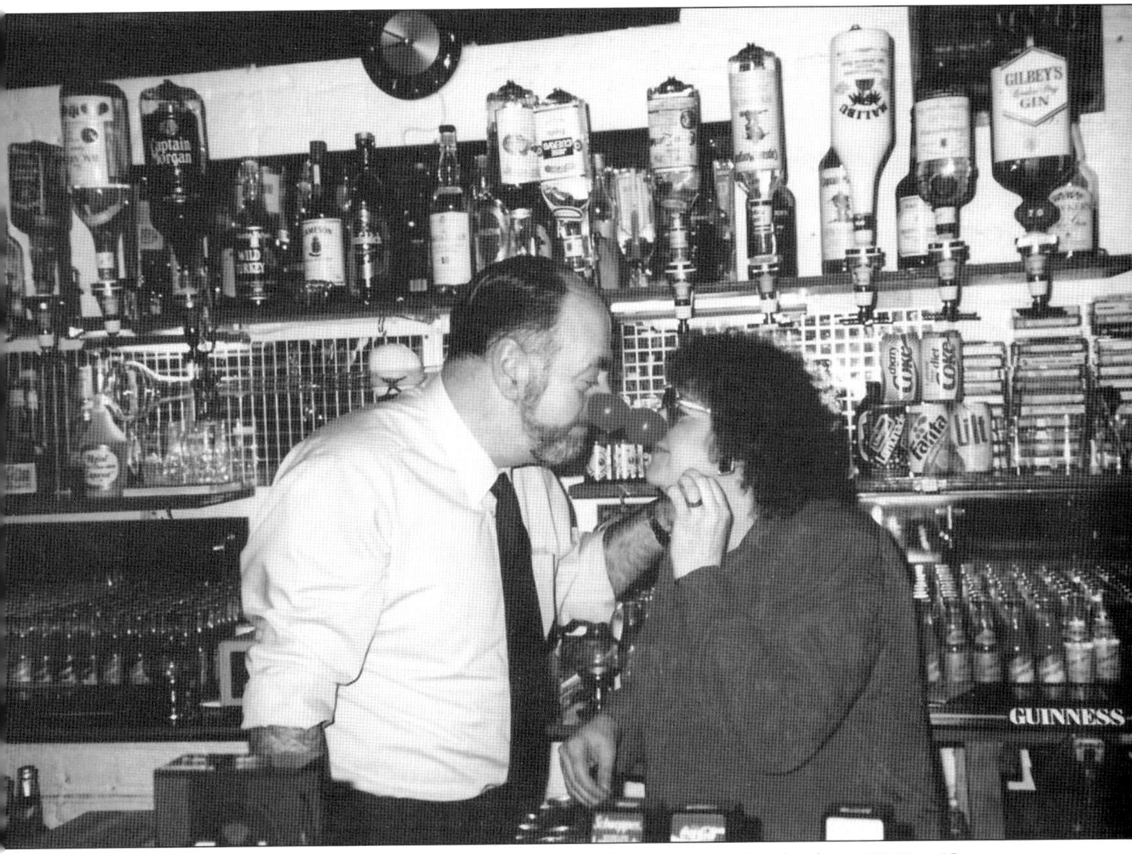

Bill and Margaret Eckford ran the Tortington Arms Pub starting in the late 1980s. (Courtesy of Nancy Weinheimer Rowlatt Wilson.)

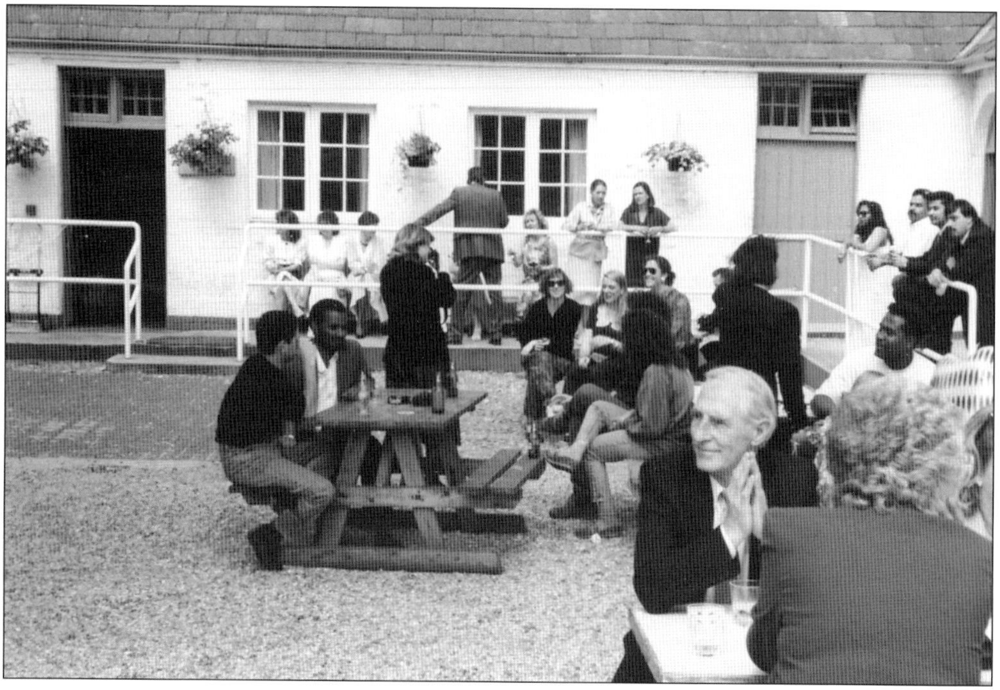

The Tortington Arms Pub opened its doors on warm days, and the crowd spilled outside onto picnic tables in the courtyard. Arundel students enjoyed conversation with Arundel faculty and staff over a half-pint or pint of lager, ale, or lemonade.

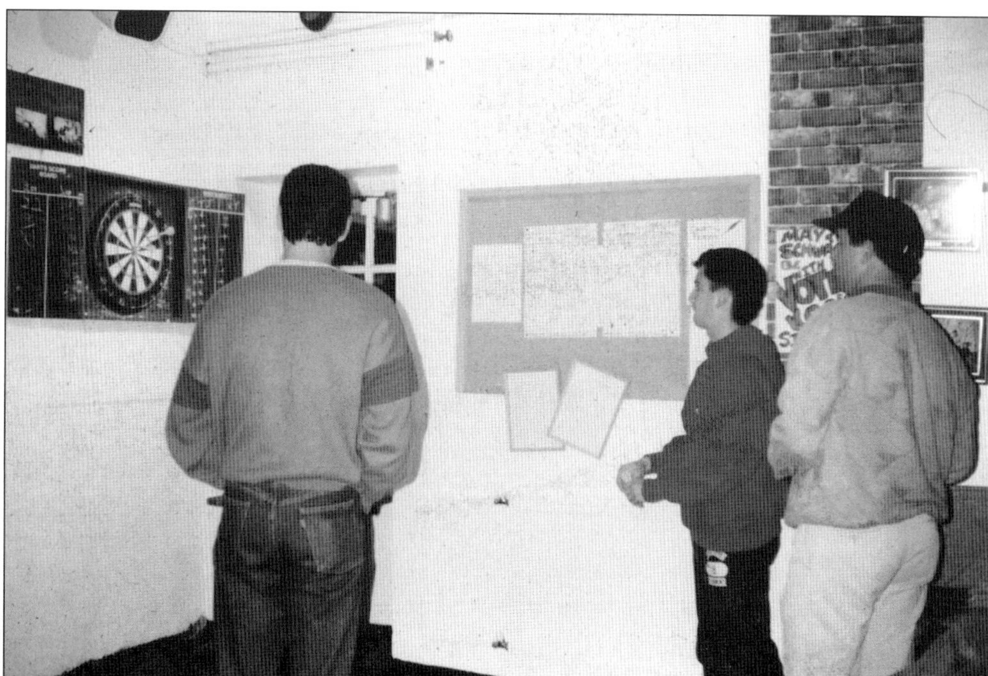

Many students first tried the British games of darts and snooker in the campus pub. Dartboards were a favorite souvenir of the Arundel campus.

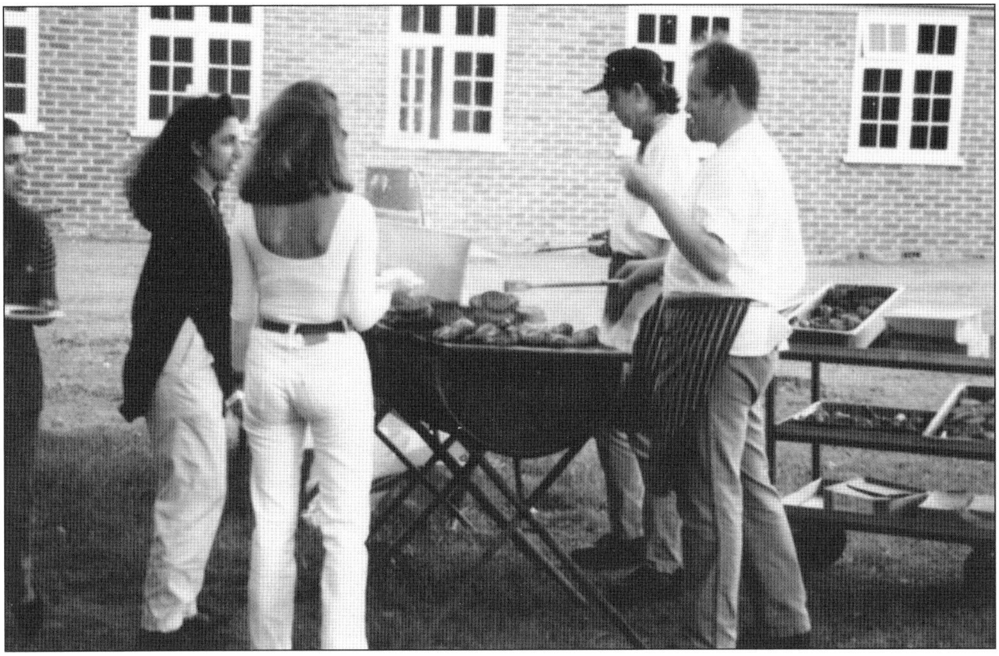

American-style cookouts, featuring burgers and hot dogs, were enjoyed by all during summer sessions. The kitchen staff enjoyed cooking outdoors for a change on warm days. Feral cats that lived off the kitchen's scraps also enjoyed the leftovers.

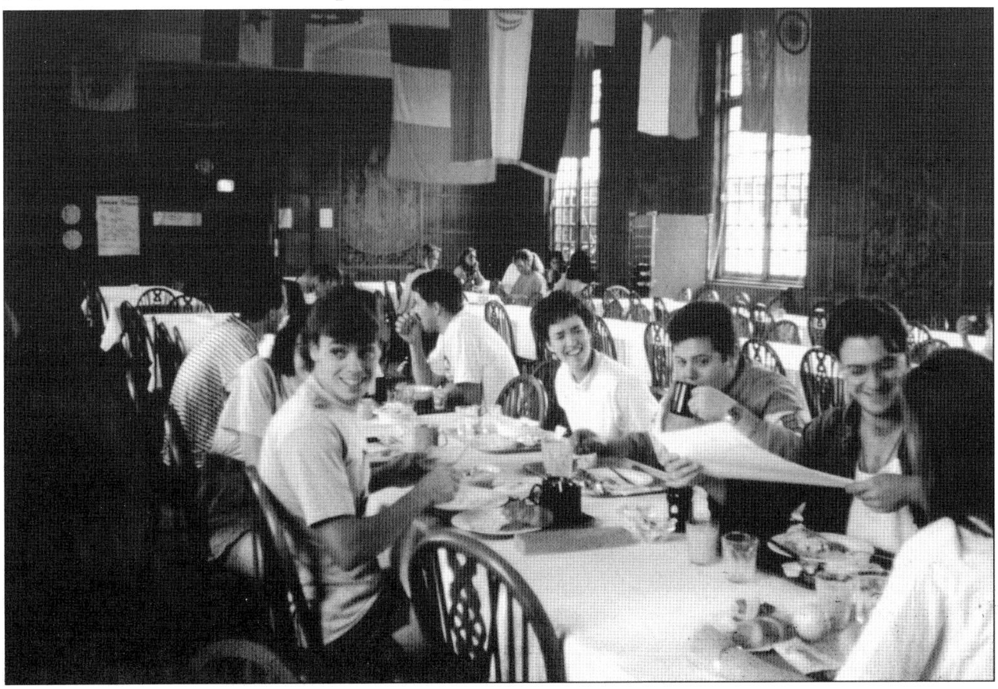

The tradition of international students donating flags from their countries to hang in the dining hall began at the Arundel campus. When the campus closed, all the flags were sent to Henniker. After several decades of this tradition, there are too many flags to hang all at one time in Gilmore Dining Hall.

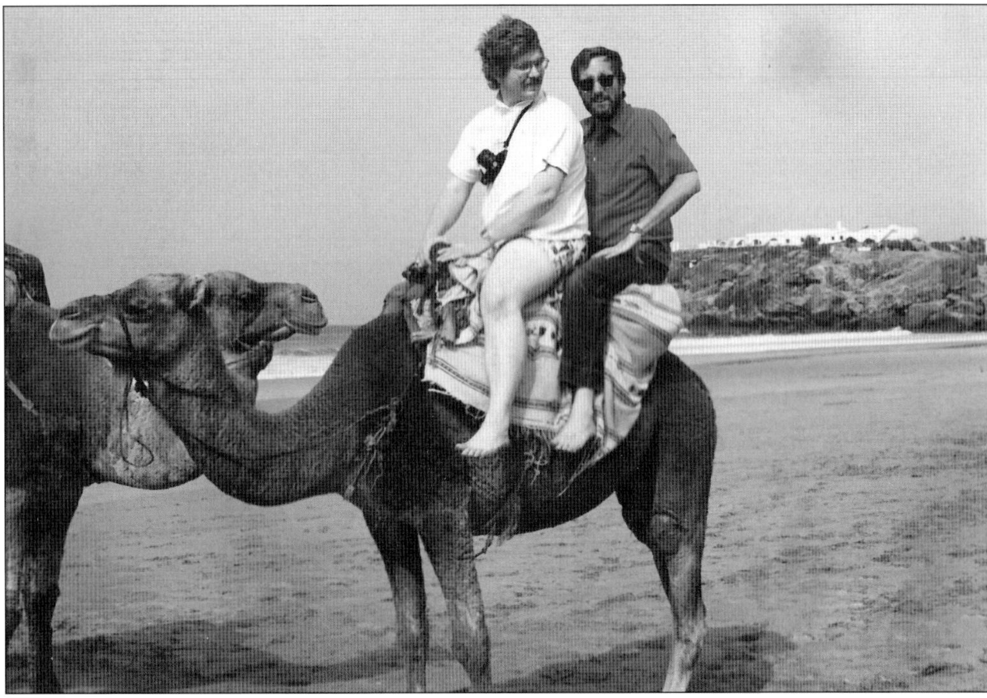

Travel was an important part of the Arundel campus experience. Many courses included day trips to castles, great houses, archeological sites, museums, and plays. Longer weekend and weeklong trips were enjoyed by faculty, staff, and students. Here are Donald Ivanoff (left) and Kevin Coyne, dean of students, riding a camel in Morocco in 1989.

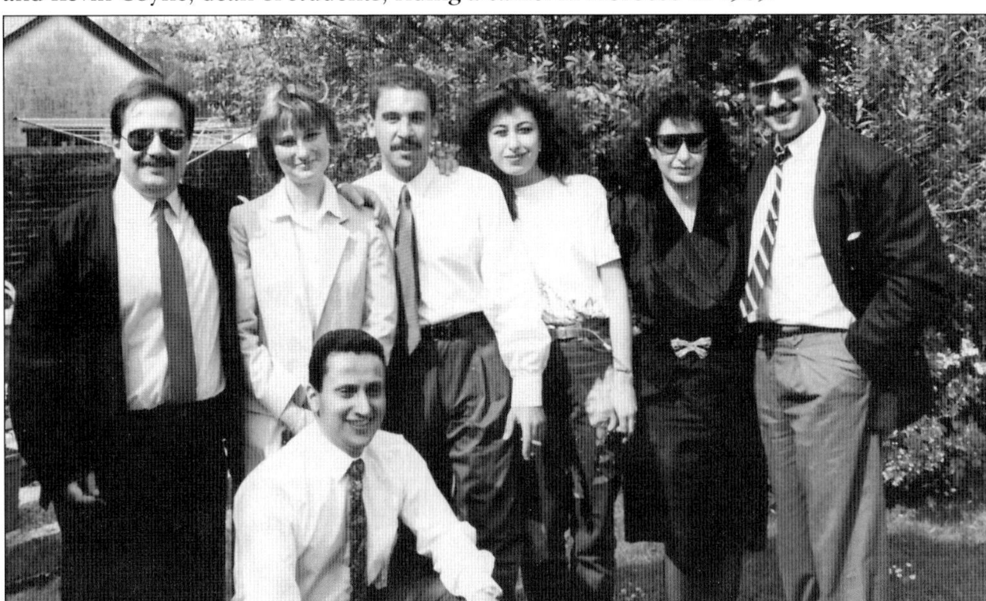

Pictured here is the author (second from left) with six senior students, around 1988. Each of these students came from a different background. A multicultural class like this provided unique opportunities for dialogue and challenged students and instructors alike to consider issues from multiple perspectives.

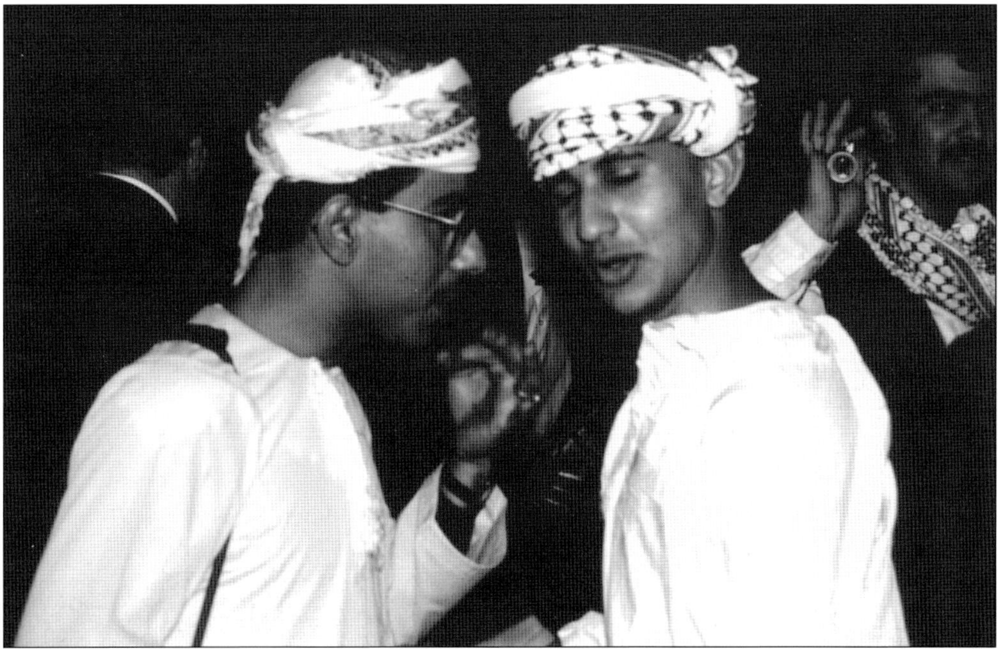

Some of the Arundel students were Americans who came from the Henniker campus or other institutions. Other students hailed from Africa, Asia, Europe, and the Middle East. They came for a few weeks, a semester, a year, or for all their undergraduate years. The highly diverse student body offered unique opportunities for intercultural learning 24 hours a day, inside and out of the classroom. International Night was an opportunity to share and celebrate native dress, food, music, dance, and other forms of entertainment.

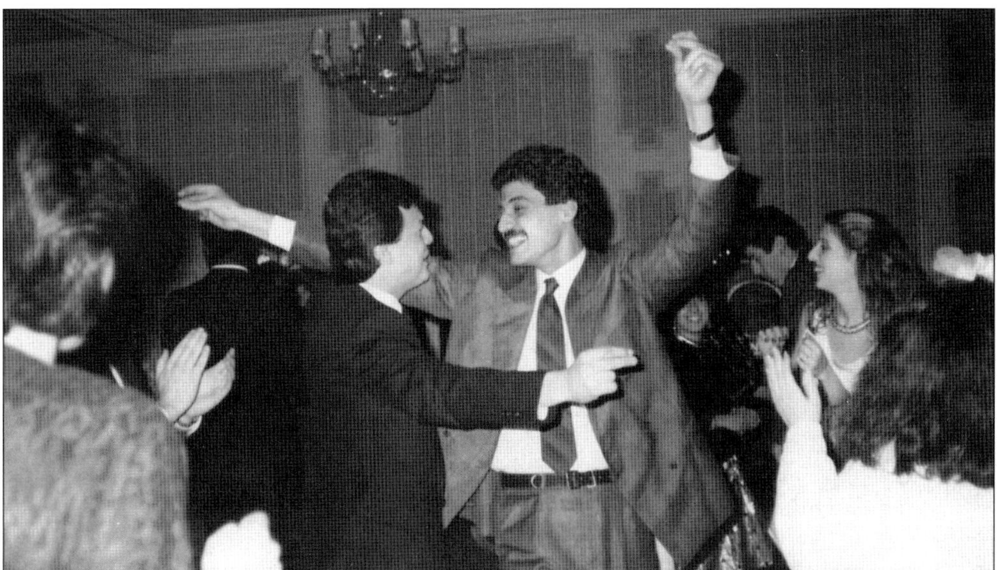

The Arundel campus, located south of London, east of Chichester, and west of Brighton, offered proximity to posh off-campus venues for the annual Senior Class Dance. The Senior Class Dance in 1985, shown here, took place in London. (Courtesy of Nancy Weinheimer Rowlatt Wilson.)

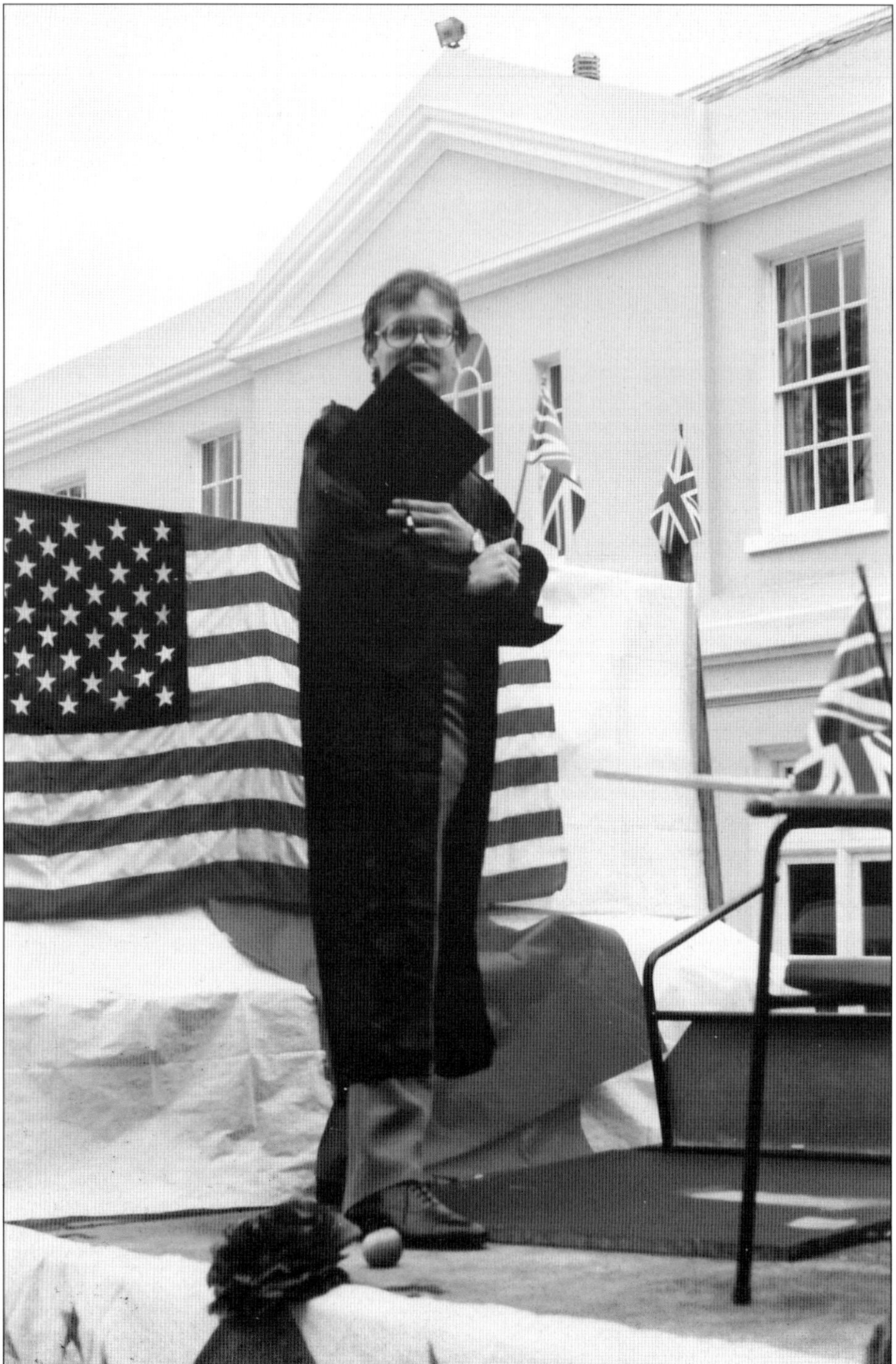

In the words of colleague Sue Lewey (formerly Taphouse), "Dick Sargeant was a legend! Always slightly dishevelled, nobody sure when or if he slept! Inevitably with a cup of coffee and a cigarette in hand. Papers and books everywhere, but always there for his students! An inspirational teacher!"

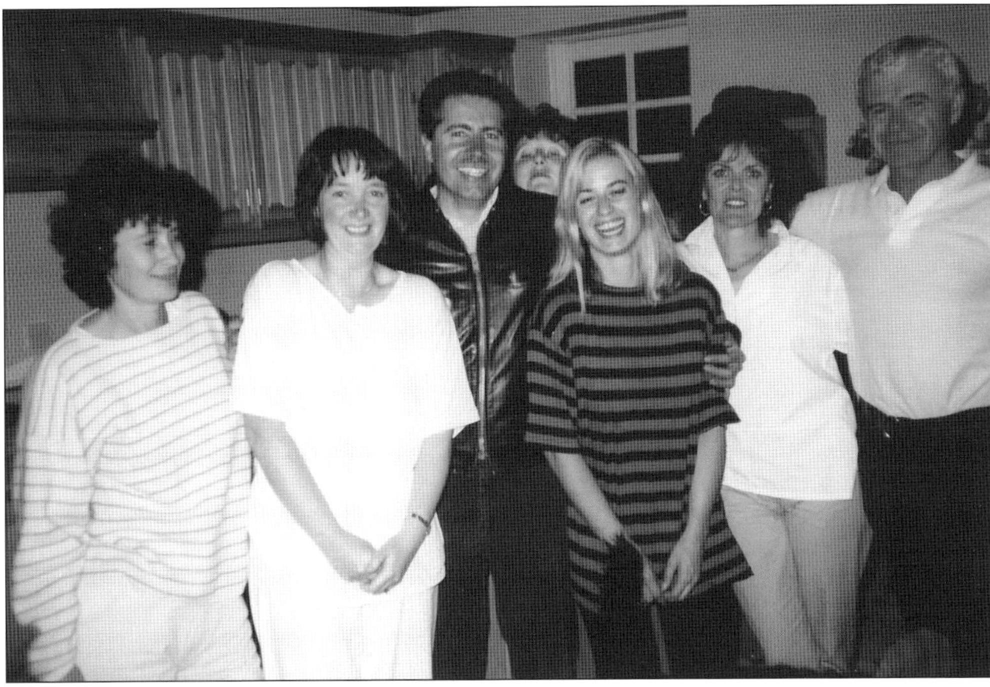

From left to right are Teresa Taylor, Sue Taphouse, Wally Pineault, Caroline Harmon, Nancy Rowlatt, Vanda Ashman, and Joe Considine.

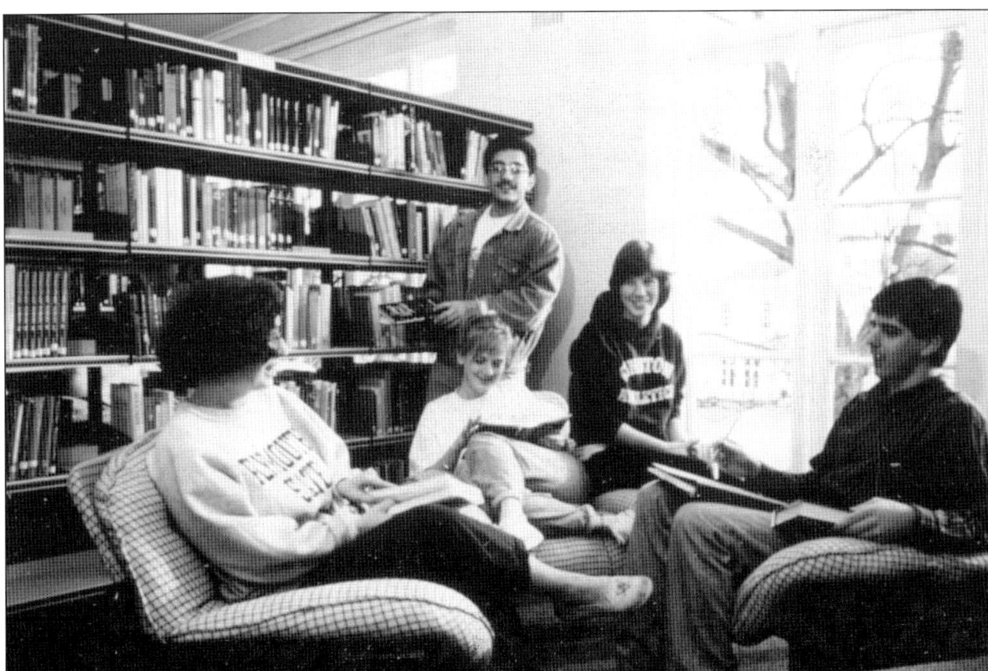

The Arundel campus library overlooked the central courtyard and had comfortable chairs that encouraged impromptu, informal, and friendly conversations between students from all over the world.

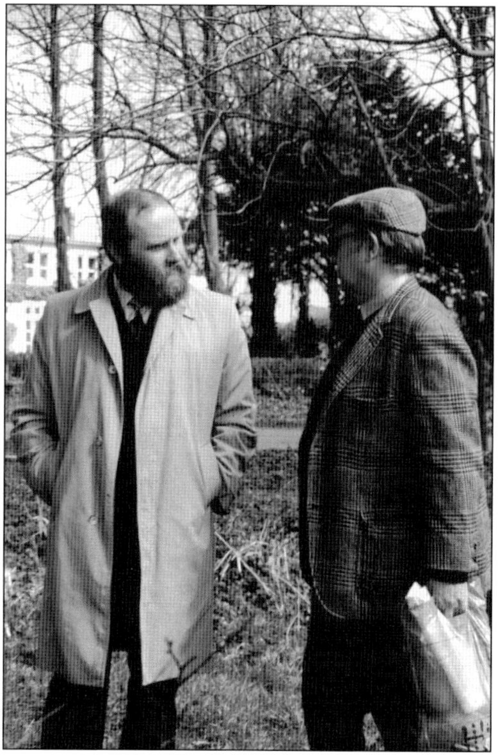

John Halcomb (left), shown here chatting with a colleague, was a patient and successful instructor who specialized in the needs of students for whom English was a second language.

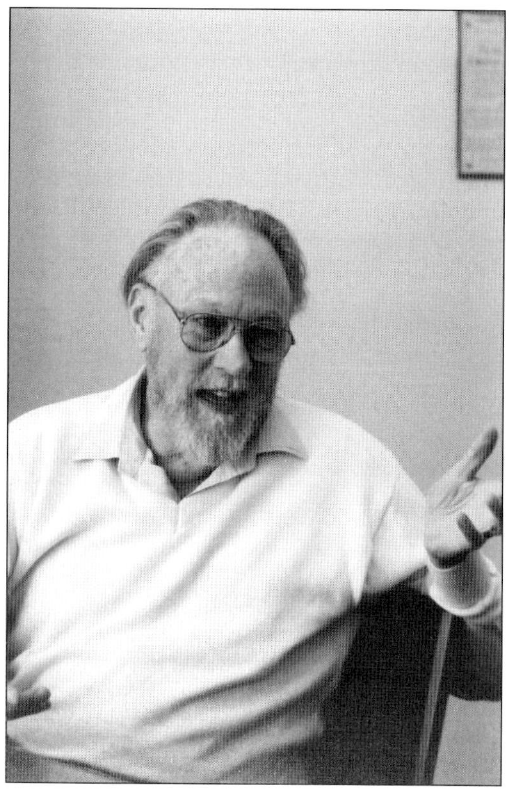

John C. de V. Roberts joined the faculty in 1977 and taught international studies. He was beloved not just for his broad knowledge of a wide range of topics but also for his genial personality.

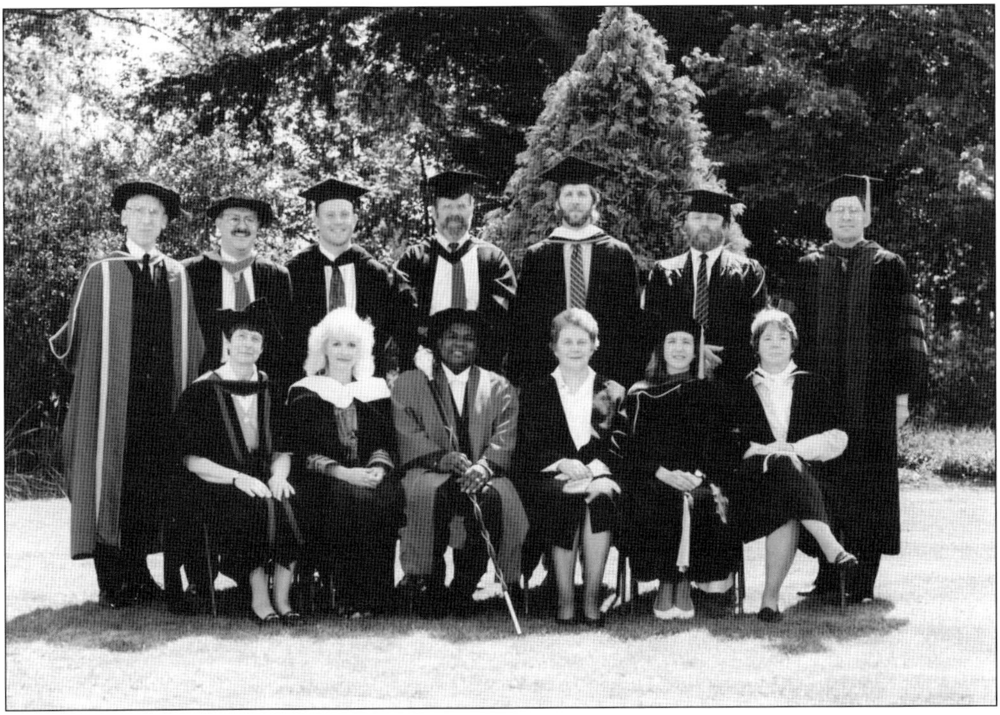

The Arundel faculty is pictured in the front garden at commencement in the mid-1990s. From left to right are (first row) Annette Barker, Elizabeth "Lizzie" Oakley, Austin Chakaodza, Margaret Birkinshaw, Mary Brydon-Miller, and Elizabeth Alexander; (second row) Brian Hopkins, Paul Latawski, Eric Braun, Robert Stock, Bronwyn Miller, John Halcomb, and Gary McGrath.

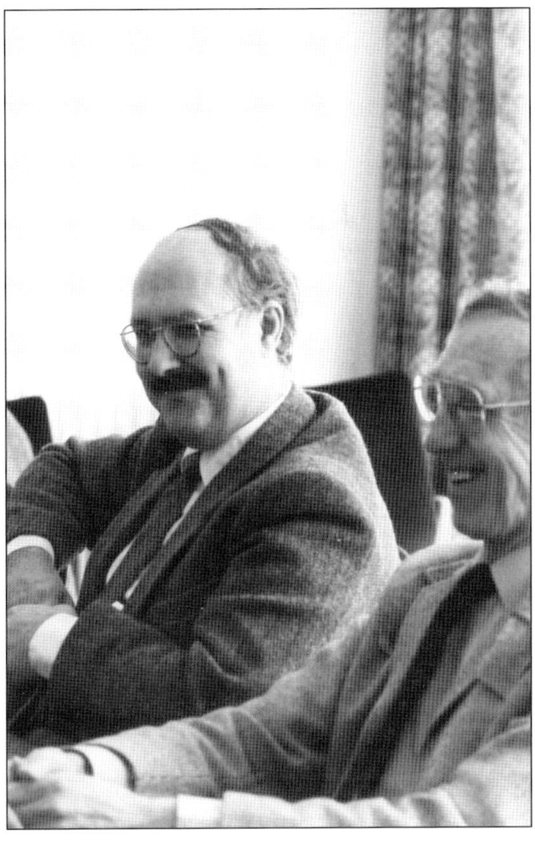

Paul Latawski (left) taught political science, particularly focused on Eastern Europe. Brian Hopkins (right) joined the faculty in 1971 at the opening of the Arundel campus and taught ecology.

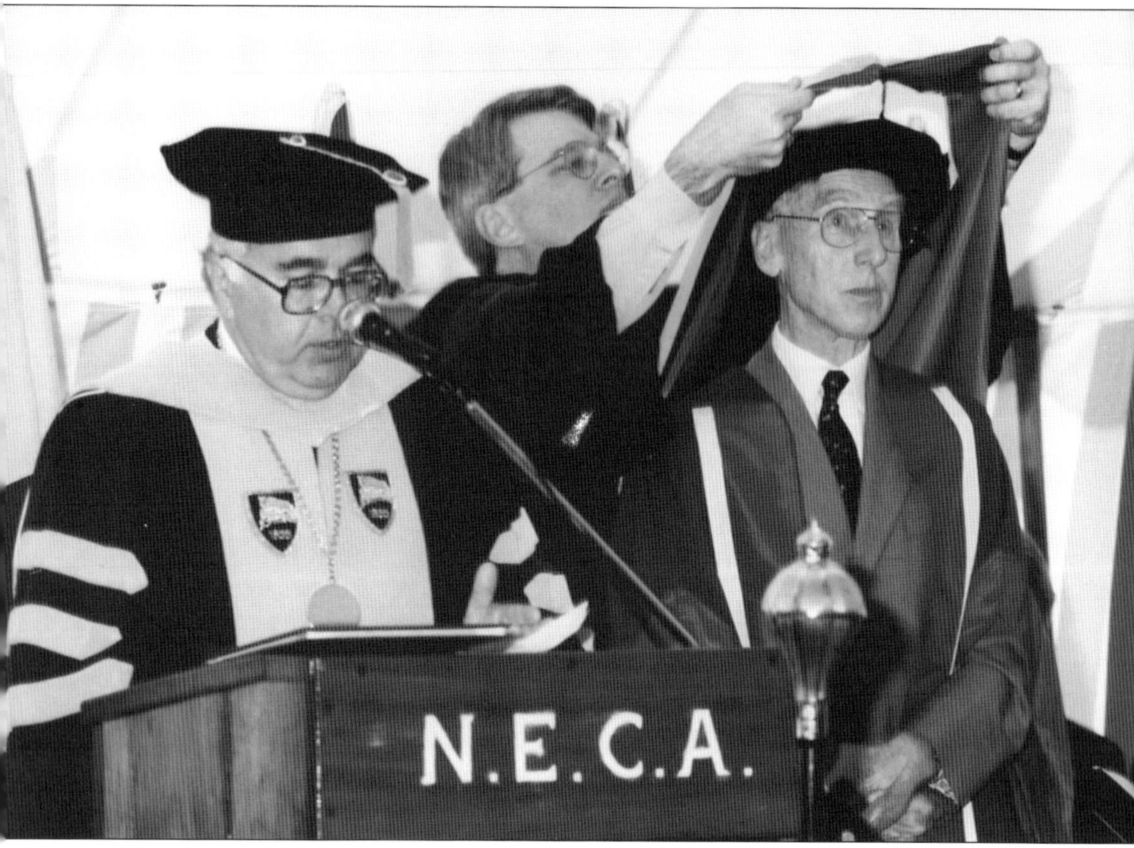

From left to right are Pres. William G. Ellis and director Gary McGrath, who conferred an honorary degree on Prof. Brian Hopkins at the last Arundel commencement in 1996. William G. Ellis served the college as president from 1995 to 1997. Hopkins was a member of the faculty at the Arundel campus from its opening year in 1971 until the campus closed. McGrath was the last director of the Arundel campus.

Seven

Of All Our College Days, Dear NEC

Relationships to Last a Lifetime

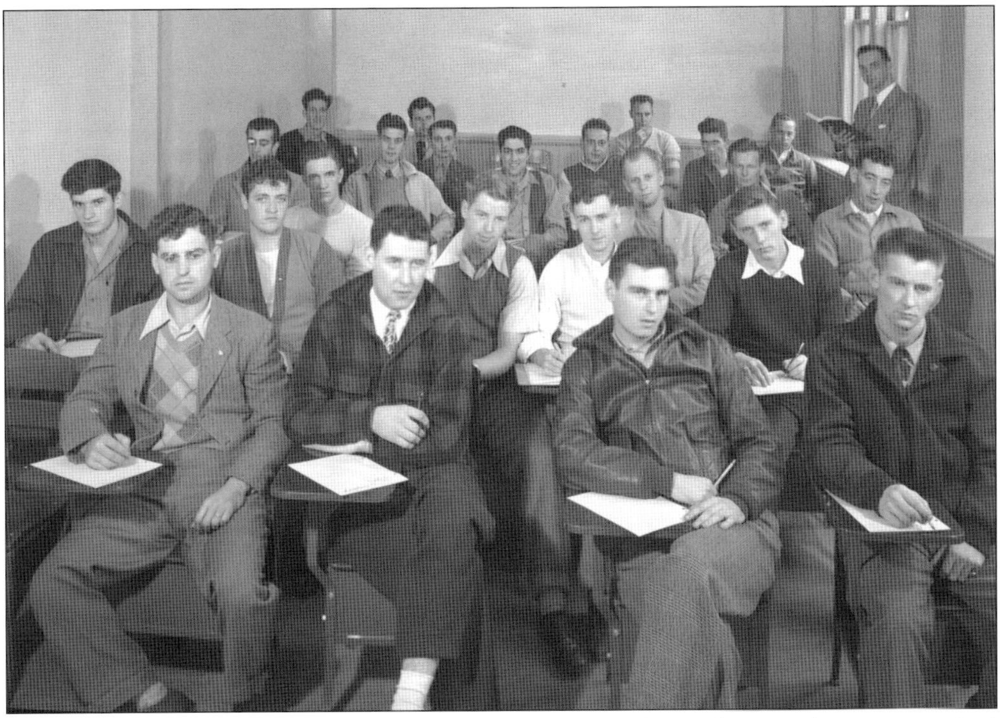

The entering class in the fall of 1946 was all veterans, shown here with instructor Carl French. There are some legendary stories about this class, like the one about the veteran having difficulty sleeping who shot out the bulb in the streetlight outside his window and the one about students who borrowed a fire engine to buy liquor in nearby Hillsborough. But in general, the veterans adjusted quickly to small-town life. They also contributed labor and creativity to improving the comfort of classrooms and residential space. (Courtesy of Hillsborough Historical Society.)

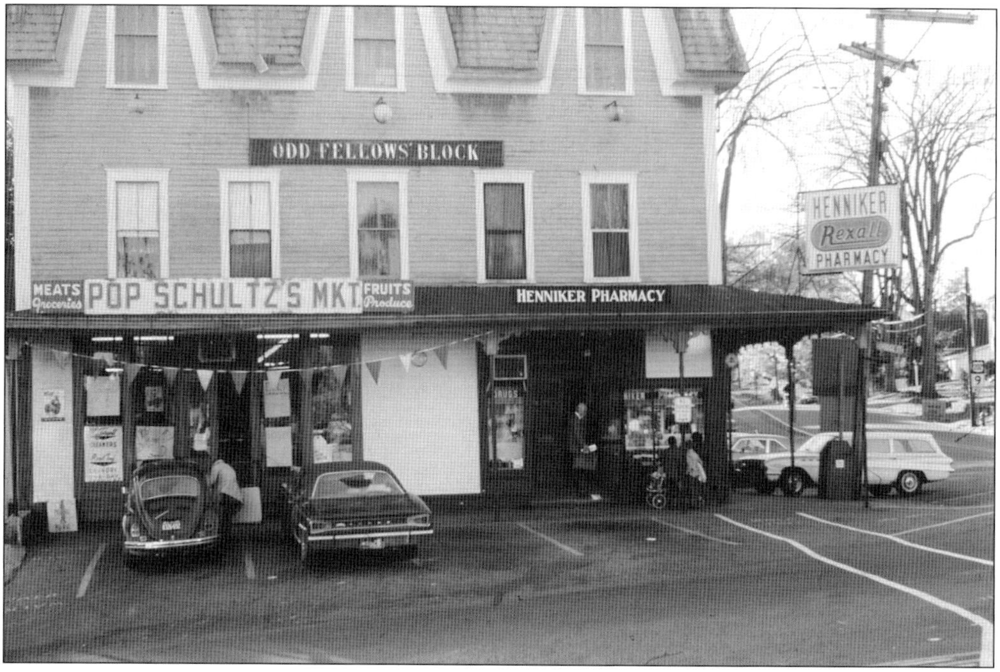

"The college brought different cultures and ethnicity to the town. Different accents—'where are you from?' opened many conversations. The answer easily could have been Brooklyn or the Bronx. When I worked at the drugstore, boys would come in and ask for an egg cream. What in the world was an egg cream? They introduced us to cherry cokes and a new popular treat for New Hampshire—pizza," recalled Deborah Spring Reed ('60).

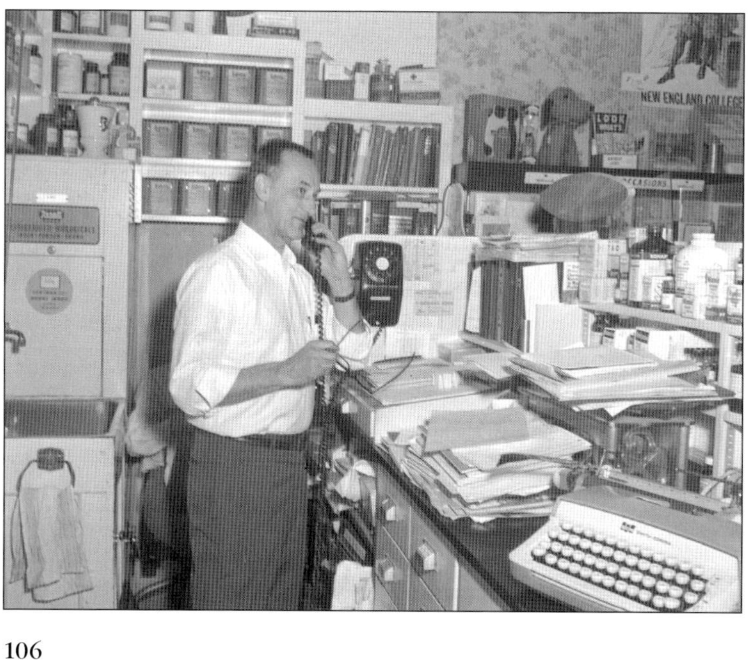

Norm Parmenter, owner of the Henniker Pharmacy, was an avid supporter of New England College athletics.

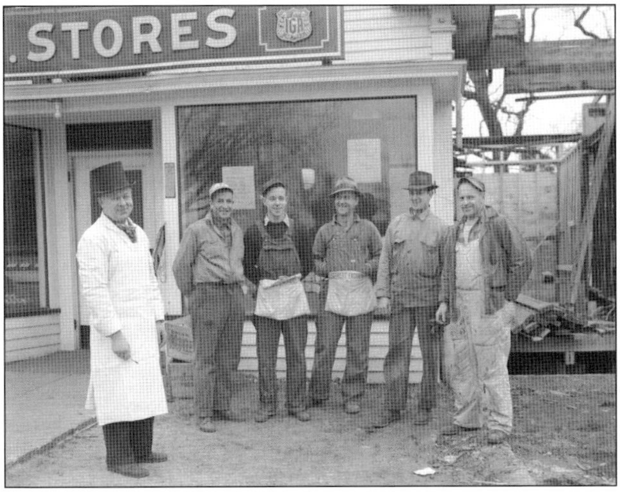

"Henniker had three small grocery stores: the IGA owned by Arthur Kendrick [left], the First National owned by Stan Bracey and Chase's General Store, adjacent to the drug store. Saturday was shopping day when the people who farmed came to town for supplies," recalled Deborah Spring Reed ('60). (Courtesy of Hillsborough Historical Society.)

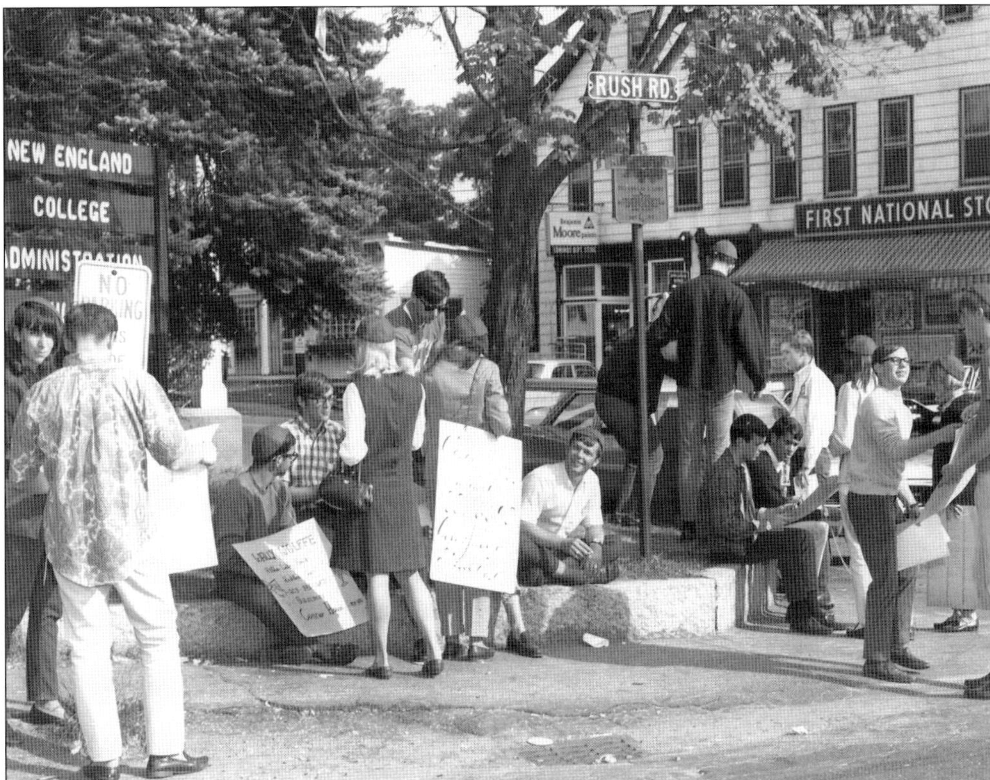

Freshmen wearing beanies, along with fellow students, hang out on a sunny day at the corner of Rush Road and Main Street by the Administration Building. Deborah Spring Reed remembered, "Edmunds opened a department store . . . ladies upstairs, hardware for men, down. Almost anything one could want was there. . . . There were three gas stations and three restaurants. . . . The Rock Garden served homemade meals such as meatloaf. The Nook had fried foods, steak, etc." In back, from left to right, are the Nook, Edmunds Hardware Store, and the First National grocery store, which closed in 1968. (Courtesy of Henniker Historical Society.)

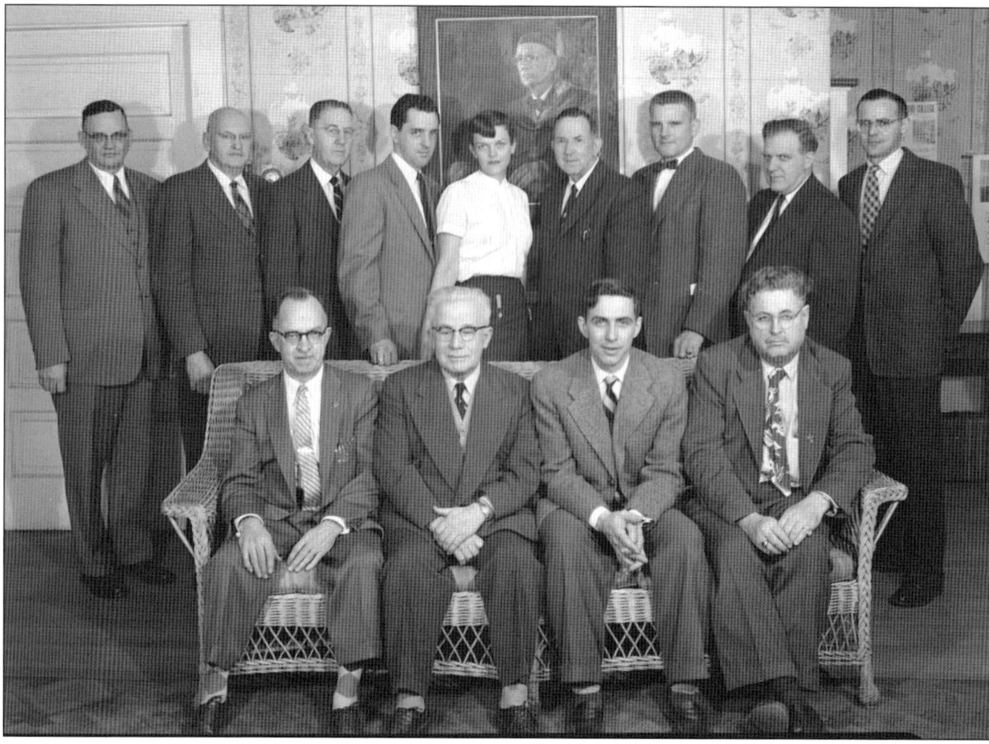

The 1957 faculty of New England College is pictured in front of a portrait of Laurie D. Cox, the first (1947–1950) and third (1952–1955) college president. From left to right are (first row) William Nairn, Vincent Gatto, David Shelton, and Cyril Abbott; (second row) Robert Lewis, Ralph Manville, Fredrick Calkin, John McMorrow, Nancy McMorrow, Henry Otten, Gustave Bochert, Ralph Edwards, and Raymond Smith. (Courtesy of Hillsborough Historical Society.)

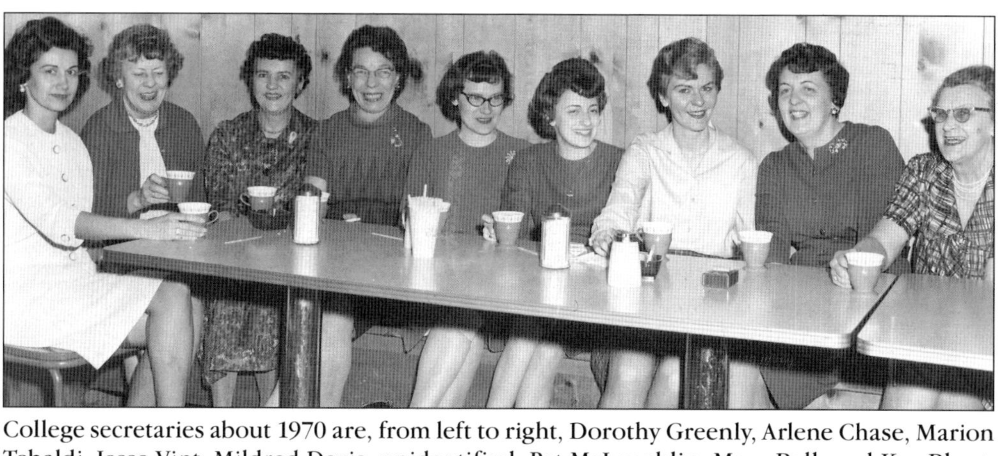

College secretaries about 1970 are, from left to right, Dorothy Greenly, Arlene Chase, Marion Tebaldi, Jesse Vint, Mildred Davis, unidentified, Pat McLaughlin, Mary Ball, and Kay Blunt. (Courtesy of Henniker Historical Society.)

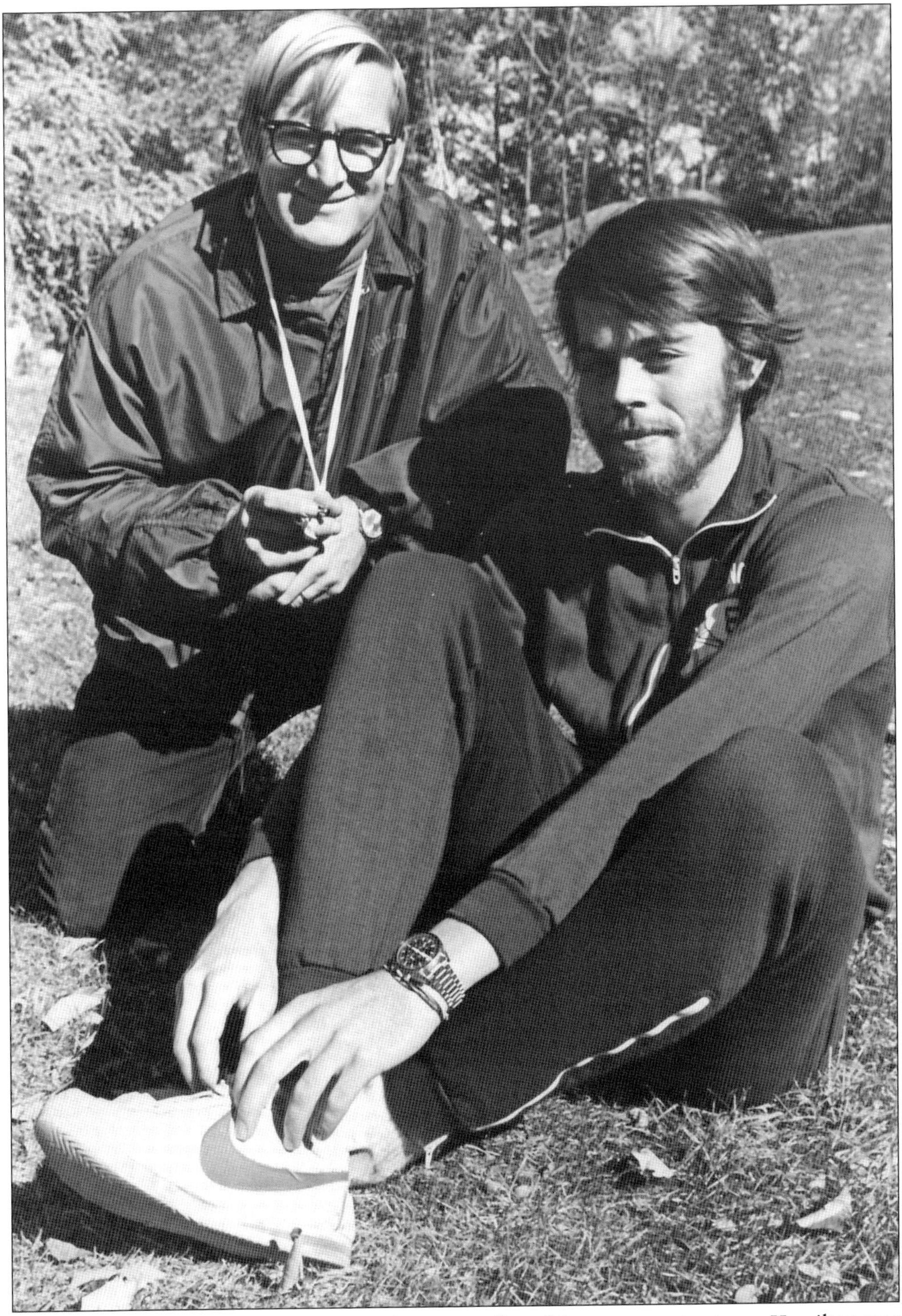

Coach George Hamilton is seen here with a runner from his cross-country team. Hamilton was a long-term and multisport coach at New England College. Numerous trails on college-owned and public land are used by enthusiastic runners and athletes training for other sports.

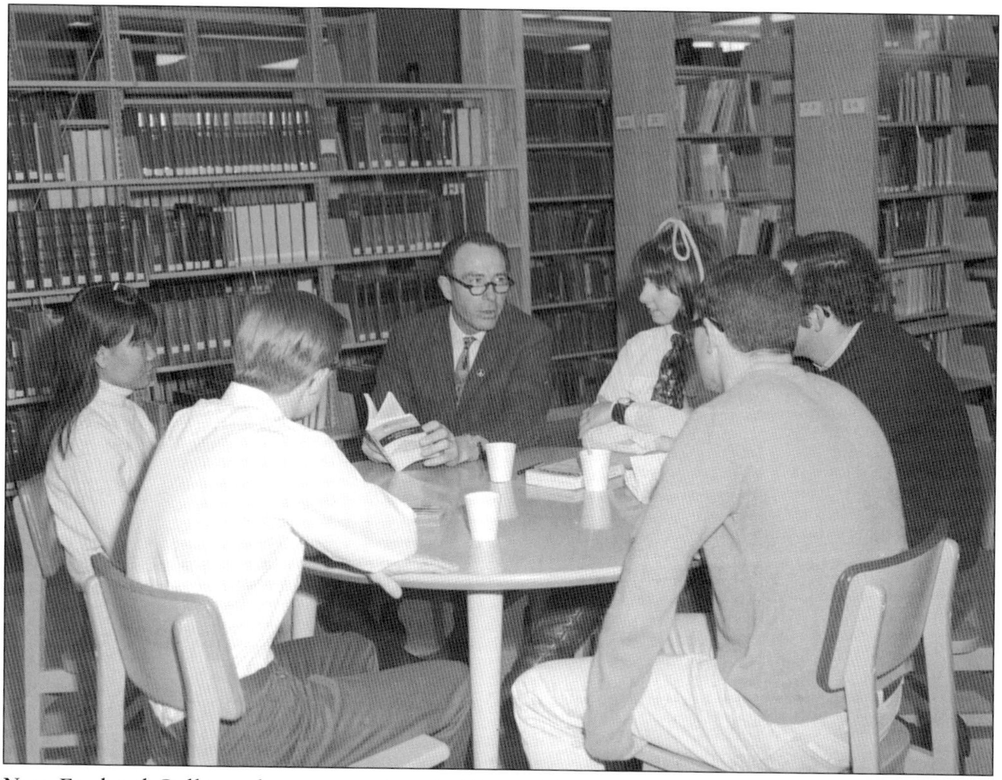

New England College classes are often held outside traditional classroom settings. Shown here is a class in the college library that took place around 1969.

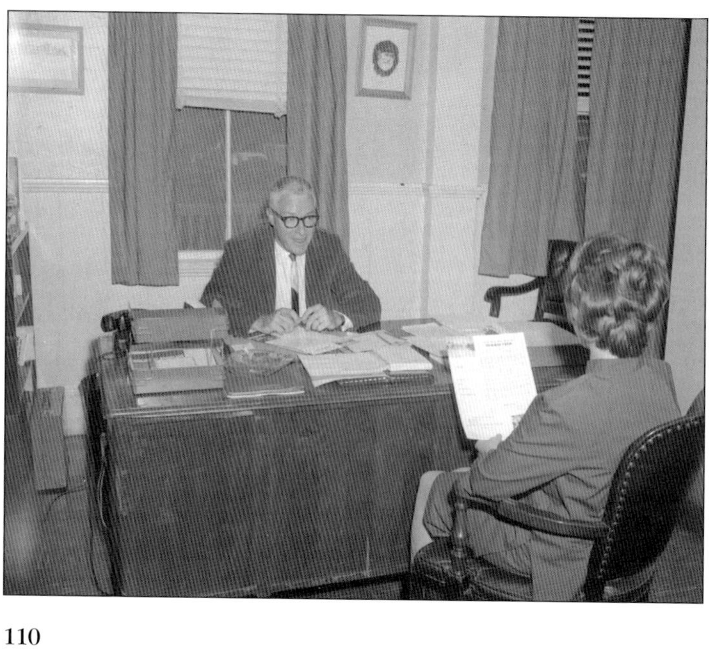

Walter K. Robinson joined the education and humanities faculty in 1963, two years before this picture was taken. He and his wife, Angela "Angie" Robinson, who taught music at the college for many years, touched the lives of many students. Walter started a shop called Book Farm, in homage to the utopian Brook Farm. The business was later continued by Gary McGrath. (Courtesy Hillsborough Historical Society.)

Dr. Jere A. Chase teaches a class about 1968. Dr. Chase served as president of the college from 1969 to 1973.

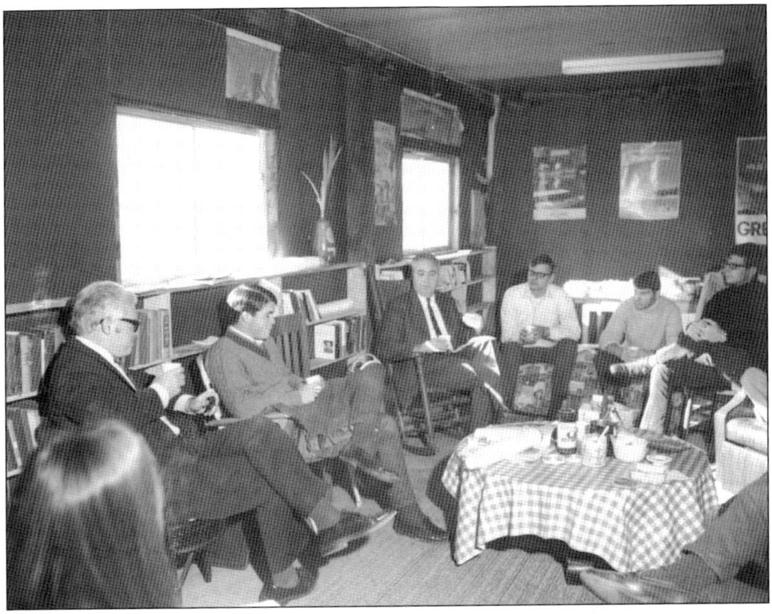

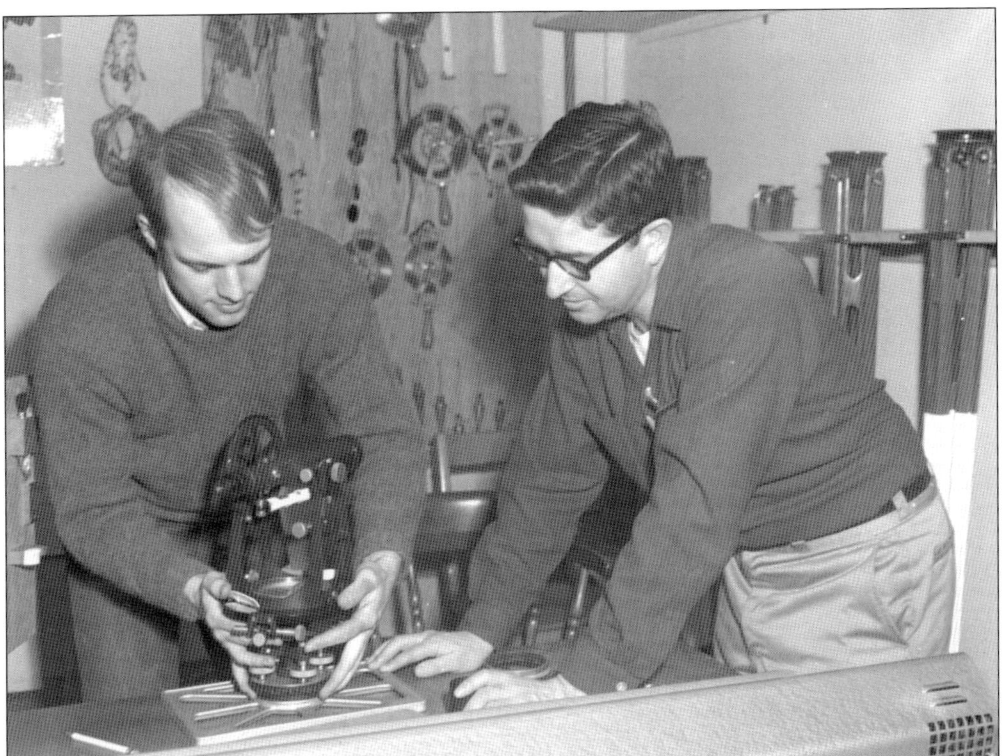

Donald G. Blanchard (right) joined the engineering faculty in 1963. Here, he is shown teaching an unidentified student in 1969. His low-key and practical problem-solving approach to engineering helped generations of students find their way into the engineering profession.

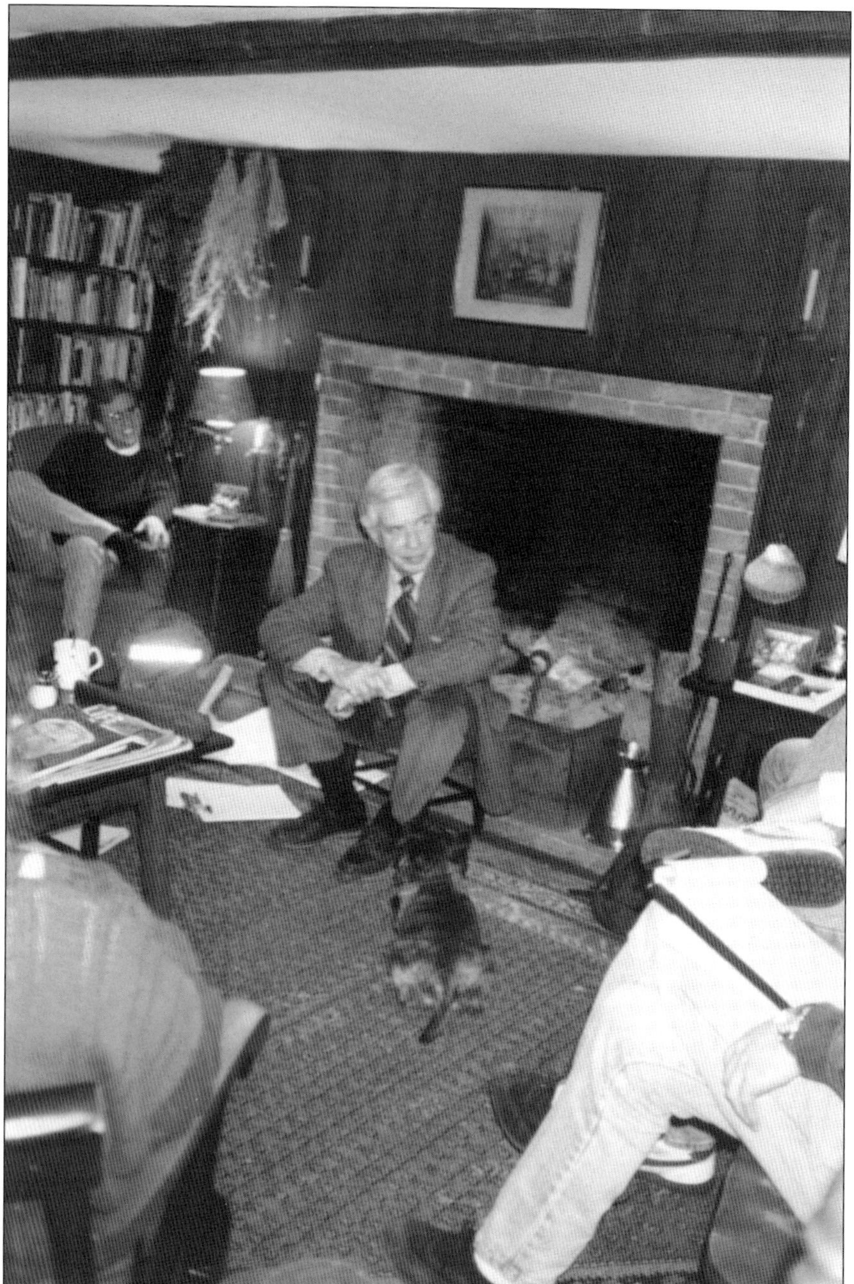

"New England College is nothing like high school. You are not in my class, or in college, because you have to be. You are here because you chose to be here. The only thing I care about is that you care about the choices you make. I expect you to care about what we are doing together. I have something to tell you. And I expect you to listen and respond. But you also have something to tell me. You can get a lecture at any college. For a good discussion, the kind where we are looking at an issue from every possible angle, and where voices might be raised, you need a class like mine. You need a school that regards this kind of learning as important," says Prof. Montford Sayce, JD, PhD. (Courtesy of Athena "Anne" Sayce.)

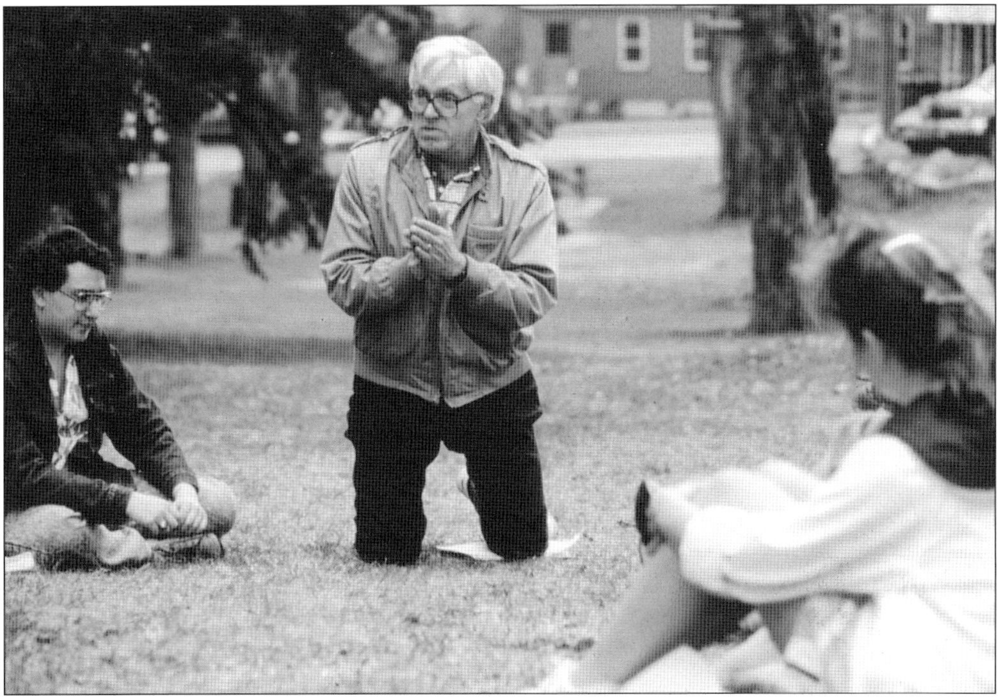

Michael Wireman joined the sociology faculty in 1970. Here, he is teaching outdoors, a common practice at New England College in early fall and late spring.

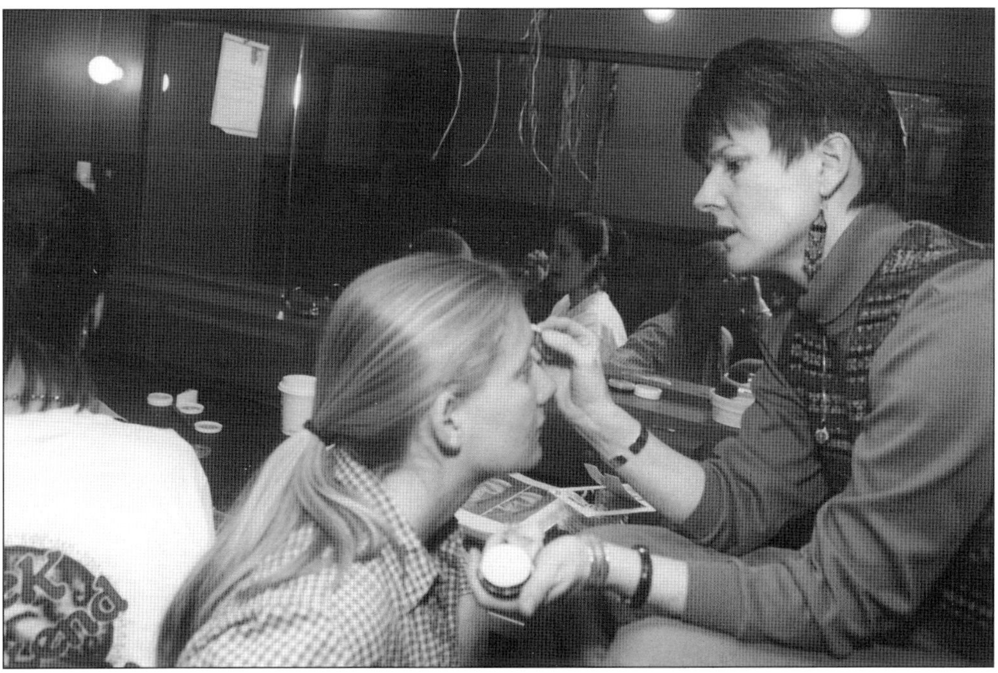

Sharon A. LaJoie joined the theatre faculty in 1991. Here, she is assisting a student with makeup before a production.

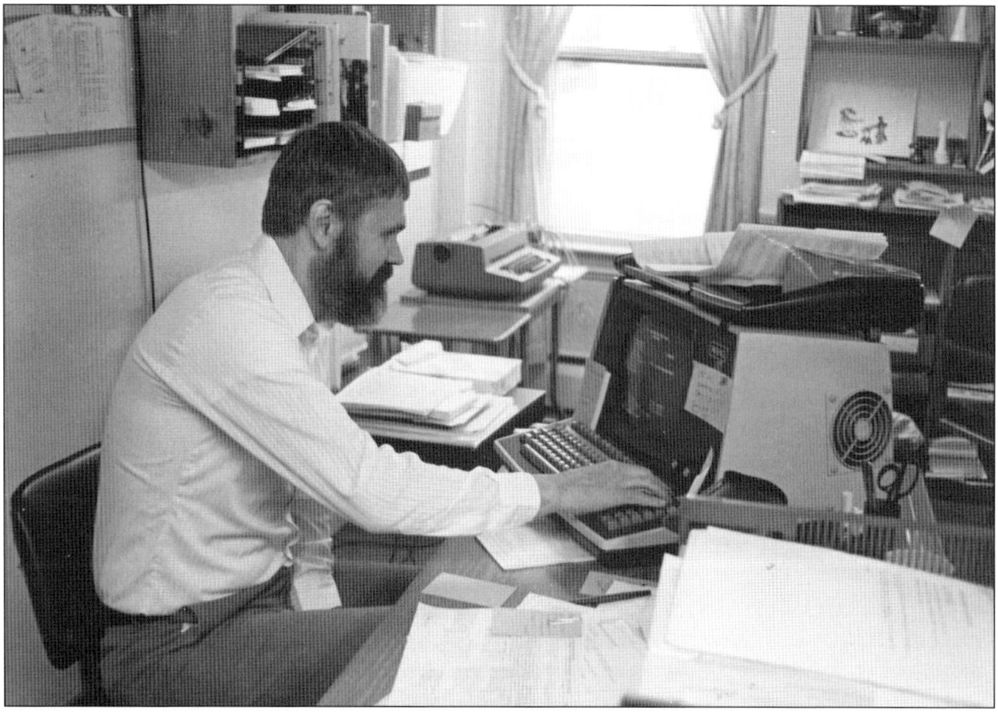

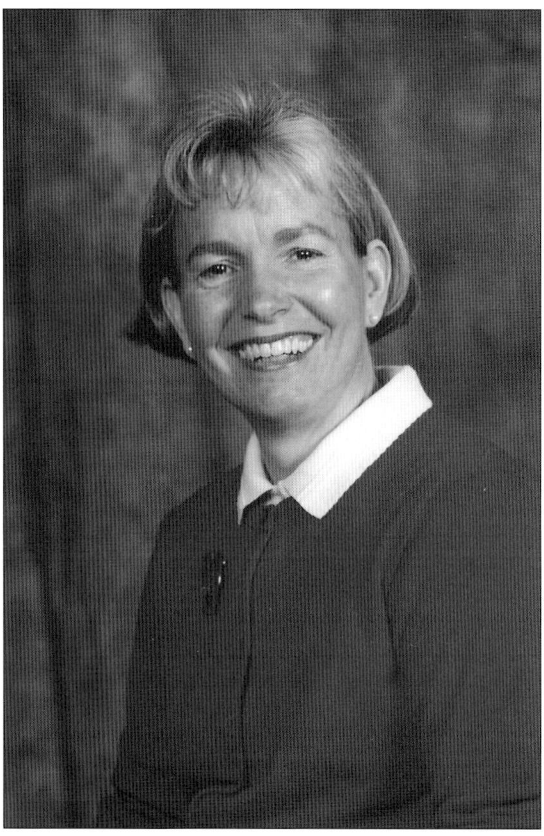

Frank L. Hall served as registrar of the college for several decades and unfailingly provided accurate numbers, institutional memory, good common sense, and grace under pressure.

Prof. Katherine Van Weelden joined the library faculty in 1981 after completing an AB at Dartmouth College and an MLS at the State University of New York at Albany. Van Weelden is not only a gifted library administrator, but also an accomplished alpine skier and ski instructor. At the time of her retirement in 2012, she served as director of Danforth Library.

John O'Connor joined the business faculty in 1988 and was called to serve in a variety of administrative roles despite his preference for teaching in the classroom. Amongst other accomplishments, he effectively campaigned for a strengthened institutional commitment to experiential learning and travel/immersion courses open to all students at no additional cost.

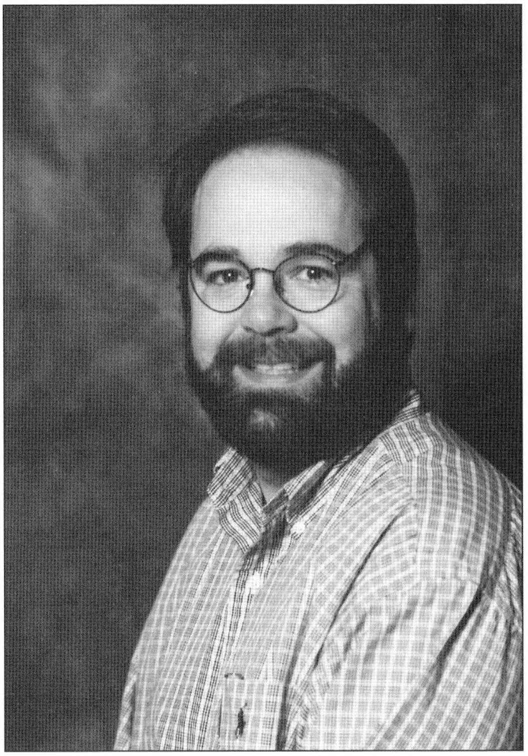

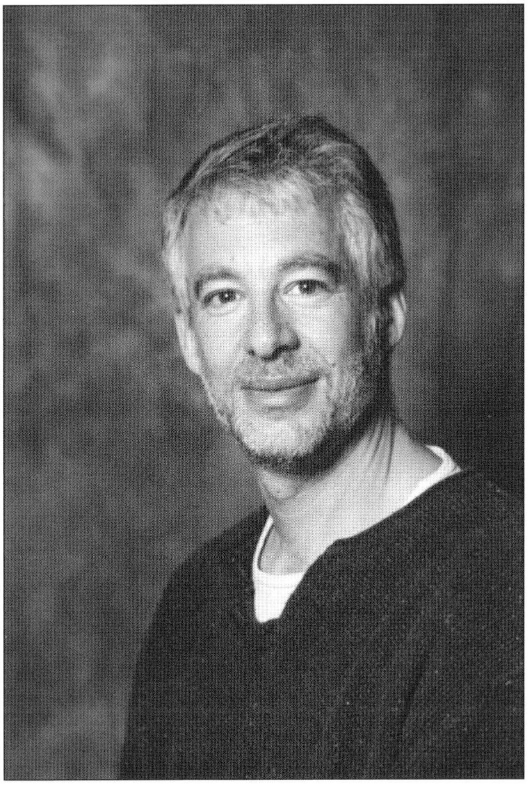

Laurence I. "Larry" Taylor joined the psychology faculty in 1977. An ardent champion of internship and community service programs, he inspired and connected hundreds of students to future careers in social service professions.

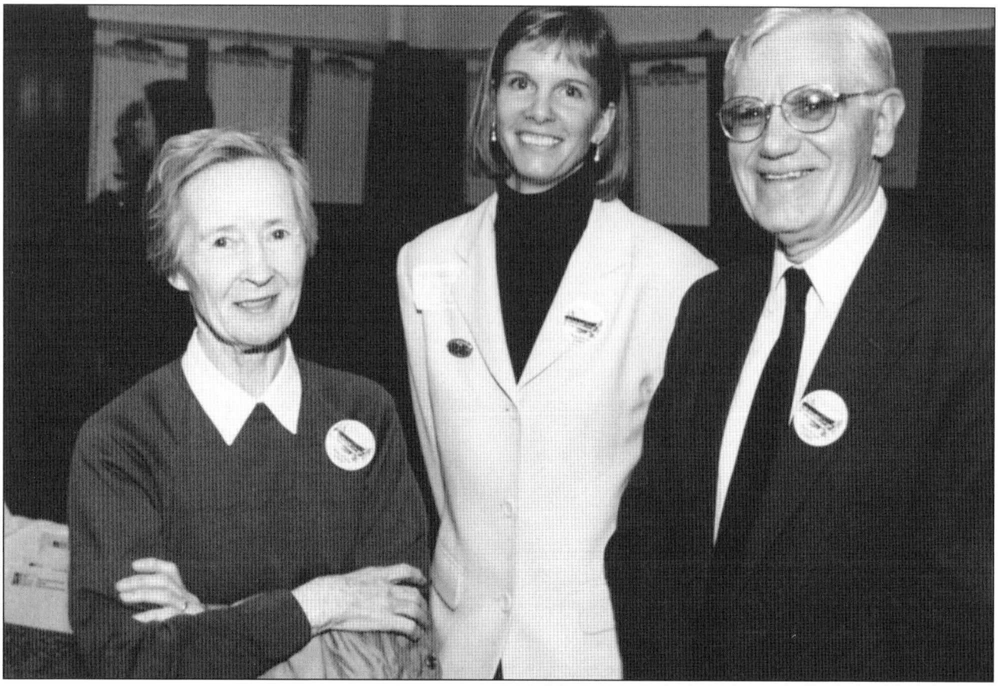

Alumna Katherine Grieves Perkins (center) has served the college in a variety of staff positions in admissions and in the college's academic mentoring program. She is shown here with college president John S. Morris (1997–1999) and his wife, Enid Morris (left).

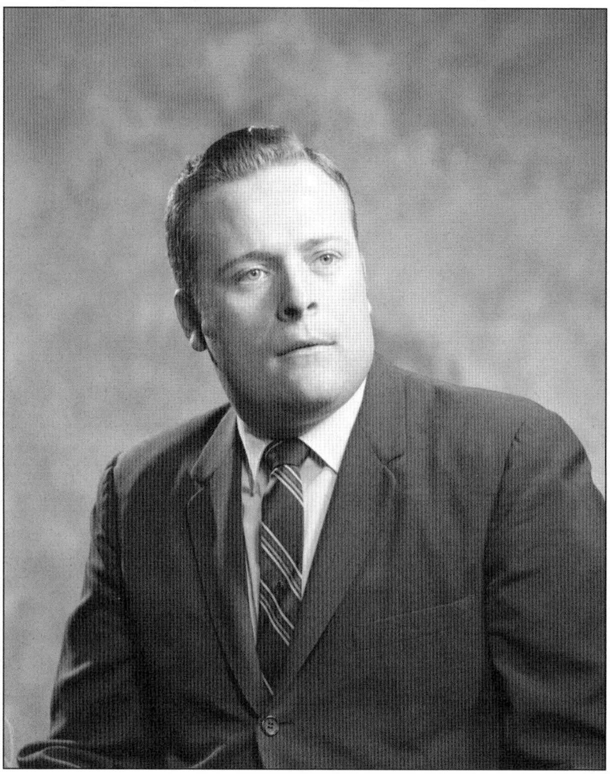

David P. "Dave" Currier ('72) founded the Henniker Brewery and Bound Tree Medical. He has served as a state senator and state representative for New Hampshire. Currier Alumni Center is named for him.

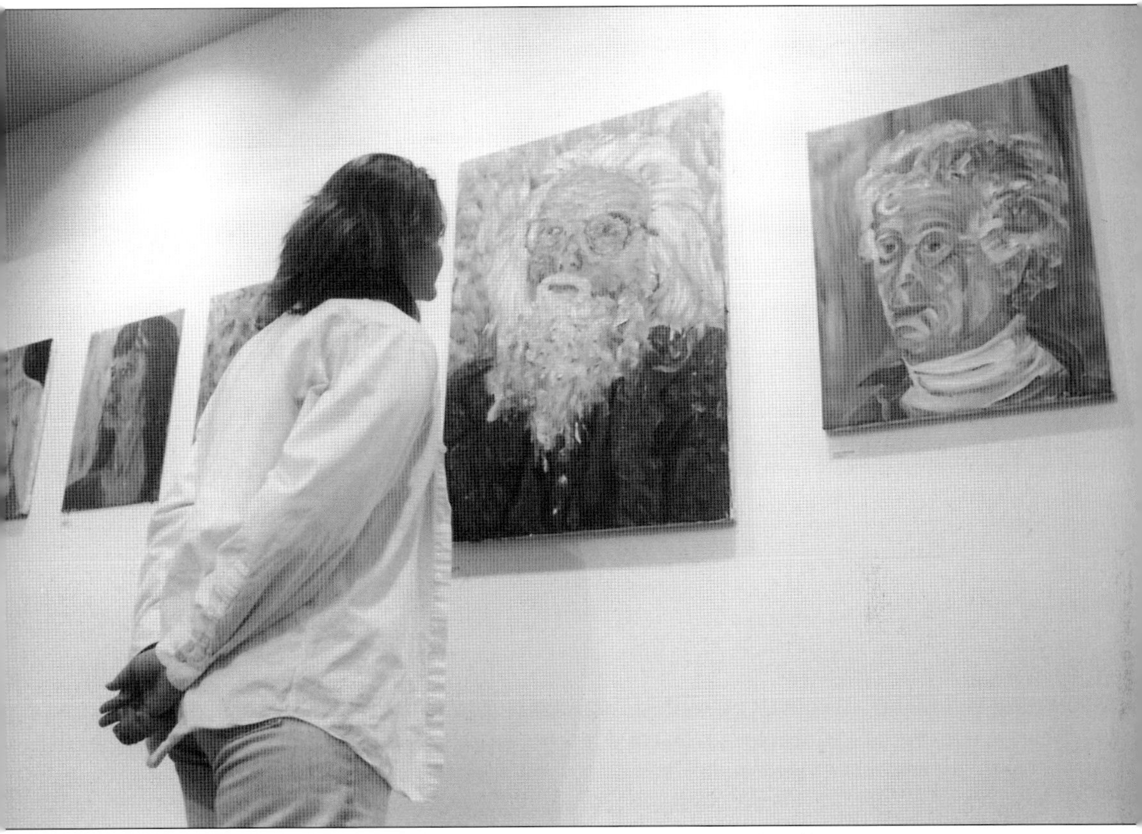

There are many connections between members of the New England College community. Here, in the art gallery located in Preston Barn, a visitor to the senior student show contemplates portraits of Prof. Don Melander (left) and Athena "Anne" Sayce ('74) (right), wife of Prof. Montford "Bunny" Sayce.

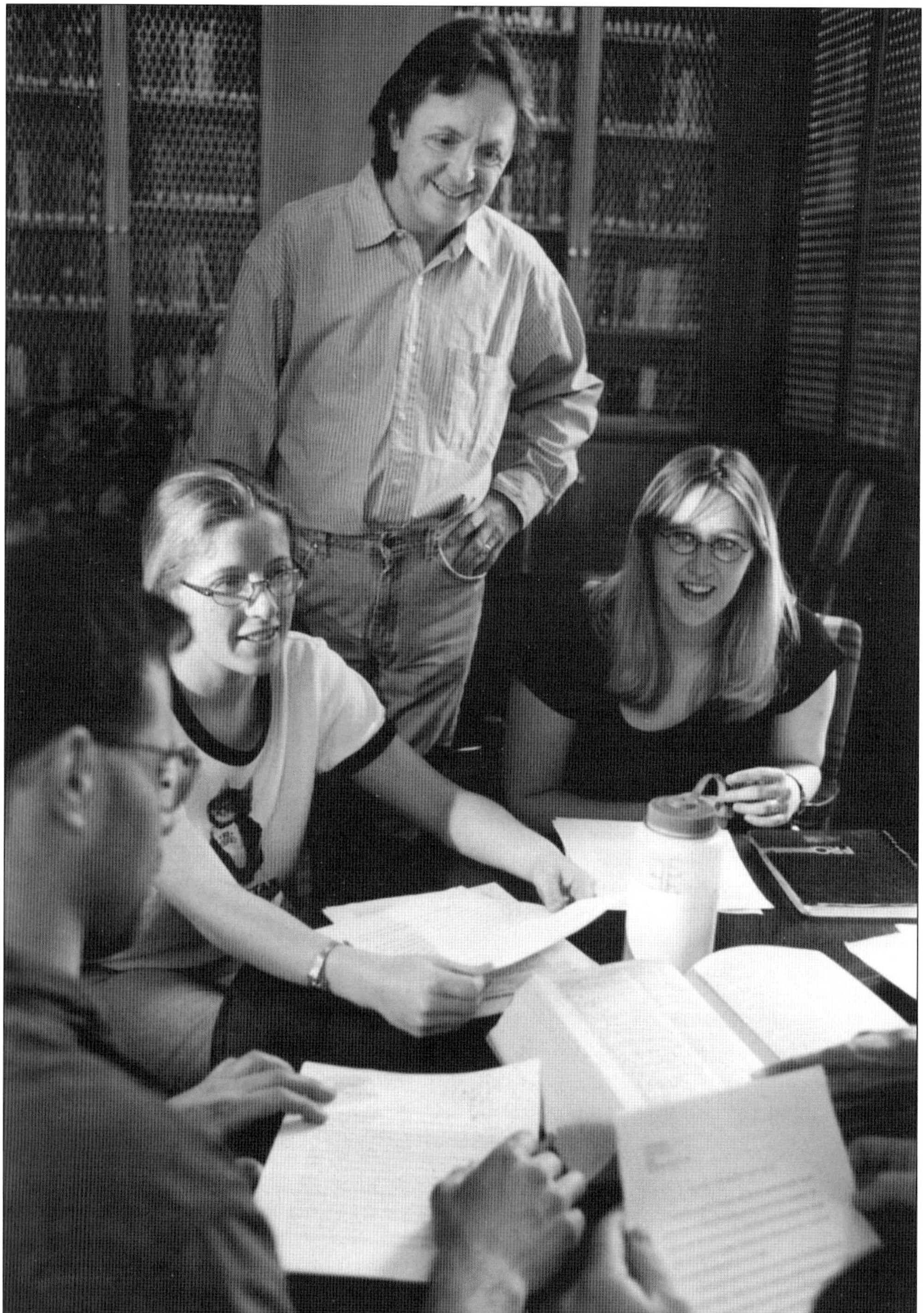

Prof. Kevin Harvey, shown here in the New England Room of Danforth Library, joined the faculty in 1988 and fostered the love of creative writing in generations of New England College students.

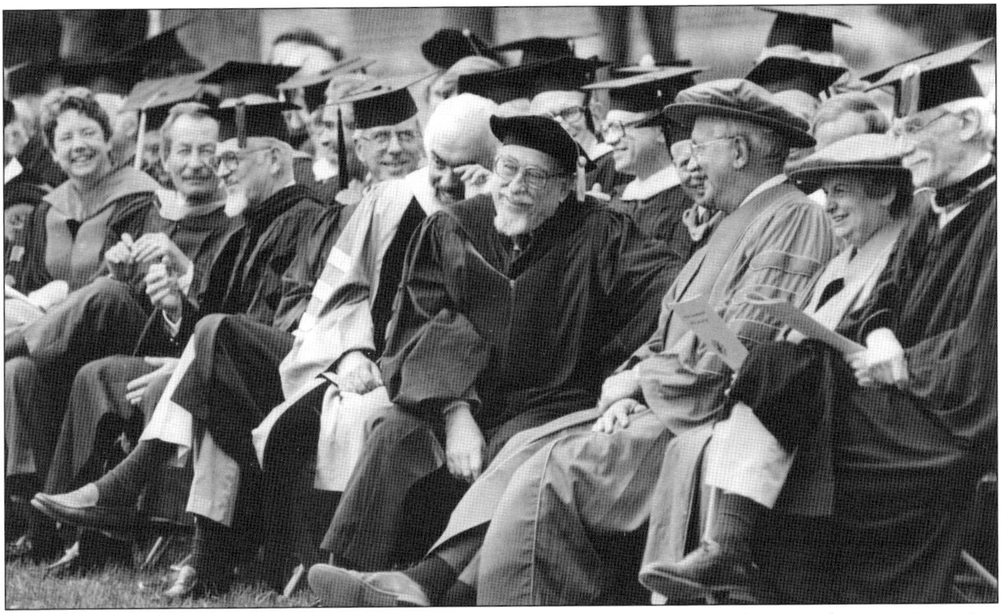

Faculty includes, from left to right, Elizabeth Alexander (English), George L. Fearnley Jr. (business), J. Kenneth Cummiskey (psychology and education), John Lyons (business administration), Marvin A. Seperson (education), Marvin Braiterman (law and public policy), Merle Hagen (business administration), Thea G. Braiterman (economics and business), and Joel Oppenheimer (communications).

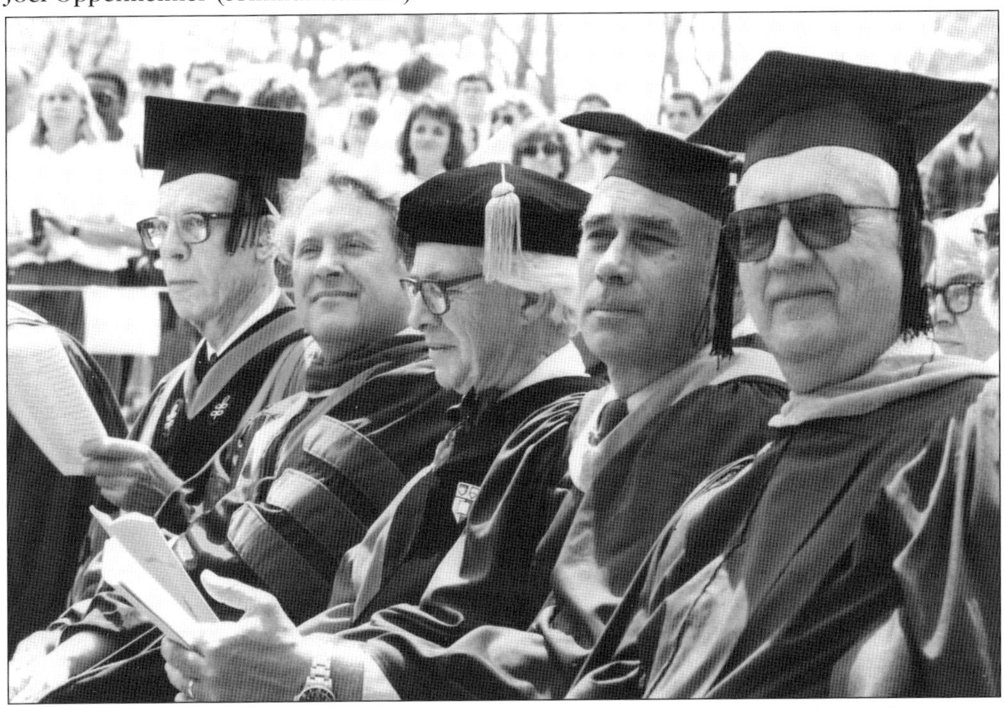

Faculty members pictured here at this graduation during the 1980s are, from left to right, Richard A. Martin (education), Alan L. Moberly (history), Montford Sayce (international administration), Taylor Loop (geology), and Merle Hagen (business administration).

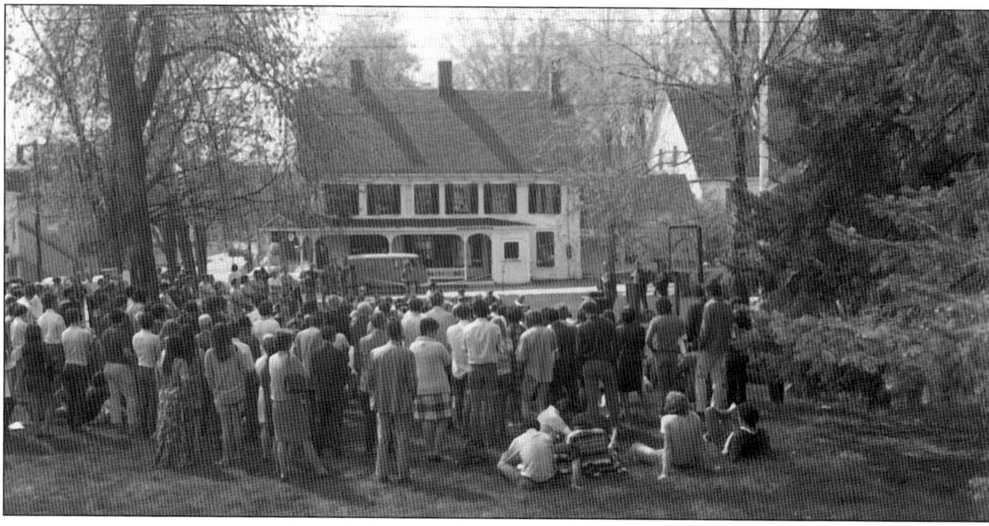

Prof. Don Melander joined the college in 1969 and remembered that the "spring of 1970 was the first of three annual spring student/faculty strikes in protest of the Vietnam war. During the strike, we faculty members who supported it did not hold classes, though we met with students who were not involved in the strike. I held classes on the lawn. We worked with student strikers on teach-ins, publications, marches, transportation to regional or national protests, and so forth. I think during those strikes we faculty who opposed the war and supported the students must have put in 12-hour days on campus. Heady times!"

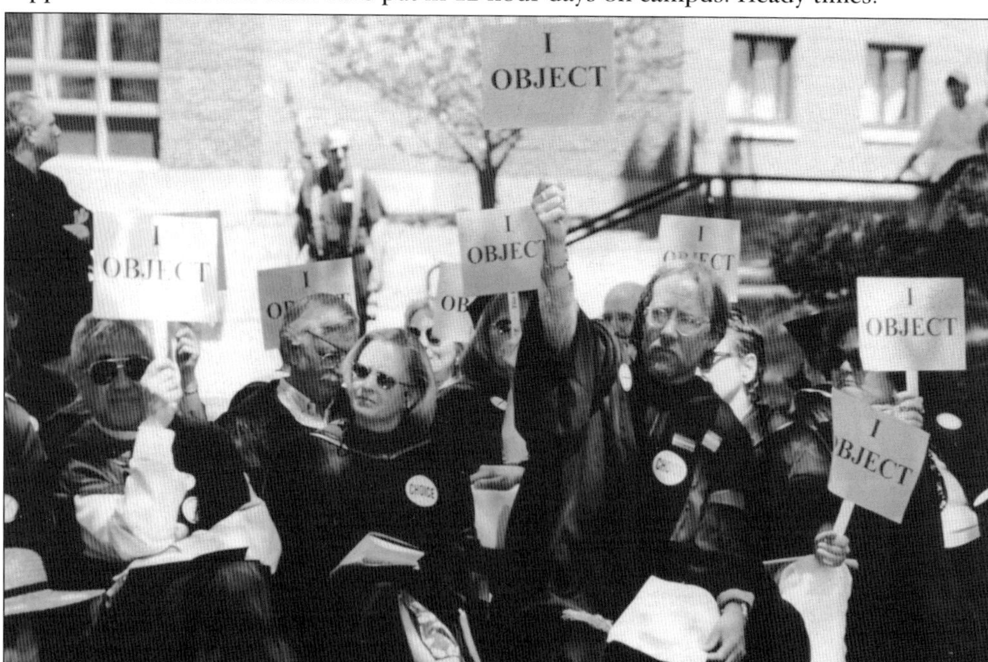

Academic freedom is cherished at New England College. At the 2001 commencement, the college awarded an honorary doctor of laws degree to US senator Bob Smith and some faculty expressed their objections to the senator's opposition to gay rights and pro-life position on abortion. In the foreground, from left to right, are professors Farid Haddad (art), Debra Nitschke-Shaw (education), and Christopher Dale (sociology).

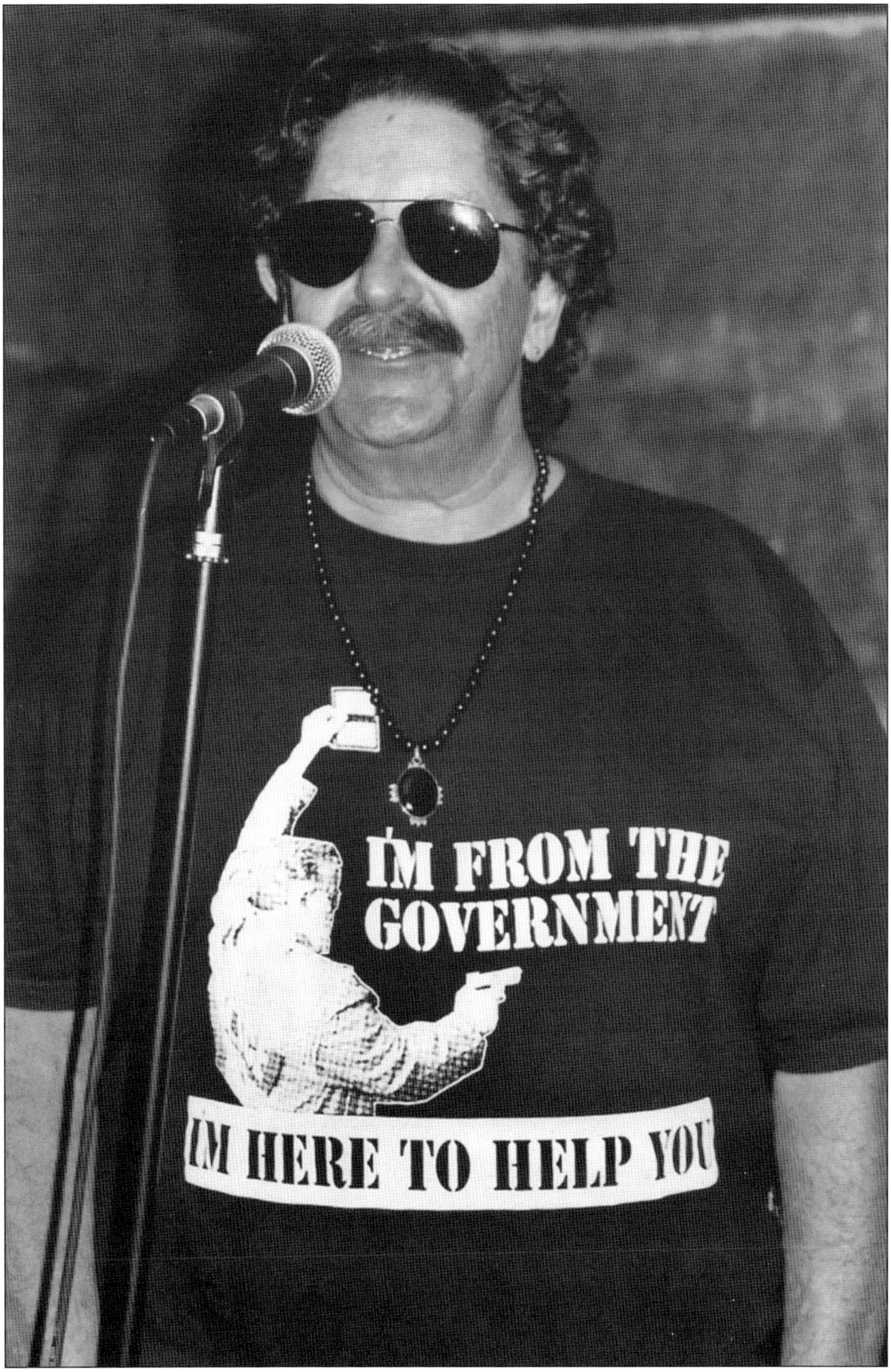

Through the years, many students accompanied Paul S. Daum, professor of history, to the National Baseball Hall of Fame while taking his course on the history of baseball. Daum encouraged students to think critically and challenge authority on matters of principle.

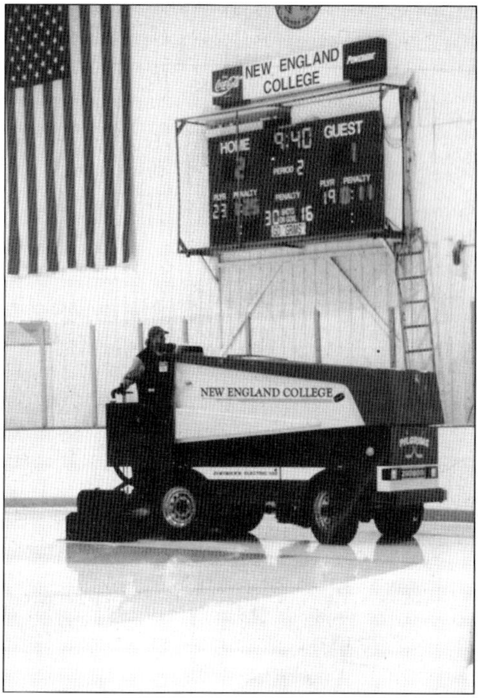

George W. Ward ('77) is most often seen in public refinishing the ice between periods at every hockey game. He is a versatile staff member who has seen the college through many decades of changes.

Dan Freese ('94) has been involved with New England College radio station WNEC since his student days. He is a true jack of all trades who can improvise, adapt, and overcome any technical challenge. He has had a long career in various staff positions at the school, most recently in the area of informational technology.

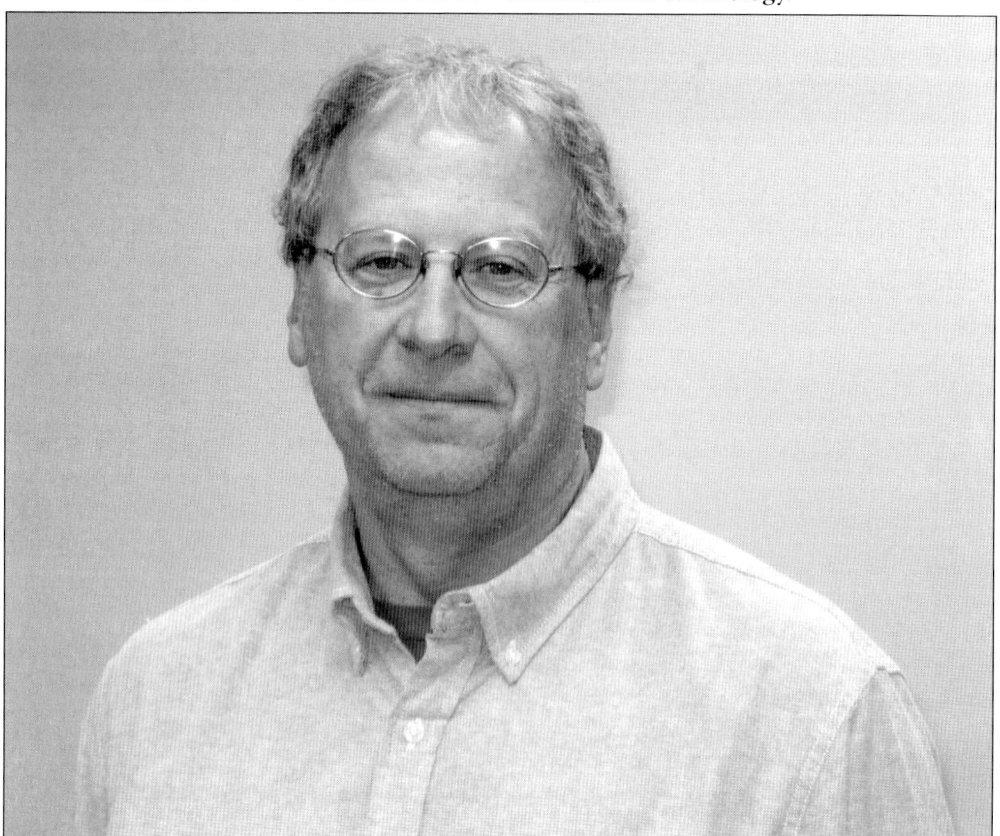

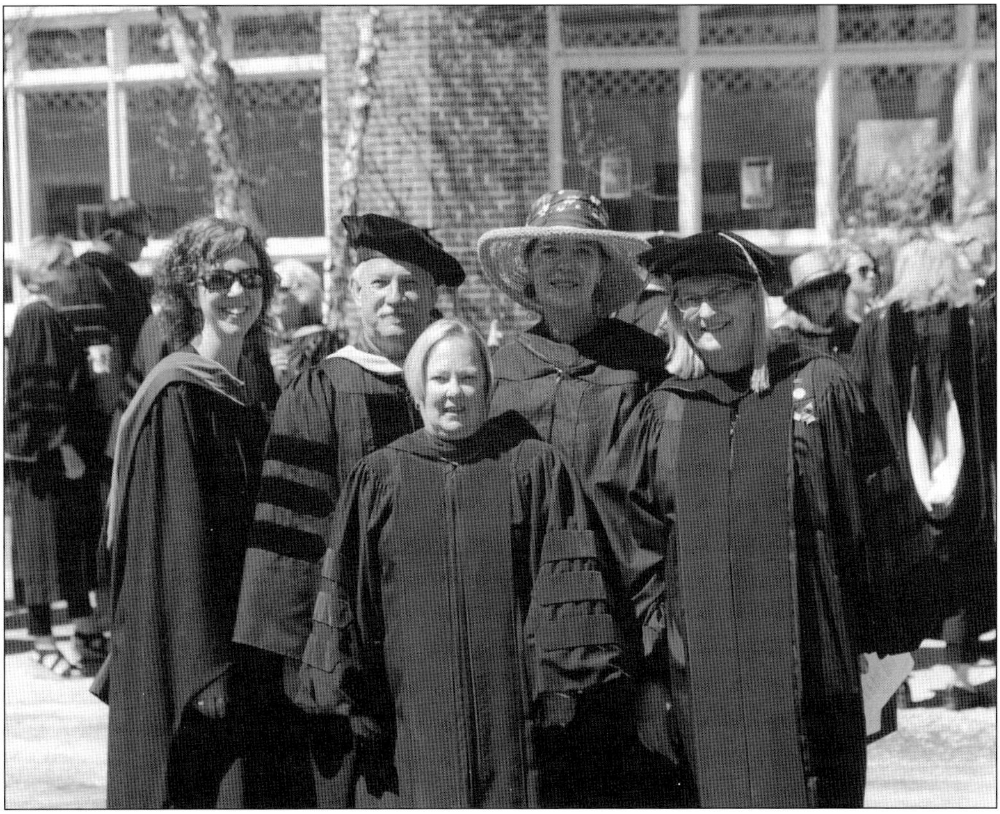

Alumni faculty at commencement in 2016 are, from left to right, S. Alexandra Zielke Picard (theatre), William Preble (education), Debra Nitschke-Shaw (education), Maura MacNeil (writing), and Debra A. Dunlop (biology).

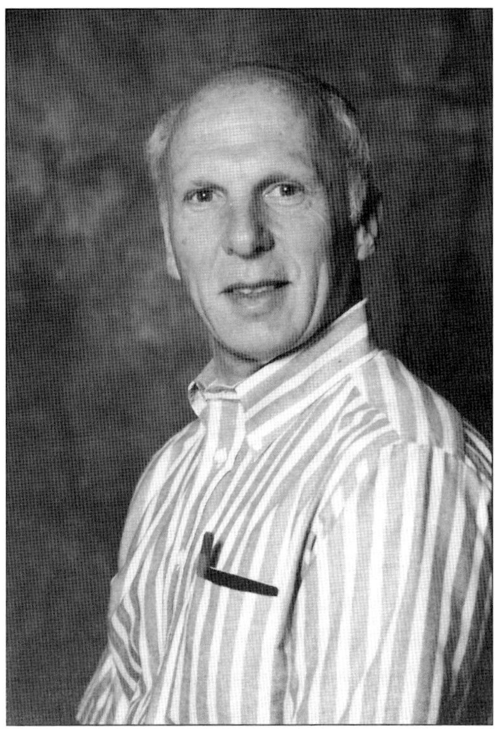

Alumnus Robert B. Seaman ('65) joined the engineering faculty of New England College in 1971. He also appears on the cover of this book.

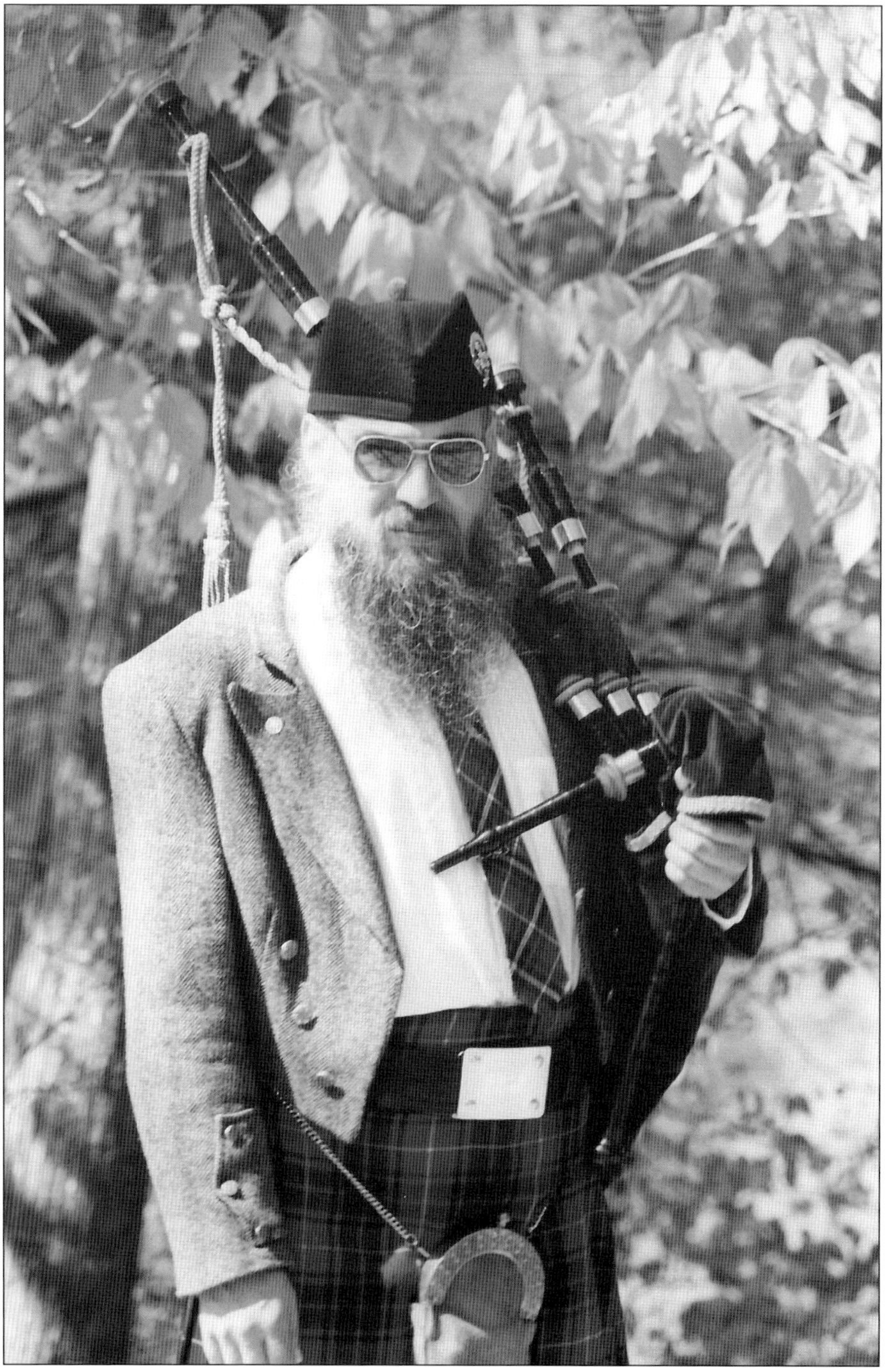

Bagpipes lead academic processions at convocation and commencement. "Hail thee New England! How can we part from thee? We are the loyal ones, faithful and true. For thee we sing thy praise, for all thy glorious days. No other can we love, save thee alone. To thy dear portals, we came to seek our fame, firm was our faith in thee, pride in thy name. The happy days are o'er, we have the memory, of all our college days, dear NEC." The college anthem was adapted from "How Can I Leave Thee" by Robert Wesley Feero ('51).

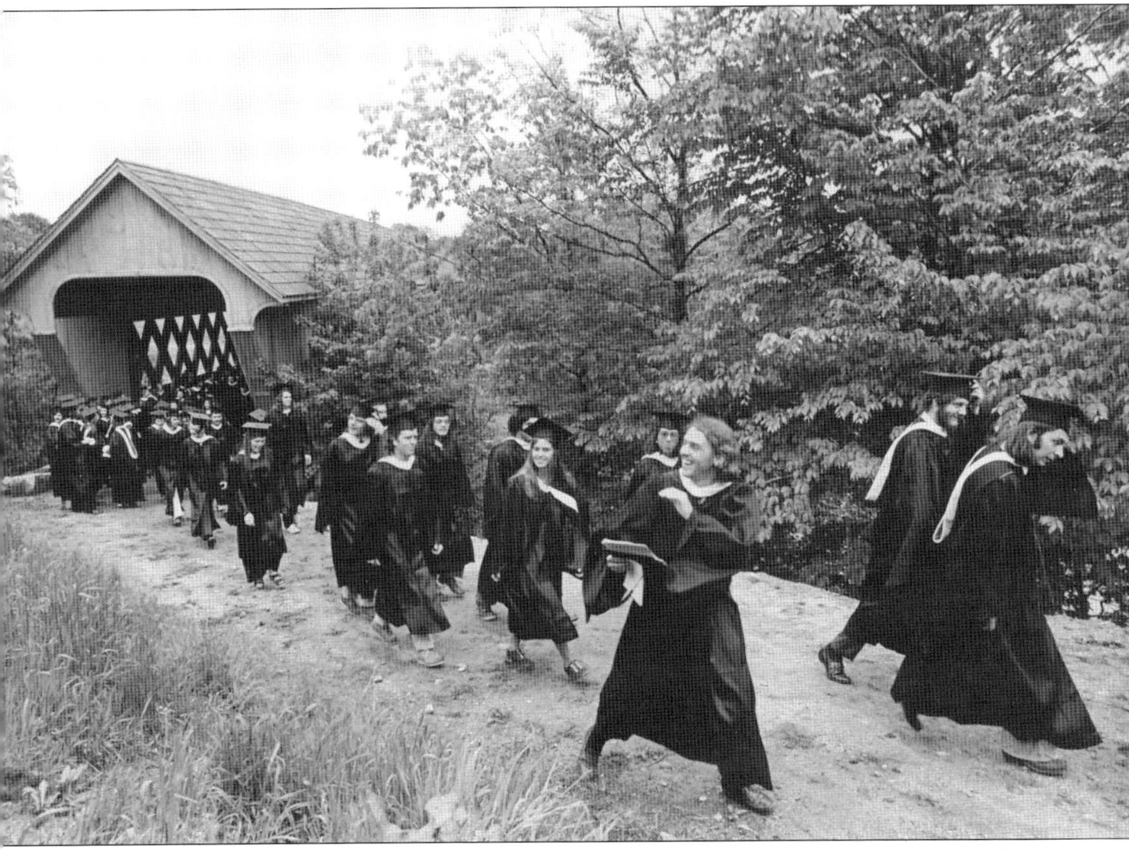

"Throughout its history, the bridge has played an important role in the traditions and life of the College. Every May, students in the graduating class gather on the bridge to bid farewell to their classmates before marching on to commencement," recalled Pres. William O'Connell on May 10, 1992.

Bibliography

Gilbert, Peter J. *Henniker Old Houses and Family Name*. Unpublished manuscript in the collection of Henniker Historical Society, Henniker, NH, 2006.

———. *New England College the First Ten Years*. Unpublished manuscript in the collection of Henniker Historical Society and New England College Archives, authorized by New England College, Henniker, NH, 2003.

Ginsburg, Philip E. *Voices: New England College 1946–1986*. Henniker, NH: New England College, 1987.

Henniker Historical Society. *The Only Henniker on Earth*. Canaan, NH: Phoenix Publishing, 1980.

Holton, Andy. *Some Memoirs*. Unpublished and undated manuscript in collection of Henniker Historical Society, Henniker, NH.

The Pilgrim (yearbook), 1950–present, Danforth Library, New England College.

Reed, Deborah Spring. *A House of College Boys*. Unpublished manuscript in collection of New England College Archives, 2016.

About New England College

Mission Statement

New England College is a creative and supportive learning community that challenges individuals to transform themselves and their world.

Description of Mission

New England College emphasizes experiential learning as an essential component in the development of an enduring academic community. Building upon a strong liberal arts foundation, we challenge our students to reach their full potential through informed discourse and the pursuit of excellence in a framework of academic freedom that reflects the following values:

- Imaginative, innovative, and creative approaches to all endeavors
- Respect for self in the development of personal, social, physical, and intellectual abilities
- Caring and collaborative relationships among members of our community
- Respect for the varied qualities of individuals, communities, and the world
- An appreciation of beauty and elegance in the search for truth
- Inquiry into and the pursuit of social justice
- Ethical and responsible citizenship, including service to the community
- The pursuit of ecological sustainability
- Continuous learning and a lifetime of personal achievement

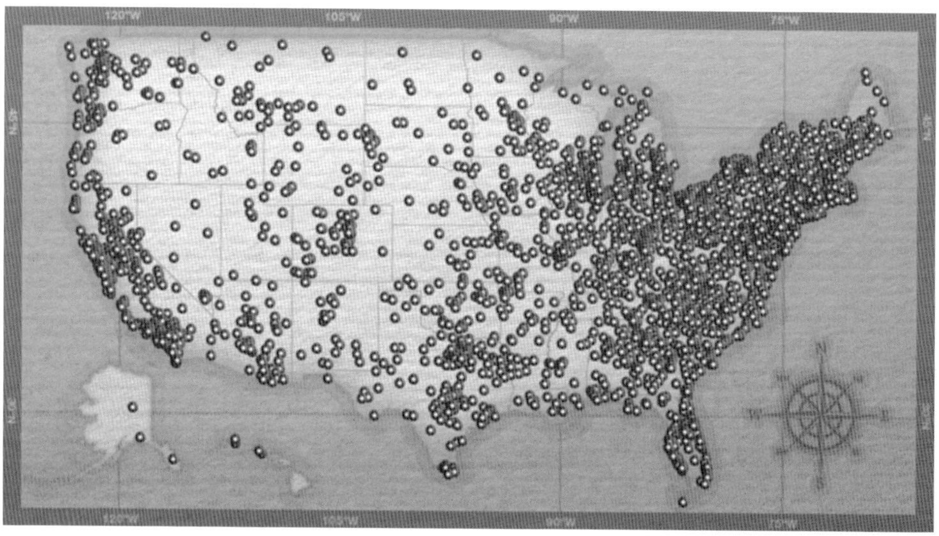